This book is
presented to you
as a gift.

May you receive
God's love, joy, peace,
and blessings.

Andrea Jaeger

first service

Following God's Calling and Finding Life's Purpose

Former Tennis Star
Andrea Jaeger

Health Communications, Inc.
Deerfield Beach, Florida

www.hcibooks.com

Scriptures reprinted from the Spirit-Filled Life Bible, New King James Version, Thomas Nelson Publishers.

"Jesus Freaks" excerpt used by permission of The Voice of the Martyrs at *www.persecution.com*.

"Teen Teaches Life Lessons" by Christopher Cogley, Douglas Country News-Press. Web interview, C.D. Baker, author, *Crusade of Tears*, River Oak/Cook Communications, Colorado Springs, Colorado.

Library of Congress Cataloguing-in-Publication Data is available through the Library of Congress.

ISBN 0-7573-0169-X

Publisher: Health Communications, Inc.
          3201 S.W. 15th Street
          Deerfield Beach, FL 33442-8190

Cover photo courtesy of the West Australian Newspaper. Taken January 1995, Perth, Australia, at a children's hospital. Andrea visited a young oncology patient, Shaun.
Cover design by Larissa Hise Henoch
Inside book design by Lawna Patterson Oldfield
Inside book formatting by Dawn Von Strolley Grove

With love, I dedicate this book to God

CONTENTS

Acknowledgments vii
Introduction xv

One. 1
Two 11
Three 19
Four 29
Five 41
Six 47
Seven 63
Eight. 73
Nine 83
Ten 95
Eleven 101
Twelve 111
Thirteen 121
Fourteen 129
Fifteen 137
Sixteen 151
Seventeen 159
Eighteen 169
Nineteen 181

Twenty 199
Twenty-One 209
Twenty-Two 217
Twenty-Three 223
Twenty-Four 231
Twenty-Five 241
Twenty-Six 257
Twenty-Seven 267
Twenty-Eight 277
Twenty-Nine 287
Thirty 301

Epilogue 307

ACKNOWLEDGMENTS

Father God, Lord Jesus Christ and the Holy Spirit: Thank you for your constant love, guidance, protection, saving grace, blessings, support, divine relationships, gifts and fruits of the Holy Spirit as well as providing the calling and purposes you have placed on my life.

Heidi Bookout: Your divinely gifted leadership, faith, wisdom, love, patience, humor, guidance, generosity and kindness have been such blessings to me and all the children you have helped. Thank you! What an incredible gift God gave me by placing me under your angel wings for the past eighteen years. I look forward to continuing with you in the eternal partnership and calling God has placed on our lives! You are a priceless treasure that glows with the Holy Spirit!

Pat Theissen: What a gift from above to have you teaching me the Word of God, the ways of the Lord and how both are lifelong lessons and gifts that need to be opened and fed daily. Your prayers have been greatly appreciated as has the very special friendship you have given to me.

Ted Forstmann: You are living proof that angels walk amongst us. Thank you for your generosity, friendship and love of helping children. You were certainly right when you declared that things change a great deal when you get involved. You have children cheering on Earth and in heaven because you have cared enough to make a difference.

Michael Bloomberg: The world will never truly comprehend the depths of your heart and philanthropy. God knows and the crowns you will receive in heaven are many. Thank you for caring about the little people in such big ways. What a blessing to have your friendship and support.

Faith Hill: The glory and love of God, the light of the Holy Spirit and the beauty of Christ live with you and shine upon everyone you meet. Thank you for making the world a brighter and better place.

KC: What a joyful partnership God divinely arranged for us. Thank your for your unconditional acceptance and love. I am eternally grateful that your presence lingers on as the anointed and appointed Holy Spirit messenger for which God has chosen you. Here's to kindred spirits, joy so engaging the mouth and sides hurt from laughing, sunsets and oceans coming together, snowflakes falling, blessed callings and purposes and the glory of God revealed in such a wonderful gift—you.

Ms. Barbara Cox Anthony: There is so much to say about your generosity of heart, spirit and way of life, that it could fill a library of books. Thank you for your passion in making such a positive difference in the world. It is with great thanks and tremendous honor that I can call you "my friend."

John McEnroe: I first met you as a child, and you were special and endearing then. Thank you for being a warrior, contributor, friend and loud voice in getting people to donate and support the Silver Lining Foundation. You will forever be a champion on and off the court.

Maja Muric: Through all your caring efforts you have brought a special joy to our programs, adventures and experiences. Your talents have released such fun and laughter to the children, kept us moving through trenches and shined brightly on everyone with

God's love. Thank you for always jumping in with abundant faith, purpose and love.

Fritz and Fabi Benedict: We know you hear the laughter and delight from the children. Thank you!

Cindy Crawford: What a generous heart you have! Thank you for sharing it with us and the children time and time again. The way you give of yourself in order to make days brighter for children of the world is greatly appreciated.

Chris Wyman: What a great partnership Heidi and I received when you came on board. Wow! Thank you for your hard work, honesty, character, loyalty and genuine love for us and for all the enormous responsibilities involved in keeping the Silver Lining Foundation, Ranch and us running smoothly. Your assistance in every project and program we take on is a blessing that is greatly appreciated.

Paul Newman: Thank you for being real. I have greatly enjoyed learning from you in all the adventures we have experienced together. Your wisdom and humanitarian walk have certainly changed the world for the better.

Bill Dwyre: That clear day in California when we first met had more than the sun shining on me. God gave us such a wonderful gift in you. Thank you for caring enough to step out for me, the children and everyone involved in the children's cancer programs. The Los Angeles community and the entire world are fortunate to have such a wonderful ambassador.

Bill Plaschke: Your heart transcends through in your walk, column and words. Thank you for letting us be part of all of them.

Beene Smyley: Your friendship has been a blessing in my life. Thank you for stepping out in faith with Heidi, me and the Foundation from the beginning. Your efforts in providing fun times to the children, their families and people all over have been incredibly special!

Kate Anderson and Mary Darden: Thank you for being part of our grassroots start-up team. Your friendship and advice is always appreciated!

RJ Wagner: Your friendship has been so wonderful. Your beauty radiates throughout the world. Thank you!

Kevin Costner and the entire Costner family: Thank you for giving so much of yourselves. Your sheer joy in providing fun and laughter to the children of the Silver Lining Foundation is greatly appreciated.

Members of the media: Thank you for bringing the Foundation's work to new heights. You supported me in my tennis tour days and have been a major partnership and force in building our Foundation family to help children around the world. Thank you for serving the public with honor, integrity, truth, fairness and care, all qualities that you have so aptly provided to me and the Foundation programs. God bless you all.

Daphne Astor: Your stellar wisdom and humor have touched so many! Thank you!

Jen Lamb: Thank you for giving your all toward our programs. Your detail-oriented work has helped bring countless smiles, fun and laughter to the children. Part of our job is to provide services without people seeing how much work goes into every single detail. You have accomplished that wonderfully. I also thank you for your research support on this book and for bringing a cheerful attitude to all the tasks you take on.

Candis Tai: Thank you for your expertise and grand efforts in the office. Every member of the Foundation team is important and we are thankful you are part of our mission to help children.

Petra Crimmel and the rest of the Silver Lining Foundation/ Little Star support team: Thank you for your care, compassion and support in all the work that you do.

Yanaris Nieves: Thank you for joining in on the journey. Your loyalty, hard work, efforts and prayers are needed and appreciated. Steve Lampman and everyone at Monahan, Lampman and Hays: You are all so wonderful and we are thankful for your years of guidance and support.

Dr. Joel: Thank you for taking care of all the little and big patients with such gentle ways. Your guidance, knowledge and honor in which you hold the patient is a tribute to how you care for all of God's children.

Tamara Manero: You are an inspiration. Thank you for all your loving support and for being such a wonderful ambassador in God's kingdom.

Dick Peterson: Thank you for being a faith-filled lawyer who cares about teaching your clients the Word of God. It has been enjoyable learning from you.

Rick Stone: You have always wonderfully stepped in to help us in a variety of ways. Thank you!

Ed Scott, Sid Smith and Bill Ziereis: Thank you for your expertise and care. Your help is greatly appreciated.

Pam Barr: Thank you for helping watch over Rancho Milagro.

Mary Dixon: Thank you for always going that extra step to help women, children and families. Those dig-down-deep efforts make a huge difference over generations for everyone, men, women and children alike.

Stephen Goldberg: Your guidance and support have had a special impact. Thank you!

To Andre Agassi, Pete Sampras, Gabriela Sabatini, Pam Shriver, Michael Chang, Anna Kournikova and all the tennis players that have supported and celebrated our children's programs: Thank you for being champions on and off the court. Your humanitarian efforts are full of the light and love in which you walk in everyday life.

Mrs. Helen Schallerer: What a teacher! Your influence has positively affected countless children. Thank you.

James Myers: Thank you for being you and for all of our fun times; canoe, asphalt and ranch chats included. Your ambassadorship in serving God is inspiring.

Don Otis and Creative Resources: Your joy in serving God comes out in all your correspondence and efforts in helping people. Thank you for partnering up with us to help the children while advancing the Kingdom of God.

Forrest and CLS Transport: Thank you for all your special ground transport assistance.

Esther Pearlstone: Thank you for bringing us into your huge heart, loving home and generous circle of friends.

To the family God created for me: Thank you!!!!!!

PL Houston: Thank you for sharing your life, your love and your passion for books and writing with me.

Peter Bodo: Thank you for always believing in me as a person, with or without a tennis racket in my hand.

Peter Vegso: Thank you for your vision, for believing, stepping out in faith, and supporting this book and the children's programs with your vast knowledge, generosity, compassion and heart. It has been an honor and privilege working with you, and everyone at Health Communications, Inc.

Christine Belleris: What a blessing it has been working with you! Thank you for opening your heart to me and this very special book project. Your friendship, editorial expertise, guidance and humor certainly made those twenty-hour work days full of complete enjoyment. I look forward to having a lifelong friendship with you and your family. God's blessings to you for giving your all in everything you do.

Gary Seidler: Thank you for all that you do in making the world a better place.

Allison Janse: It has been wonderful working with you on all the editing and processes of bringing this book together. Your kind, engaging and informative ways and wisdom have been heaven sent. Thank you!

Kim Weiss: Thank you for bringing your cheerful spirit and heart to all of the processes involved in making this book possible.

Nancy Burke: What a joy to have your wisdom and talent on this project. Your round-the-clock copy editing support and sharing of thoughts have been greatly appreciated.

The HCI publishing team: What fun! Thank you for the love and purpose in which you handled this book.

To the past and current advisory board and board members: Thank you!!!

To every donor, contributor and supporter: Your love, support, donations, heartfelt notes and prayers have been felt and they make such a difference in bringing joy to the children. Thank you! God's blessings to you and thank you for partnering up with us to help children all around the world.

To the families and caregiver system: Thank you for being you. May God continue to bless you with the ability to carry on for the children.

To the children: Thank you for showing the world how God's love comes in angelic, heroic, gifted and incredibly special packages.

To all: Peace, love, light, joy and God's blessings.

INTRODUCTION

The idea of God, enshrouded in mystery, evokes a multitude of opinions and beliefs. For those who passionately seek God's heart, the truth is simple and easily discovered: God exists. I have always known this, and in writing this book I discovered just how intricately He is entwined in the lives of believers and nonbelievers alike. From searching souls to devoted followers, atheists to fundamentalists, God watches over all of us.

I didn't come from a religious background. My faith chose God. Once I released that decision heavenward, God set me on a journey that proved His miraculous ways in a powerful and graceful fashion. I was called upon and led by God, who transposed His majesty on my heart and spirit. Embarking on fulfilling my destiny, maneuvering through one adventure after the next, I was held tightly in God's loving embrace.

Unknowingly chosen as a child, I experienced amazing manifestations of God's glory as He communicated with me. I honored my purpose without realizing the significance of these often-dramatic occasions. Meandering my way through the years with constant prayer and soul-searching, it struck me that God was orchestrating every moment of my purpose and calling: to protect and help children. This calling was clear and unmistakable. God set a course that was carved in stone.

As with many of our lives, we seem destined for one path, which is really a springboard to another place. A teenaged tennis phenomenon with pigtails and a mouthful of braces, I entered the professional tennis circuit at the then unheard-of age of fourteen. Startling a great number of people, I rose as high as the number-two female player in the world. I was showered with accolades, media attention, prize money and endorsement earnings in the millions of dollars. I traveled the globe and learned about people and cultures distinctly different from my own. I gained discipline and focus. God was preparing me, not for greater victory on the tennis court, but for the much larger purpose of running a foundation that would enhance the lives of, and give long-term support to, children with cancer.

When I was a teenager on the pro circuit, I persuaded the transportation representatives at a tournament to take me to a toy store. I wanted to buy presents for children who were hospitalized. It was something I felt drawn to do. Eagerly entertaining the children at a pediatric oncology playroom, I felt a sudden shift in my thinking. At that moment, I knew that tennis would eventually fade to the background while I discovered my true calling. Destiny pointed me in a new direction. From that point on, my purpose was set in motion: providing much welcome assistance to children in need. I continued this practice by reaching out to children in unfortunate circumstances in the cities that I visited.

This new focus could not have been more different from my life as a professional athlete, where competition and winning at all costs is paramount. To leave my tennis career, when I could swing the racket with power and ease, beating opponents many years my senior, would have seemed unthinkable to many people. I felt that God was showing me the way through my heart and spirit to a different path.

My strength and abilities yet to peak, I seriously injured my shoulder, which effectively ended my career just a few months shy of my nineteenth birthday. Seven unsuccessful surgeries and a nearly fatal car accident sealed my fate as a *former* tennis player.

From meager beginnings, and initially funded solely by my tennis winnings and pension, the vision of helping children provided to me by God has grown exponentially. Today more than four hundred children a year, along with their families, take part in programs operated by the Silver Lining Foundation, a nonprofit organization I jointly head that is based in Aspen, Colorado. The children who enter the program hail from all walks of life and from states coast to coast—even crossing international borders.

In one of our many programs, children participate in weeklong sessions at our 18,000-square-foot permanent facility, the Benedict-Forstmann Silver Lining Ranch, built in Aspen specifically for children with cancer. For these youngsters, weary of sterile hospitals, painful procedures, and the loneliness and trauma of dealing with a life-threatening disease, the Ranch and activities provide a welcome relief amid the beauty and serenity of the Colorado Rockies.

While countless children are from loving families with great community and parental support, others can arrive from foster care and harsh, broken family environments. These particular children are more used to the sound of bullets at night than chirping crickets. Some must take buses, alone, to their chemotherapy treatments, and many need a great deal more assistance to get them through their illnesses. The Silver Lining Foundation and Ranch programs provide long-term support in a variety of ways that help children find peace, have fun and share the similarity of their experiences with fellow cancer patients. They explore the quaint Rocky Mountain town, ride horses, go river rafting, play tennis, fish, explore artistic gifts, share stories, ski and display their unique talents in a closing-night talent show.

For the staff and me, every session is different and every child special. Even though many of the children succumb to their cancer, we do not feel defeated. We know that we have spread joy, helped forge friendships, and brought smiles and laughter to the children's lives. Over the years many angels, from both heaven and Earth, have joined in on this personal pilgrimage.

Recently, I stood in the departure lounge at the Aspen airport, sending off another group of children at the end of their weeklong session. Amid the tears and farewell hugs, the group presented a carefully created picture and message book. The kids surrounded Heidi—the Silver Lining cofounder and vice president—and me, encouraging us to read the heartwarming words written together by the entire group.

I read one message out loud: "Andrea, you've helped make a new world: one in love. I promise to keep in touch and come back. Keep up your smile and love, Brianna."

The enclosed photos brought back priceless moments of warmth and laughter. The children's faces beamed with happiness.

Constructed with great care, another message stated, "Andrea, thank you so much for everything! You are such a wonderful person and an inspiration for me to help people. You are so sound in your faith and glow with love and caring. You are an amazing person—and I don't mean just your tennis skills. I appreciate all you do and I love you so much. Love, Anna."

Asal wrote: "Andrea, thanks for giving me some of my most precious and lifelong memories. You are an angel and you have touched my heart. Love you always, Asal."

Moments like these remind me that regardless of what cancer or any hardship takes, in terms of years and dreams from lives, it can never diminish the spirit of a child—or any person—who walks in the light. No grim prognosis, or depth of struggle, abuse, pain or suffering, can crush the spirit or curtail love. And love, when given purely, always returns unexpectedly to attach to the heart. Every child is a cherished treasure. I have been blessed many times over from doing this extraordinary work, and I feel honored to have been called by the Lord to perform in His service. Children are our future and, most importantly, they are our responsibility— to protect, provide for and support. All over the world, children are suffering, whether through abuse and neglect, or disease, poverty and hunger. But we each have the power to change that. When we equip children with God's Word and unconditional love, we release power to the purposes He intended.

The instant I committed to fulfilling my calling, I became part of a global effort to heal, protect, help and make whole what God had placed in my hands—making a difference in children's lives. The glory is all God's as I, as His vessel and servant, work with children.

God loves all His children regardless of their backgrounds or strength of faith. During times of hardship, pain and confusion, God is always there to help shoulder the burdens that test our souls. The choice to follow Him always rests with us. He is connected to us in times of joy or suffering. Whether we hunger for a spirit-filled life or shun the kingdom of God, the choice to walk with God is ours.

Mine is a story of what anyone can accomplish when we let God be our guide. Much has been done to make the world a better and brighter place for children, but there is still so much left to do. I hope that you, too, are inspired to follow in God's footsteps and find your own special calling.

Chapter One

Before I formed you in the womb I knew you;
before you were born I sanctified you.

—Jeremiah 1:5

As with many Americans, I was a child of determined immigrants seeking freedom and a better life in a new country with countless opportunities. My parents, Roland and Ilse Jaeger, longed to leave their native homeland of Germany, where everyone they knew told stories of the ravaging effects of two world wars. They had both lived through horrors of their own, and this added to their personal strength and determination to make a new life for themselves and, eventually, a better life for the family they hoped to start.

My father was a gifted athlete, but his frequent bouts with sports injuries curtailed his dreams of becoming an international soccer or boxing superstar. As much as this disappointed him, these injuries might have saved his life since they prevented him from being drafted into the German military.

War had been difficult for the Jaeger family. While my dad's father, my grandfather, was fighting at the front, his mother battled the ravages of a brain tumor and died in the prime of her child-rearing years.

1

My dad's father was then taken prisoner by the Russians and held captive for four years. Filled with sorrow and despair, my father was determined to keep the remains of his family together to rise up against the death and decay all around him.

My mother had a fateful encounter during the war that, if acted upon differently, would have altered the course of many lives— including mine. In the pastoral German countryside, in view of the Rhine River, a soldier broke into my mom's home at the end of the war. French troops had captured the town of Brennet, Germany. The Americans were in Berlin. The Nazi regime was falling. As in all wars, bullets, mortars and bombs bring down innocent bystanders. Soldiers have to make split-second decisions to spare and take lives, including their own. This particular soldier was securing the perimeter around my mother's home when his attention was drawn to a noise in the kitchen. He made his way inside.

My mom sensed a presence behind her and turned from the kitchen counter where she was undertaking her daily chores of preparing a meal. Startled by the invasion, her eyes locked on the soldier. She feared for her life. He slowly came closer to my mother, lowered his firearm and withdrew a long blade. The soldier lifted the knife high in the air, apparently ready to slash my mother, but she didn't flinch. She watched the knife slice through the air. If it was her time to die, she certainly wasn't going down as a coward. But rather than harming my mother, the soldier decided to smash the knife down on the counter. In a mark of compassion, in the blink of an eye, the soldier spared my mom's life.

Staring at my mother, the soldier expressed that this was not her time to die. She had her own destiny to fulfill. Long seconds passed as they stared at each other, taking in how quickly life can turn to death and vice versa. The soldier made the next move, slicing himself some cheese, and then proceeded to quietly make his way out the door, never to be seen again. With the life-threatening situation over, Mom, in her typical no-nonsense fashion, continued about her chores. Nothing would deter her from her duty of making sure the family had food on the table.

My parents survived these rough challenges and more harrowing ones as well. No one lives through war without scars—emotional, spiritual or physical, or worse yet, all three—but it gave them an even stronger will to succeed and more reason to focus on their future and fulfill their hopes and dreams.

My mother's aunt lived in Chicago. Roland and Ilse, in love but not yet married, were encouraged by her stories of life in America—the land of prosperity. With few possessions, but a wealth of dreams, they set sail for the strange new land that would soon be their home. They had to travel separately, as my father had difficulty getting a visa from the German government, which wanted to keep as many of its citizens as possible—especially the men—to help in the rebuilding effort. In February 1956, undaunted by the challenges of traveling alone, my mother bravely ventured by boat to the United States of America, where her aunt met her in Chicago. My father finally joined his teenaged sweetheart in November of that same year. By January, they were married.

Roland and Ilse sought their own version of the American success story as they started their new life together in Skokie, Illinois, a suburb of Chicago. Knowing little English, they jumped with blind faith into a culture they knew almost nothing about.

With a clean slate, and their inherent dedication and never-give-up attitude propelling them forward, my parents hit the ground running. They learned the language and acquired skills that would help them build promising careers. My father began in construction, eventually becoming a foreman. This ultimately provided him with the leadership skills and financial resources to fulfill his real desire: opening his own restaurant and bar.

Ilse helped Roland in his quest to own a restaurant by working as a beautician to help save money. Being a hairstylist alone did not satisfy my mom's drive for success, and with her own determination and fortitude she eventually opened up her own beauty shop. In just over four short years, my parents saw their dream realized. The Postillion Lounge opened its doors in 1961. Roland and Ilse treated their American customers to a family restaurant with a definite European flavor. They were proud to be Americans, but held fast to their heritage.

In spite of these accomplishments, Roland and Ilse felt that something important was missing from their lives. They longed to start a family. In 1962, they received their wish with the birth of my sister, Susy. Another dream was fulfilled.

My mom said that Dad cared for his newborn as if "the sun rose and set with Susy." And she loved that about him. He would put his daughter on his new red Corvette, proudly wrapping his arm around her as my mom snapped away with the camera. The Jaegers were the quintessential immigrant success story: a young, beautiful family proudly living the American dream for all it was worth.

Susy, an ideal child, made life easy for them. While some parents could never think of taking their young child out to dinner, my parents could take Susy anywhere without a fuss. She behaved well beyond her years and never cried or threw temper tantrums in public places. Even at home, Susy was well-mannered and rarely needed discipline.

This atmosphere gave my parents reason to expand their family. When Susy was nearly three years old, my mother became pregnant with me. Very quickly, my parents learned how different children born of the same parents can be. As my mom drove along Lake Shore Drive, on June 4, 1965, her labor pains began fast and furiously. From the outset, I had a sense of urgency to get things done in a style all my own. Through the pain, Mom somehow safely drove herself to the hospital. It was a difficult labor for my mother.

She was a small woman and I was a large baby. Fortunately, the doctors managed to remove me with a minimal amount of damage while using forceps to safely deliver me. My mom survived the ordeal with few problems, but I came into the world looking decidedly unlike the Gerber baby. Pronounced forceps marks on my head, along with a bruised face, led my parents to hide all delivery and hospital photos.

Susy was charming and persuasive from the start, always looking and acting as if she was born to lead more than just our family. She was a child model, featured in many catalogs and magazines with great success. She was also highly intelligent, easily reading books written for adults even as a child.

I was completely different from Susy. While she was an extrovert and liked being in a crowd; I was shy and preferred to play alone. It was as if I was in a world of my own. Susy was charming and entertaining, while I "disappeared" into fascinating internal ventures. Susy could always be trusted to do the right thing and behave impeccably, making people feel welcome. I was being trained by unseen forces to follow my spirit. This made me appear aloof, indifferent and unresponsive to others.

My parents had a perfect built-in babysitter for me in Susy. I fondly called her "Foofin" until I could properly pronounce her name. I was enthralled with trying to crawl, walk, run and even bike to have fun with Susy and then excitedly escape to my own retreats. I found it very entertaining to watch Susy captivate people with her colorful intellect and considerable beauty. This eventually served me well since one of my favorite activities became studying how people interacted with one another.

As do all successful restaurateurs, my parents worked long hours. But this hard work made it possible for us to visit our relatives in Germany every year. Since countries in Europe are so near to one another, my parents would always add scenic and educational side trips along with our visit to their home country. They wanted us to appreciate the culture and history of all of Europe.

The scenery and European way of life thrilled me. It seemed that every nook and cranny in the quaint little villages that dotted the countryside were somehow historically important, and conducting business always took a backseat to something as simple as eating lunch. And unlike America, where we were the newcomers, every place we stepped here was part of my family's history. The butcher, baker, neighbors, grocery store owner, wine merchant, restaurant staff, even gas station attendants, all knew my parents. We were treated as visiting royalty. The butcher gave us free snacks; the baker, samples of his tastiest dessert. Every merchant grabbed a handful of his or her favorite delicacy and handed the morsels over to Susy and me, lovingly placing them in our tiny hands.

I would spend mornings picking strawberries along the Rhine River with my grandmother. This lovely woman, whom I affectionately called "Oma," had a smile as sweet as Swiss chocolate. That smile was permanently etched on her face. Everything she did, every memory I have of her, is with that beautiful smile. Perhaps she was so cheerful because part of her purpose was to sprinkle our lives with great joy.

Oma's entire English vocabulary consisted of "ya-ya," "so-so" and "thank you."

I would ask, "Oma, do you want to go with me to the river and pick strawberries?"

"Ya-ya," she'd answer with a jolly lilt in her voice.

I would inquire, "How do you think this area looks to pick from?"

"So-so," she'd reply, blue eyes sparkling.

The language barrier never bothered us. We had our own special relationship because love, spoken through the heart, transcends all boundaries, languages and cultures. It has its own way of communicating. I never learned to speak much German—unlike my sister, who was quite fluent, picking up my parents' mother tongue quickly—and Oma never learned any more English, but our relationship was strong and immovable.

After picking fresh strawberries and gazing at the swans delicately making their way along the crystal clear water, my grandmother would say to me, "Thank you." Then we would turn toward the road for the leisurely walk back to the house, winding back and forth on a meandering pathway, our spirits playfully enjoying the moments spent together. It was there, in these quiet, intimate moments with my Oma, that I started honing my skills to carry on conversations without having to speak at all. It was comforting to me to be able to retreat like this and not be forced to talk.

When it was time to leave Oma's chalet, she would stretch herself out the window, waving as if her hand reached right into heaven. Tears streamed down her face, but her bright smile still shone through the sadness of watching us leave, comforting us and reassuring everybody that we would all be okay until our next visit. It was this way every time until my grandmother died in 1995.

Back home, as the warm summer air began to take on the briskness of autumn, it was time for me to start preschool. While separation anxiety is common among youngsters who leave their mothers for the first time, mine was acute. Right from the start of my academic career, I never felt a sense of belonging in school. I enjoyed my own internal world and wanted to keep it intact—my conscious thoughts uninterrupted and the inexplicable pull on my spirit strong.

Leaving her baby daughter for the first time was difficult for my mother, but she put on her game face for my benefit and gathered herself for first-day introductions. "Andrea, this will be fun for you," she said positively. "Look at all the children, and oh, look, here comes your teacher!" Her peppy speech notwithstanding, I was mortified. The classroom was a chaotic mix of unfamiliar sights, sounds and smells. Children gleefully played in ways that startled me. They yanked each other's hair, ate crumbs off the floor and shrieked loudly. This was as different from my quiet, comfortable world as it could be. From the start, I was miserable. I would never get used to being there.

I reached up and pulled on my mother's protective sleeve, preparing a speech that would save me from a place I didn't feel I belonged. My mom was concentrating on hearing the drop-off and pick-up information from the teacher. I gazed sadly across the room again at the organized unruliness. A precocious and inquisitive child with insatiable curiosity, I knew, even at this young age, that I would not learn anything here. I would spend most of my time watching others being calmed down and taught simple activities. I wanted more than what the nursery school class could provide.

I turned to my mother, prepared to plead my case for returning to the car and finding another school. Despite her valiant attempts to stay strong for me, her lips quivered with emotion. Tears welled in her eyes. My heart sank. I couldn't add to her anxiety. I silenced myself and, without hesitation, voiced my feelings to God.

That's when it started to click: My uncomfortable introduction to school unlocked the first door into what was urgently driving the spiritual portion of my life. What I thought was talking to myself in an internal dialogue, was not that at all. Finally, the spiritual longing that cycled through my thoughts daily made a solid connection. All along, I had been reaching out to God, searching for a purpose and a protection that I knew my parents couldn't satisfy. I took my request to the Creator.

This innate connection with God was natural. I was born

believing in Him and fully acknowledged that there was a reason
and purpose behind everything, whether I favored the outcome or
not. In my spirit, I instantly felt a sense of comfort to help me deal
with this overwhelming situation. Not wanting to attract attention,
I whispered under my breath, "God, I know I am not supposed to
be at this place. I will put up with it for now, but this will have to
change."

Many people think that God only listens to people but cannot
reply. This fallacy stops relationships from going to another level
with God. I expected responses. I knew that God provided results
and would always assist me. This declaration of faith was critical to
God opening our two-way communication system. It was unlike
anything I experienced with any person.

God soon answered my prayers. Not long after, my parents
decided to move our family farther out into the suburbs, where we
could have a spacious house with a big yard, shaded by an abundance of trees. Along with a nicer house, my parents wanted us to
be in good schools that would challenge and inspire us, satisfy our
craving for knowledge and help us attain our own dreams.

Mom and Dad loaded us up in their shiny blue Cadillac and drove
about thirty miles north of Skokie to the picturesque town of
Lincolnshire. I marveled at the change of scenery. Cement play-
grounds turned to ample green fields. We took the toll road, but soon
four-lane highways gave way to country stores and wide-open vistas.

Among the houses we saw, 6 Sheffield Court turned out to be the
perfect one. My parents made an offer and soon it was ours. The
brick ranch-style home contained three bedrooms and two bathrooms with ample living and dining space. There were so many
trees in the front and back yards that I would often lose track trying
to count them. Enormous old willow and oak trees surrounded the
neighborhood, standing sentinel and making us feel safe and
protected. The driveway had a slope perfect for sledding in the

winter, and skateboarding and roller-skating in the spring, summer and fall.

Laura B. Sprague Elementary School was within biking and walking distance from our home. Susy and I would walk to school every morning until my parents—whose bank account was depleted from buying the new house—could afford to buy us new bicycles, since we had long outgrown our old ones.

Susy continued her role as older sister, mentor and babysitter to me with endless patience. It was a big job for her, as my curiosity continuously sidetracked me on our trips to school. I searched for monarch butterflies, caterpillars, milkweed, frogs, birds, bunnies and anything that moved in the countryside's natural kingdom.

Lincolnshire was more than our new home; it was a kid's paradise.

Chapter Two

Trust in the Lord with all your heart, And
lean not on your own understanding;
in all your ways acknowledge Him,
And He shall direct your paths.

—Proverbs 3:5–6

B y the time I was eight years old, hearing God's voice was a
central part of my life. It became like breathing, a natural part
of my existence. A combination internal compass, barometer and
soul-checker emerged within me, helping me balance the two
worlds unfolding before my eyes. One world involved communication with God and listening to children's spirits; the other was the
life of a dutiful daughter and schoolgirl, growing up while obeying
her parents, teachers and other authority figures.

Hiding the best of who I was became the norm. I could speak
loudly without ever saying a word, and take part in conversations
while never revealing a thing: abilities I learned to use with great
efficiency. This isn't unusual for children. God talks to the spirit
inside a person. It is like any skill that requires practice. Mine
was slowly developing, and I met each improvement with great

excitement, never allowing any of society's contradictory messages to mute my sense of communicating with and belonging to God. I learned useful lessons in my private conversations with God. Suffering and spiritual survival, I discovered, were two distinctly different subjects, in which God was equally present. Most importantly, I learned that things may not come easily, and that anything is possible.

I loved the spiritual life. Holy influences were a regular part of my childhood, and I welcomed them with open arms. I made a lifetime commitment to God, and in return, he guaranteed me celestial surroundings. I joyfully chatted to God with full faith and love. God was more than my Father above; He was my best friend.

To hear God, I was often silent. For the most part, this was neither understood nor appreciated by my peer group or adults trying to make a connection with me. I was often called "supersensitive" when I didn't respond to people; in reality, I was just trying to listen to God. People dismissed episodes of divine intervention as coincidence or dumb luck. These attitudes only encouraged me to shelter the parts of my life that I loved the best. At a young age, I understood that my childhood was different. It was a playground with miracles, signs, visions and wonders. God's frequent communication was familiar and made me feel warm and welcome rather than fearful and timid.

My parents raised me the best way they knew how. Coming from a foreign background, we did not participate in many of the traditions other American children did. We didn't sing nursery rhymes and rarely had slumber parties. As a family, we straddled both cultures, attempting to stay true to our European heritage while assimilating into life as Americans. My parents knew the value of strict discipline, which, to outsiders, might have appeared militaristic. However, this was their way of building character, solid work ethics and tenacity.

Roland and Ilse valued education, in and out of the classroom. Any voids in learning were replaced with fascinating educational experiences. We discussed nature and animals, current events and history. Eventually sports became important because of my parents' own athletic accomplishments in Europe and the United States, and their interest in providing a healthy activity we could all participate in together.

My eighth birthday was a major turning point in my life. I had a big party in our backyard, which was turned into an all-out festival with bright, happy decorations. Mom draped the trees with beautiful bows and streamers, and balloons were everywhere. The entire neighborhood, it seemed, had been invited to the gala in my honor. I unwrapped presents, appreciative of the generosity of people, some I barely knew. One box contained a complete badminton set. It immediately caught my attention, and I became completely taken with the contents.

Mom politely explained that I needed to turn my attention to the remaining unopened presents. I obliged her request and rushed through the rest of the birthday activities. The moment the last guest said good-bye, I raced to the front yard to play with my newly acquired badminton set. For hours, I played right hand against left hand, rarely making contact at all. I hardly noticed the time passing, I was having so much fun.

At one point, I noticed my parents pushing the drapes aside to see what was holding my concentration for so long. Eventually it was dinnertime, and I still did not want to be disturbed. I ignored my mom's pleas to come see the special birthday dinner she had made. I was fully engaged in the competition of making contact with the birdie.

My mom called out, "Roland, she is not coming in." From my

dad's demeanor, I figured I was going to be taught a lesson. "It looks like you are having fun with your badminton set," he said.

I nodded in agreement as I chased after another birdie thrown in the air. "Would you like me to teach you tennis?" I immediately stopped. Susy and my mom had learned the game from my dad, who had taught himself by studying tennis matches on television. I was always left out of their practices, because they felt I was too young. Now, at eight, my opportunity showed up.

I envisioned the big tennis court and whacking the balls with power over the net. My dad said, "We don't want to waste court time until you can hit a ball, so I will start teaching you tomorrow in the driveway." My shoulders dropped in disappointment. "The driveway? What about a real court?" I asked.

As my father walked away, he quietly murmured, "Maybe one day, if you are good enough."

That remark motivated me to make tennis, not badminton, my new interest. I proudly walked in the house declaring that very soon I would make it to a real tennis court. Susy had advanced in her tennis endeavors. Her progress in local tennis tournaments allowed her to join a summer-long sleepover tennis camp. Excited to join in on the fun, I eagerly awaited my lesson.

The following day, my father and I hit the driveway. It was apparent from the start that talent wasn't going to surface for some time: a swing and a miss followed a swing and a miss. This continued for hours. I thought Dad was going to blow in frustration. He never did, and that helped calm my anxiety about my inability to make any connection at all between the racket and the ball.

It started getting dark. I refused to go inside. "Come on Dad, one more," I kept saying. I could tell this was wearing thin. Finally, after countless attempts of swinging and missing, I made contact. The ball dribbled forward, but to me it was progress. A big smile crossed my face. I shouted, "Dad, did you see that? I hit it!"

My dad did not think a tennis champion was born that moment. He expressed his congratulations but he was more excited about using my "victory" as a transition into the house for dinner. "Great shot, Andrea. That is a perfect one to end on." I skipped inside knowing I would progress even further during the next day's lesson.

We continued our driveway drills every day like clockwork. After one of the instructional periods, pupil and teacher entered the house. My mom asked my dad how things were going. "She hits her forehand like she is swinging a bucket. She will never make it." Being from the old school, this was perhaps Dad's way of motivating me. His disapproving reinforcement encouraged me to attempt the insurmountable. This psychology seemed to have an extra effect on my passionate need for producing results, so despite this strange strategy of guiding me that some might find counterproductive, I improved faster. I lived in a world of "I can," not "I can't."

Change wasn't automatic or immediate, but eventually, after hitting thousands upon thousands of balls in the driveway, my dad announced it was time to head to the courts. From that point on, my progress increased so rapidly that the entire family could compete together with enjoyment. Our disciplined household rearranged its schedule to include tennis training. Because of my father's love of soccer, I became a dual participant in sports programs. During the summer months, I played tennis five days of the week and concentrated on soccer for the remaining two, removing soccer altogether in the winter.

As my family guided me in tennis instruction, I longed to have mentors and teachers of the spirit. Athletic and scholastic endeavors were given the highest priority in our household. Spiritual or religious focus was placed in a vacuum. The mere mention of God or religion was quickly and quietly swept away, as if it would somehow pollute our minds.

Mom and Dad loved and cared for Susy and me deeply. They

gave every ounce of energy they had to provide us with a wide range of opportunities. They took great care in passing along the values of their ancestors. What they did not do was school me in Christ. I didn't understand why people ignored the subject of God and His kingdom, most especially my parents. We did not go to church and my parents did not own a Bible. I was aware of a presence directing my path, but the only mention of God, Jesus and the Holy Spirit came from my prayers.

I don't blame my parents for this. Neither of them was brought up in a Christian-based home and they were unaware of how God's presence, with infinite possibilities, could affect the family. Susy and I were grounded in discipline. We were taught the fundamentals of the importance of education. Morals and values were paramount, yet the principles of following God were never taught to us.

Occasionally, I would quiz my parents about why we didn't go to church. The answer was always the same. "The demands of our work involve late nights and early mornings during the week and weekends, Andrea. It makes it very difficult for us to get to church for services."

Even without having a family committed to Christ, God's light and love came to live in me. In my childlike manner, I believed that there was something bigger than me, my mom, dad and sister—even the world. I believed the bigger thing was God. I received confirmations of this from the peace and joy in my heart and spirit during and after completing my prayers. I didn't have a Bible or a manual on how to communicate with God, but it happened naturally. No one taught me how to pray; I received those lessons from above. Faith ignited a fire in me, making me feel safe, complete and connected. It embraced me, providing me the most sacred times of my day.

Praying as a child brought me closer to God. Still, I somehow felt like I had to hide this from my parents; I didn't want them to interrupt the sanctity of my time with God. Fortunately, I had my own room and it provided me a private sanctuary in which to pray. My bed served as the platform to reach out to God. Every night, I firmly clasped my hands together and stretched them upward, as if each inch made a difference in touching the presence of God and His angels.

In prayer, I always felt at peace. Discomfort melted away. Fears dissipated and vanished. Confusion turned into certainty. Darkness gave way to a soothing light. I strived to broaden my horizons during prayer. I stepped forward into the wilderness of life, accepting the challenges, knowing full well that God would protect me.

Once, as I was silently thanking God in my special prayer position, I heard my bedroom door creaking open. I froze. I thought about hiding, but I knew running would be a cowardly act. I did not want to deny God His time with me or my time with Him. Thinking that I would be less visible if I held my breath, I gulped in a pocket of air and stayed in position. My eyes tightly closed, I could feel the tension build from my toes on up.

I heard a foot quietly step into my room. I waited to hear laughter, or perhaps even a question about what I was doing; none came. I could sense someone looking at me, taking in the situation. Then the door broke the silence, creaking as it shut. I opened my right eye, easily adjusting to the darkness, and caught a glimpse of my mom exiting my room. I continued pretending that I did not notice her presence. Thankfully, she saw me in my private moments with God and left with no interruptions.

The following morning, I prepared to confront my entire family about my faith. I walked to the kitchen ready to answer any question. I was anxious about how my prayers would be received—if they were accepted at all. The topic never came up. I waited for the inquisition. It never arrived. I was given the freedom to express myself in prayer. It was a milestone.

Normally, any activity in our house had to be presented to my parents for permission. This obviously proved to be an exception. As my childhood progressed, I felt the tug of war increase as several different worlds unfolded. Education always remained a priority, but my tennis talents were virtually starting to dictate my entire family's schedule. I was becoming the center of attention in my home, school, town and the junior tennis environment. I couldn't grasp the concept of everyone thinking I was special because I hit tennis balls. What was more exciting to me was the discovery of spiritual communication with God.

chapter Three

And you shall remember the Lord your God, for it is He who gives you power to get wealth.

—Deuteronomy 8:18

On the way to my first junior tennis tournament, no one in my family could have predicted that the road we were on would bring a wealth of knowledge and wisdom, riches and success. I entered my first tournament at the age of nine. Who would dare speculate that within five years I would be good enough to turn professional, break records and earn millions of dollars? Of course, God knew—He had those goals in mind for me.

I was small for my age and playing girls much bigger, older and stronger; this in turn made my parents hesitate to let me play in tournaments. Susy had been entered in events for years, and I was getting bored always sitting around watching. Finally, my begging paid off. My mom challenged the situation. "Roland, she is too young to engage in such hard competition."

My dad responded by trying to teach me how to keep score. "After fifteen comes thirty, then forty." Susy's role consistently involved trying to calm my parents down, explaining I was not going off to war, I was only going to play a tennis tournament.

Three conversations rambled on at once in the car heading over to the tennis club. Over and over again I was told, "Losing is not a disappointing result. Just try your best." Inside, I was laughing. The concern my parents had for my emotional well-being was humorous to me. I took Susy's perspective: It was not a big deal; it was only a little game.

My first match showcased my inexhaustible storehouse of energy. I switched sides on the odd changeovers as if I was racing to catch up with a soccer ball, while also using the time to wave to my family through the glass viewing area. I won the match and the entire tournament easily. The most stunned people in the tennis club were my parents.

The victory and small trophy ceremony didn't impress me. I had not gone to bed the previous night dreaming of winning. I certainly didn't feel different as a tournament champion.

Many other victories followed this tournament success. Still, even after my first twenty tournament wins, there was no discussion of the financial prospects unfolding before us. Thankfully, my parents didn't look at me as a meal ticket. Tennis still remained an enjoyable family activity. Winning was fun, but I had nothing to compare it to. It made some people happy, others distraught. Overall, chasing the ice cream truck on summer afternoons or finding monarch butterflies was more challenging.

I loved training but beating opponents didn't ignite a greater passion for the game; in fact, in many ways it disturbed me. Watching facial expressions and body language change on opponents as they went down and eventually lost left me terribly conflicted. The point of all my hard training was to win, obviously, but the fact that someone else had to lose hurt my spirit.

Soon my tennis life began to fall into predictable patterns. My parents had nervous anxiety in their stomachs at every competition, apprehensive that I was playing too far up in age groups. I played, won matches and a tall person would hand me a trophy. I was starting to get bored with the routine.

My dad decided to raise the stakes to make the tournaments more interesting. We created all types of games to keep me entertained. At one tournament, the goal was to not lose a game; at a few matches the challenge was to not lose a point. Other times, I created strategies of my own, which I kept throughout my pro career. In one of these, which I called "shot clock," I put restrictions on my game: For example, I had to win the point immediately before or after a certain number of strokes were hit. My parents also raised the bar by dangling interesting rewards that went beyond the tennis trophies I was obtaining. Prizes included having a family bowling outing, inviting friends over for special occasions, getting a skateboard, bringing home a dog, going to the movies and other inventive ways to keep me motivated during easy victories.

The local tournaments grew into sectional ranking events. Before we all knew it I was competing on a national stage. Being the number one under-twelve national champion did nothing in terms of pumping up my ego. It only served to isolate me from my peer group because I was defeating kids older than me. Eventually I moved up age groups, crossing borders, so by the time I was thirteen years old I was competing in collegiate and adult professional tournaments in order to be challenged. My dad's coaching skills were phenomenal. He certainly brought an edge to my performance that no other competitor I played against possessed.

Although losing was a rarity, my parents were worried about me experiencing dreadful defeats in the higher age brackets. I descended on any competition as if it was a science experiment, making sure the result would prove satisfying for audiences interested in my tennis talents, who wanted to discover how far they could push the envelope. In my case, it was farther than anyone had gone before.

Setting records as the youngest player to win prestigious

national and international competitions didn't captivate my attention. The games my parents added in older age groups were the reason I stayed so interested in the sport. In tennis rankings, the age categories ran from national twelve, fourteen, sixteen and eighteen before entering the twenty-one, collegiate or pro events. I was number one in the national twelve-and-unders; fourteen was just as easy. I skipped most of the sixteens' schedule to concentrate on under-eighteen competitions. At thirteen, I was number one in the country in the under-eighteens'—an unheard-of accomplishment.

The Orange Bowl, Easter Bowl, Seventeen Tournament and Grand Slam Cup were prestigious international competitive events. I succeeded in carrying home first-place trophies while beating players much older than me. These successes were not racking up a huge number of friends for me. Jealousy and resentment from fellow competitors surfaced in a variety of ways. For example, players and their families often complained that my place was in my own age group competition. Recently beaten opponents gave interviews, often lying about the facts, using me to get their own time in the spotlight. It was disappointing to see this ugly side of human nature.

I went into the new playing environments hoping not to make enemies because I was so talented, and to do well enough competitively to keep everyone happy with my progress. Ironically, the more successful I became as a tennis player, the further I isolated myself. Fortunately, I had Susy to protect my best interests like a mother bear guarding her cub.

Life became a strange mixture of good and bad. Children in school started poking fun at me because of my sporting achievements. *People* magazine, *Life* magazine, *Sports Illustrated* and numerous other major media came to visit my home, school and training center. I transcended into a place where I became a spectator in my own life. Animosity and anger leapt out at me from places that I was not expecting. Still, the positive far outweighed the negative. I was grateful that my tennis practice comrades at the local tennis club didn't get as enamored with all my press as most everyone around me did, children and adults alike. Besides, God still controlled the best part of me, and I was blessed with tremendous opportunities, which were blossoming all around me.

Pursuing tennis training without dislodging my relationship with God was imperative. It was apparent that God had a hold on my life as He provided ample gifts and taught me essential lessons while I was competing as a child. My tennis racket became a valuable instrument. In a bizarre way it became my voice, and it helped me get to worldwide locations where I was able to learn and research what was important to children from other places.

I flew to Australia more than ten times to play tennis. I was ten years old when I went the first time, as a member of the United States junior team. I was so small I could barely carry my tennis racket bag, but I was thrilled with the invitation and opportunity.

Thousands of miles from my home and family, at the international baggage claim area, my team inadvertently reminded me that God was always with me. As my green suitcase came into view, one of my teammates made it a point to loudly announce how the bag was held together with staples. I was dumbfounded. Before I had left home, I had watched admiringly as my parents gave me their suitcase, securing it with more staples so I wouldn't lose anything inside.

Now, I listened as the other players joined in on the humiliation, laughing and ridiculing me about my battered green suitcase. I turned inside myself, trying to think positively about this trip. For one, I was grateful my parents gave permission for the Australia trip, so that I could represent my country. They worked double shifts to give me care packages and money to buy Australian souvenirs for myself.

I thought back to my send-off. My dad, never a poster boy for showing love with physical affection, sent me off at the departure gate with a firm, "If you get homesick at any time, you can come home."

Susy hugged me and whispered in my ear, "If you need me to come out, I will be there."

My mom, on the other hand, was far more demonstrative. She brought enough love to light up the entire state of Illinois over the Christmas holidays. I had settled into the very last row in the back of the plane, listening to the flight attendants' preflight announcements, when I suddenly heard incredible sobbing noises coming from the front of the aircraft. We were only moments from shutting the doors and taxiing down the runway.

I poked my head around the seat in front of me and caught a glimpse of a frantic woman running down the aisle screaming, "Where is my baby?"

The hysterical noises had a familiar tone, I thought, but I pulled myself back into my seat. Then it dawned on me who it might be. "Oh my God," were the only words I could mutter as I shriveled into my seat. My mom was running down the aisle with tears flowing down her cheeks, arms flailing, determined to find her youngest daughter. Passengers watched in complete amazement. By the time my mother reached my seat at the very back of the plane, every passenger and crewmember had his or her eyes pasted on me. I was completely and utterly embarrassed.

"Mom, what are you doing? I said 'bye' to you at the house when you left for work." My mom, still nearly hysterical, said, "I couldn't let my baby go without saying good-bye again." Suddenly, I didn't feel humiliated any more, because people all around us were getting teary-eyed from the touching moment.

The pilot then announced on the intercom that all nonticketed passengers would have to leave the plane. It was the 1970s, and plane travel allowed for nontraveling parents to come on board to see their children off safely. "Mom, the pilot is saying you have to go now. Thanks for coming."

My mom asked a flight attendant for one more minute with me. She then handed me the biggest bag of comic and puzzle game books and candy that I had ever seen. She lavished hugs on me and made her move to depart the plane. Her entire walk down the aisle was backwards as she waved and kept eye contact.

Now, thousands of miles away in Australia, I had reached my destination—far from my family's love and protection—and was enduring disgrace from my own United States team members. I had packed the bag with pride. I saw love holding it together, not staples. However, I was the youngest competitor there, by years, and certainly hesitant to speak up to those more senior. Still, I was angry and felt the need to defend myself. As I was about to release the first barrage of words to shut up the group around me, God gently nudged my shoulder to get my attention. I kept hearing, "Resist yelling, resist yelling. There is a better plan."

I hesitated. Backing up for a minute, I waited for a confirmation. I really wanted to let loose with a few remarks of my own. God adamantly told me, "Don't react now. There is a plan that will bring great gifts to you and your family. Let it go, because the plan in store is better."

It was not my conscience talking. Even my conscience wanted to sound off. Instead of reacting with hurt and anger, I backed off. I murmured under my breath as I walked away from the incident, "God, they are all yours." Sure enough, true to His word, God provided.

The Australian Junior Tennis Federation in conjunction with the Bonne Bell Cup tournament sponsor gave every member of our team spending money. I was able to purchase and bring home several presents for my parents and sister in the green, stapled suitcase that I had come to love.

God must have anointed that bag, because it was a miracle it stayed together on such a long journey. I never had a doubt that the staples would hold on the way home, because inside were prized possessions made possible by God's helpful and giving nature.

Throughout my childhood, finding reaction skills when I was picked on unmercifully occupied a great deal of my time. I was challenged on how to obtain results—working at 100 percent of my capacity—without hurting other people's feelings. At times, it seemed difficult, if not impossible, to keep everything in balance. If I worked hard on my studies and received good grades, other students became upset. Training diligently helped me achieve success on the tennis court, but it disturbed my peers.

The uncomfortable reactions were from children and adults alike. Watching how disappointed competitors, parents, adults, peer group individuals, and associates became when I won or did well was tricky enough. But to endure the trauma of how a loss or negative result affected someone else was excruciating. It tormented me to see anyone disappointed because of what I could do well.

Children being yelled at and beaten up because their forehands or backhands were not up to par seemed to be a ridiculous price to pay. One fellow competitor, who sported a cool, red tennis racket, became so distraught after her tennis losses, and with life in general, that she committed suicide. It was a scary scenario to see how people around me placed tennis as the number one and only valuable thing in their lives. Watching and taking in the "get to number one at all costs" atmosphere caused me to withdraw from others, and it became a major force in how I would develop and carry myself.

The best comfort zone I could retreat to, given my circumstances, was to increase my interaction with God. I could always be true to myself and never have to worry about hiding who I was with God. I knew God loved me whether I won or lost a tennis match. He kept His outstretched arms around me if I received an A or a C on a school assignment. I didn't have to perform as a tennis player or a student for God to love me. He loved me because of what He was made of and who He was, not because of what I was doing or not doing.

Chapter Four

It is doubtless not profitable for me to boast.
I will come to visions and revelations
of the Lord.

—2 Corinthians 12:1

My early adolescent years were cataclysmic for me in several areas of my life. It was a time of character building and further enhancement of my relationship with God.

Playmate after playmate from school disappeared because of my tennis training demands and increasing notoriety. I was in many ways relieved, and responded by retreating to my bedroom and pouring my energy into homework.

My parents were focused on keeping me out of trouble. I would frequently overhear my father explaining to my mom, "The time Susy and Andrea spend on the tennis courts is time they are staying off of street corners and far away from drugs, violence and guns. When they are done training they are too tired to do anything stupid to get them into trouble and that is how it should be."

While tennis might have shielded us from street crime, it wasn't the ultimate protective canopy. Within the dictates of this etiquette-laden sport, I learned many lessons about human nature, and they were often ruthless.

For several years in the junior doubles competitions, I teamed up with an enormously talented player. We were like a wall—nothing got by us. We racked up title after title and we seemed unstoppable. The problem was I hated it. Our victories were hollow.

My partner was often cited for cheating. I had the unfortunate experience of dealing with the situation firsthand in singles matches against this girl. My dad changed my game plan to hit a few feet inside the lines because of concern that I would be cheated out of victories. From the sideline, I would catch glimpses of a large figure menacingly walking the sidelines. I felt for the child under the threat of this man, and he wasn't even my father—he was my opponent's dad.

After one grueling match of protesting line calls against this particular player, I said to my dad, "I don't get it. You taught me that anyone who cheats, also steals and lies, and you expect me to play doubles with her?" My dad, in his obey-me-or-else voice, replied, "She is the best player. You both make a great team. We will request a line judge in matches, so no one will get cheated a point."

I knew what that tone in his voice meant. My dad was a big believer in discipline.

This discipline helped me grasp many lessons: Respect your elders, work hard and diligently, pull your own weight and don't talk back. The problem was I often forgot the don't-talk-back rule. Whenever I mouthed off to him in a "I think it's like this" or disrespectful tone, I would get a scolding or beating and that solved the problem for a while until I forgot again. There was always a purpose behind my father's discipline and I respected it. He gave me a lot of leeway, and if I pushed the envelope, he was there to remind me of my place.

I believed that my doubles partner's father didn't necessarily follow a principle with his discipline. His purpose was the awful "win at all costs" attitude. So rather than get in trouble for losing, the girl tried to win by cheating.

In my book, cheating was wrong for three reasons: First, if I cheated, participating in an act I knew was morally wrong, my dad would take the belt to me; second, I knew God would have seen it and been extremely disappointed in me; and third, cheating was unfair, regardless of the reason.

During one doubles match with this girl, our opponents refused to partake in the traditional post-match handshake. They were angry about all the balls that the umpire corrected, making us either replay the point or giving the point outright to our opponents.

After the match, I protested vehemently to my dad, practically getting on my knees and begging him to let me get a new partner. His response was a resolute, "No!"

Loyalty to a cheating ship seemed a little past my responsibilities as a partner. Finally, the day came when I was given permission to pick a new partner and I jumped with excitement. I chose my sister, because I knew I could always trust her to play fair. If Susy was at fault for anything, it was going the other way on calls. If she ever had a hesitation at all, she would give the point to her opponent. It was an admirable quality that did cost her several matches, but no one ever walked off angry with her. Susy made friends at every corner.

The sacrifice Susy made to become my doubles partner was quite impressive. Now, she was going to be stuck traveling with her younger sister throughout the year. She became my full-time chaperone, which was also beneficial for my parents because it cut down on their ever-increasing travel expenses.

The entire family made great financial sacrifices for my budding career. They gave up their lifestyle, European vacations, stylish cars and personal spending money to get the dollars together for adequate training, court time, entry fees and travel expenses. Susy and

I traveled around the world staying in housing situations with kind and caring local families who supported junior tennis events. She and I spent four years on the road together before she went to Stanford University, and I cherished our time together.

ℂℂℂ   ℂℂℂ   ℂℂℂ

As the momentum of my tennis accomplishments steamrolled ahead, I faced the typical turbulent rites of passage associated with going from childhood to adolescence. Through these often-difficult times, God held me close, and provided me with assurance of his love through incredible visions that could only be described as miraculous.

One night, I was fast asleep when God awakened me with His voice. It pierced right through me, but it was not frightening. It was strong, full of guidance, protection and love. Anytime God spoke to me it felt like an intercom system to my spirit. It would wake up everything inside of me and make me come to full attention. There was no mistaking—ever—where the voice came from.

This particular time, God said, "Wake up and look out the window." I didn't really want to. I always listened intently when His instructions came, much as I did when my earthly father gave me tennis tips. However, this took on a different dimension. I was usually awake when I heard God's commands, but now I was asleep and cozy in my warm, comfortable bed. This was going to take some effort. God understood my weariness and instead of departing, He tried to get my attention again. God said, "Wake up and look out the window."

I was curled up in a ball, facing my wall and not the picture window. I'd have to turn *and* open my eyes, again, expending more effort than I was used to at this hour. I flickered my eyes open, but my eyelids were so heavy they immediately closed again. As I struggled to wake up, I felt a presence on the other side of me, exactly at the picture window. Goosebumps appeared on my legs. Not because of fear, but because of awareness. My eyes flew open, desperate to see the image that was taking over my room. I pushed my covers back slightly and turned ever so slowly, not wanting to create an imbalance of the energy in the room.

I trusted God. If He felt I needed to look out the window, I would do exactly as He commanded. Now, my curiosity was awakened as well. I was not disoriented in the least. I turned and immediately saw a man outside my bedroom window. If I had seen the figure without God's command to look, I might have been scared. I was not frightened, however, because I knew that this man came with God's love, light and protection.

The figure faced me, extremely sure of his purpose and place. He was silhouetted against the window, with a slight, flickering glow surrounding his form. I couldn't make out details such as facial features or see what material he was clothed in. While he definitely looked human, he most certainly could have been an angel. He had a stillness about him, and a sense of purpose that was very distinct. Even though he appeared solid, I felt as though I could look through his body. His hand was gracefully outstretched, as though he wanted to shake my hand. With this gesture, God sent me this message: "Welcome my child. Come to me. I am your protector."

A tremendous sense of purpose, light, love, protection, peace, comfort and joy came upon me at that moment, which was how I could always recognize God. Darkness elicited from evil or non-enlightened energy was always heavy, disturbing and something I felt I needed to avoid. It became easy for me to tell the difference between the two. God wanted me to know that anytime, anywhere, He and His angels were watching over me. I was to call on them when needed.

I could have chosen to bypass God's instruction, quietly going back to sleep, but I would have missed out on this amazing encounter. My life changed because I followed God's instruction, because I knew that His presence was always around. This experience also helped secure the sanctuary my room provided as I tried to sort through all the changes in my life.

One time, God gave me a glimpse of what my life would become. While I was awake and inside my Lincolnshire home, I had a vision of a scene in the American West. As with other visions God provided to me, it was like receiving an image on a television screen. A large group of friendly people, wearing cowboy hats and other Western clothing, were gathered in a rather dimly lit place with rough-hewn wood floors. It was large, like a gathering hall of sorts, and was filled with laughter, happiness and celebration. Now, instead of merely watching the setting from inside my suburban Illinois home, I felt as if I was in the scene. I hid behind a pole so as not to disturb anyone.

The people's kind nature and the festive feel of the gathering drew me in. I leaned out from behind the pole when one of the people saw me. I recoiled and then froze. I didn't have a clue what to do. One of the adults, who had previously settled in to enjoy the music and company, motioned for me to join in on the fun. I meekly made my way to the center of the room. All eyes were on me, and people greeted me as if I was one of their own. Someone pulled out a chair, providing a place for me to feel free to enjoy the fun. It was a grand party arranged by God and was, indeed, a precursor of where I would live in my twenties and thirties. I did not know this at the time, of course, but I took note of this very vivid scene, because I knew it was important.

I encountered many visions like this, and I never questioned them or asked myself, "Wow, where did that come from?" To me, they were natural. It was normal for me, like the way other kids find entertainment from watching television or playing a video game. In a matter of minutes, I was back in my room in Lincolnshire, going about my business. These visions were more than entertainment, of course, and they made me realize that there was always something better ahead as long as God was the artist of my life.

While I was accustomed to having God's presence in my life exhibited in such spectacular fashion, I kept this part of my life concealed from everyone, including my family. I had ample opportunity to explain some of the things God was showing me, especially since we traveled by car to tennis tournaments, practice centers, school, soccer games and my parents' work establishments. Still, I could not find the words to tell them about it. It was awkward, and I thought it best to wait before I said anything.

While the drives may not have helped my parents understand me better, I often learned things about them I did not know. One day, my dad and I were driving from our home in the suburbs to my parents' restaurant in downtown Chicago. He had long since traded in the Corvette and the Cadillac for a more economical car, a Volkswagen. I always enjoyed these trips into the city. Chicago was so vibrant and alive with activity. I was in the middle of a reading assignment when my dad interrupted me. Pointing to a building in the emerging Chicago skyline, he said, "I helped build that."

I opened the window to get a clear view and asked, "What is it?" The brick and cement structure rose up powerfully into the sky.

"A children's hospital," he said joyfully, the words veritably exploding from his mouth. It was the first time I looked at my dad and thought, *Wow! What an important man.* Before this revelation, he was just my dad. Now, I recognized his greater responsibility in life. His purpose was not only to raise his own children to stay out of trouble; it was also to provide a safe haven for children who were sick and needed medical care.

This was another defining moment in my life. Through the bricks and mortar, out the window of my dad's car, I made a connection with the patients inside the Children's Memorial

Hospital. Without having direct, face-to-face communication, I could feel their pain, like when you meet someone and get a sense of who they are. The spirits of these children were reaching out to mine. I promised God I would always remember them. I made good on that pledge and, not quite twenty years later, the children from that facility would be the first participants in the children's cancer foundation that I started in Aspen.

Under His watchful eyes, God was positioning me for great tennis success, children's humanitarian efforts and Colorado Rocky Mountain living: events that he revealed to me in advance, but which would come together later.

By the time I graduated from Daniel Wright Junior High, I had become somewhat used to the glare of the spotlight. While an array of parents took pictures of their children during graduation ceremonies, the large lenses of the media eagerly clicked away at me. I was never intimidated by the interviews and photo sessions. Instead, I found them intriguing. This was in large part due to the numerous kind people in the media who took me under their protective wings at this early stage in my career. One such couple was Johnnie and Jeannie Morris, a celebrated sportscasting team that came into the living rooms of viewers throughout the Chicago area.

Johnnie was a former Chicago Bears football player who turned to television broadcasting once he hung up his jersey. Johnnie and Jeannie interviewed me many times, and each occasion was like visiting close relatives for a fun-filled afternoon. Their genuine and caring natures gave me a special bond with the media that could never be broken. At the tender age of ten, after one of our television interviews, Johnnie gave me one of his prized football photos. The autographed inscription read, "To Andrea, Your sparkle will add to your success."

My introduction to major print media was identical. Ray Sons from the *Chicago Sun-Times* was always respectful when he came to our Lincolnshire home for interviews. He was warm, kind and nurturing, and I easily placed my trust in him. Because of Ray, Johnnie and Jeannie, I established a special rapport with the media that I would always treasure.

In between the major changes in my life, God was stepping up the pace in my spiritual life, continuing to set the stage for my calling to come into full view. He would often drop in a dramatic message during some normal activity. Once, I was sitting quietly in my junior high classroom when God presented me with a life-changing vision. The teacher had given a reading assignment to the class and we were all quietly focused on our books. I was in the middle of a sentence when, out of nowhere, I heard children screaming for help. Startled, I abruptly straightened up in my chair and looked across the room to locate the commotion.

The classroom was as quiet as before; the teacher continued grading her papers, and the other kids were continuing their silent reading exercise. However, the screams continued. I kept turning my head, hoping to see another student who was also hearing the pleas for help. The screams changed from only an audible situation to an entire scene displayed before me as if I was at a movie. Thankfully, I was becoming accustomed to God's projection ability and power in revealing messages, otherwise I might have high-tailed it out of the class, screaming at the top of my lungs.

In the vision, I saw children wearing somewhat crude military attire, and they appeared to be going off to battle in the hilly European countryside. The cries kept coming, "Save us! Please help save us!" They were staring at me, as though they knew something about me I was unaware of. I didn't see their enemy, but way off in the distance, I sensed an overwhelming spiritual darkness and sense of danger.

God narrated in the background and told me this was the Children's Crusades.

Even before I learned the facts behind this scene, the mission was obvious. These children, thousands of them, were willing to risk their own lives because God called on them to serve. They followed an unseen force to battle against an enemy in order to advance the kingdom of God. The nobility and honor of such a prestigious position was not lost on any of the children or me. I was chosen to hear the children's pleas, not because they were scared or feared death, but because they were chosen to serve one of their purposes by directing me on my course. The children were in charge of equipping me and instructing me on my calling.

I became part of this army of children. In a ceremonial, rhythmic pattern, the children moved forward, more determined with each step. Every detail in this very real and serious vision was powerfully imprinted on my mind and spirit. I could feel the soft breeze gently on my face; the sounds of the children's movement on the grass echoed in my ears. Although it was obvious that I was the only one in my class who saw this, I wanted everyone to be part of the glory God released. It was then that I understood the message was specifically designed for me.

This vision stayed with me for the rest of my life, but I didn't research the historical accuracy of it until January 2003. Up until that point, I stood in faith that the vision was truthful; it wasn't until this much later date that God decided I needed to know more about it. Without giving any background, I asked the Silver Lining Foundation's program coordinator to find some facts on the Children's Crusades.

My staff member found the information in a Christian History Institute interview with C. D. Baker, author of *Crusade of Tears:*

What exactly were the "Children's Crusades"? He was asked.

Baker went on to explain that in the spring and summer of 1212, two separate, yet related events occurred. In France, a twelve-year-old shepherd boy named Stephen claimed he saw a vision of Jesus calling him to lead an army of children. . . . In Germany, near Cologne, a ten-year-old boy named Nicholas claimed a similar vision. In response to their calls, thousands of children began to gather in both regions to proclaim a crusade in which God would honor the innocence and purity of children. . . . The two simultaneous pilgrimages were together called the "Children's Crusades."

Wow! I took in a few major breaths. The confirmations were all there, plus revelatory explanations of what was in my vision. The facts lining up didn't startle me; rather, I felt serenity in knowing how much God was involved in guiding me to my calling. He was dedicated to my life's purpose even before I knew what it was.

Once again, God was recruiting me to my calling. He instilled in me the importance of helping children in the world. I fully comprehended that the Children's Crusades did exist, and I was to be instrumental in helping children in a crusade of my own, directed by God.

Chapter Five

"But whoever causes one of these little ones who believe in Me to stumble, it would be better for him if a millstone were hung around his neck, and he were thrown into the sea."

—Jesus, in Mark 9:42

The paths my spiritual and natural life took were the very things that kept me the most grounded. Since I worked best in forward motion, I surged ahead with determination. It wasn't easy to ignore the increased attention I received as I walked the school hallways, tried to eat lunch in the cafeteria or attempted to make my way on the pro tennis tour. At an age where everyone strives to be part of the group, I stood out. I wasn't just another kid, and if my notoriety as a sports personality were not enough, my introspective nature made me even more of an oddity to my schoolmates.

My family tried desperately to get me to fit in with other schoolchildren, but their efforts in helping with my acceptance proved futile. I had the right clothes, shoes and new school supplies every year. I appreciated my parents' actions, but no matter how they worked on improving my life, I still felt like an outsider. Truthfully,

I didn't want to fit in. I was a little different from the norm, but I viewed that as a good quality.

If I had to rank the three parts of my life at that time, it would be like this: Spiritually, I was running on all cylinders; academically, I was holding my own; emotionally, I shut down, retreating into my own world because the companionship God provided far outweighed any interest I had in anything else. At school I stopped attending casual gatherings, dances, school trips and friendly neighborhood events. I wanted to avoid more opportunities for people to stare at the girl who was a household name in national tennis media circles. In some ways, this extra time was helpful. I used the time productively, studying and training, and the results paid off in better grades, sharper tennis skills and less concern that I didn't relate to anyone on a spiritual level.

I didn't want anything more from school than to get a great education. My family and the school administration bent over backwards to help with the growing media requests and curriculum work I could take on the road. When I was in class, I looked up to my teachers and was glued to their every word, often asking for extra credit assignments simply because I enjoyed the challenge. This gave some students another reason to mock me.

Kids who are ridiculed, as I was, often take their hurt feelings out destructively, either on themselves or others. I was fortunate that God and my faith helped me choose other options. The individuals who tried to break my spirit actually helped make me stronger. They became catalysts for me to get closer to God, because He represented love, protection and truth. He helped me block out negative thoughts that my mind could have conjured up—if I had taken to heart what people were saying about me.

God presented solutions that I believed would solve my dilemmas. I was under the full understanding, as a child of God, that suffering was part of life. And I was a survivor. My philosophy was not fueled by youthful ignorance; it was rightful understanding of how God was going to take care of me. He promised to do so, and I stood on His Word that He would. Besides, compared to my parents' war stories, a few bullies didn't seem to be that difficult to overcome.

By the time I started shattering tennis records, I was not only walking toward God for my main companionship, I was sprinting. He didn't love me more when I won a match, and He certainly didn't distance Himself from me when I lost. It was a fair agenda that helped keep me sane as I watched people adore me on one side and mock me on the other.

As God's presence and force became stronger in my spirit, our relationship grew beyond friendship. He was my Almighty protector in whom I put total faith to handle all dangerous and confusing situations. Clinging to Him helped me break through experiences, rather than stay stuck and damaged in traumatic episodes.

I spent many hours of my young life practicing at the tennis club located next to Trinity University. As much as I loved the surroundings of the tennis facility, I longed to be at the college's chapel. Most of the time, I diligently made my way to the courts, practicing with great intensity. On a few occasions, I would sneak away and race over to the chapel. Every time I did, I felt God's light opening up a path for me.

I loved the peaceful atmosphere and solitude in the sanctuary areas. I happily spent my free time, between learning forehands and backhands, in this sacred place. Completely feeling God's presence, I sat and talked to my best friend, realizing He was listening, understanding and helping me more than the people I was following for direction.

Since God was so real to me, I never doubted that He could see and hear everything that was happening to me. When one of our training sessions turned ugly, God proved He was watching over me and the other children I was with in a delightful way.

One sizzling summer day a tennis instructor went on a rampage and decided to take his rage out on us. He ordered us to run until we dropped, or were told to stop, at the field separating the courts on 22 Tennis Club and Trinity's School. I was not happy about this but I kept my mouth shut and obeyed like everyone else.

The blazing sun glared down on us, its heat intensifying with every step we took. There was not even a hint of a breeze, and the humidity that day was stifling. Our clothes were soaked with sweat and we were all miserable.

I could run for hours if there was a purpose behind it, but this was plain torture. Running as punishment because someone else was in a bad mood seemed a pretty poor training technique to me. The instructor was pushing us over the edge for his personal enjoyment— and it wasn't the first time. We weren't adults in boot camp; we were children. I pushed on, knowing the end had to be near, using part of the time to concentrate on my cravings for a vanilla milkshake and crispy fries at Trinity's snackroom.

As I trudged along I heard kids who had already collapsed vow never to pick up a tennis racket again. At that point, I could not hold in my frustration any longer. I was reaching the point when I would have to voice my displeasure.

I was one of the few remaining kids in motion and the only girl still standing. Seeing this, the instructor decided to turn the torture up a notch with a competition between the sexes. The coach cruelly belittled the boys and drew them into a rivalry with me. They looked over at me, dejected. Now, they couldn't stop until I did, or they would be ridiculed even more.

My mind spun with ways to confront the coach, then drifted back to the milkshake-and-fries reward I was going to give myself when this ridiculous training activity was over. Then a startling realization hit me: I had no money. The shock of this almost made me stop. My interest in the fries and shake was the only thing helping me cope with the ordeal. I regained my composure and carried on.

The coach continued to berate the boys. I said to myself, *This is so messed up and wrong. Something has to be done to stop this man.* At that exact moment, I fell. I didn't trip in a hole, catch my shoe on a rock or get tangled in anyone's legs. The nearest runner was over ten feet away and this part of the lawn was smooth and rock-free. I fell as if something grabbed both my legs, held them and flipped me in the air. No forward motion was possible. Suspended with no base of support, I fell smack in the grass. The boys smiled in complete relief and all the children looked happy that the ordeal was over.

The instructor continued to shout, "We are done here. Be back at the courts in one hour. This lesson better have sunk in." We were all dumbfounded at his comments and no one had the energy to complain about more tennis time. The kids who had quit early made their way up and sauntered slowly over to the club. I was still on the ground, perplexed about my sudden fall. My knees were grass-stained, and I had a clump of mud stuck in my hair. I moved into a kneeling position, ready to stand up, when I noticed something next to my leg. It was a twenty-dollar bill! I grabbed it triumphantly, as though I had just won the lottery, and bolted upright.

I let out a shriek of excitement, suddenly realizing why I had fallen. My strange tumble had a purpose. I was astonished that God was watching over a thing so minor as children running in a field, but He wanted to show that He was well aware of the mistreatment going on. I was sure He didn't like it. Even in defeat, my stumble had God's grace attached to it. With the twenty dollars I found, I bought fries and milkshakes not only for myself, but also for the boys who trudged to the end with me. God made sure that our sour experience had a sweet ending!

Chapter Six

Now when Job's three friends heard of all this adversity that had come upon him, each one came from his own place . . . to comfort him.

—Job 2:11

By the time I turned fourteen in 1979, I had outgrown playing with other children at my backyard birthday parties. Instead, my summers were spent in Europe playing in tennis events. This was the year I moved up from junior tennis to turn professional. I was the youngest player at the time to do this, and I was becoming a real novelty for the athletic world.

I'll always remember the discussion my family held as we jointly deliberated about whether I would turn pro. The conversation took place in the dining area of our house. Although still a minor, I had input on important scheduling decisions, travel situations, training methods and product endorsements that could earn millions of dollars before I would graduate high school. All throughout this very important conversation, I played with my new Matchbox cars and speed ramps that Susy gave me as a special gift.

"Andrea, this is serious. Please sit at the table so we can discuss this," Susy announced.

I answered back, "I don't understand what the big deal is. We went through this already. I want to turn pro. It will be fun."

Susy, ever the mediator, continued, "Come on Andrea, we need to go over everything with you." My mom nervously sat at the table, as if the decision would mean she was abandoning her child.

"Look," I said as I sped my favorite maroon car down the ramp, "it is stupid to be winning so much prize money and having to return it all as we are chalking up tons of traveling and training expenses. And no way am I going back to juniors. To do that would be so boring. This will be fun."

Susy continued, "This would mean you could never play on a collegiate team. You always wanted to do that."

"Well, that was when it was the only way to get to college, because we couldn't afford the tuition without a scholarship. Now maybe I can earn money to go to college one day," I reasoned.

Again, Susy covered all the bases. "You will have to quit the high school tennis team."

I rolled my eyes, exasperated. "I won the state tournament for Stevenson once. Come on! Seriously, I want to do this. Can we just get on with it because it really isn't that big of a deal?"

And that was it. The Jaeger family collectively made the decision for me to turn pro, but the weight of the commitment gladly fell on me. My family never pressured me—nor did anyone else—to make this move and catapult myself into an adult world with extremely different demands.

The main difference between being an amateur and a professional competitor was the fact that I could keep the money I was earning. We could review earning and endorsement opportunities in a whole different light because we would not have to be concerned about ruining my amateur status. Tennis is an expensive sport and my parents had made many sacrifices to keep Susy and me involved. While they weren't talking about money, they were counting it, sometimes late at night on the kitchen table, scraping together everything they had to nurture my budding career.

I didn't base my decision on money, though it certainly entered into the discussion as I thought of all the prize money I had to return as an amateur. I wanted to help my family after all the sacrifices they had made, but I was determined that I was not going to be a slave to money. Earnings were never brought up as a reason to make the decision to turn pro. What ultimately led me to take this natural next step in my career was the fascination with the new challenges and opportunities that turning professional would have on my life—both on and off the court.

A couple of immediate benefits came as a result of our family meeting.

First, because of my recent amateur results in a Las Vegas qualifying professional event, winning thirteen matches consecutively, I earned my right to be part of any two professional tournaments of my choice. We were all thrilled because that meant I could start my professional career at the Virginia Slims of Chicago tournament, where I could share the celebration with my family and hometown. Second, I would still be able to attend Stevenson High School and, with extra effort, graduate on schedule with the rest of my class.

It felt right to pursue my love of the game by being challenged and having fun. It was a terrific start to an amazing career, always under the watchful eyes of God.

My first year on the professional circuit, I won the rookie of the year award. Never had a fourteen-year-old, or any teenager, come into the pros and ascended so quickly up the rankings. I never had to worry about my qualifications being insufficient to make the strict cuts to get in the tour events. I was good enough to challenge the best adult players in the world.

At the 1980 gala ceremony in New York, where I was to receive my award, I had adults all around me telling me what to say in my acceptance speech. God had other ideas for me. He wanted me to say how He was filling my spirit. The Plaza Hotel ballroom was crowded with admiring tennis fans of all ages. I didn't want to be a fraud and speak from the heart of other adults, I wanted God's words to come forth.

Wearing fancy attire and walking in heels took some adjustment. For years, I'd only worn tennis shoes or sometimes winter boots outside and socks inside, so my walk started off a bit wobbly. I practiced during the reception part of the evening and happily ended up meeting the poster child for the March of Dimes, which was the charity associated with the awards dinner. She was young and had a big smile, just like me. But we also had some big differences: She could only walk with two supportive metal braces. While her steps were labored, she never lost her smile. It was an impressive display of how the spirit can shine through even in the most difficult of circumstances.

This girl had a big impact on me. Immediately, I knew what I would say in my speech. I wanted people to remember the real champions in the room. I couldn't look at the poster child and get up on stage and talk about me being someone special because I received an award. I had a bigger responsibility than saying thank you for my award. I was determined to get the girl and other children like her more help.

It was the first time I had the good fortune to be placed on such a spectacular stage, in front of an audience full of powerful and influential people. I was going to take advantage of the opportunity. I needed the audience to remember the kids who were not as fortunate as I was. The prestigious title and pricey Rolex watch that came with it were of little interest to me; my purpose here was to convey a message for people to reach out and help children fighting diseases.

As my family and I sat through the dinner, we were constantly interrupted by people who wanted to congratulate me, wish me well and tell me what I needed to say in my speech. It was easy for me to turn off what I didn't think was useful. I didn't fault the people who offered me advice; they were only trying to ease what they assumed would be a normal fifteen-year-old's anxiety about speaking before thousands of people.

I wasn't nervous. There was no reason to be stressed. If God was guiding me, then protection, peace, confidence and comfort would surround and fill me. That was exactly what happened. As I sat there in my flowery formal attire, God said, "Speak from your heart. Share what concerns you. Don't worry about reactions; the only way to speak is from the truth I have placed in your heart."

I couldn't get on stage fast enough. I knew exactly what I wanted to express: "There is a special child in the ballroom who needs your help and it is not me." I continued, "We have the privilege of being healthy, but my new friend, who I met tonight, has to fight for her life. We need to remember to help her and others like her through children's programs." I was feeling God's glory coming out of my mouth and I saw the effects. I finished by including more information about my new friend, "The poster child who came here tonight is the true person to be honored this evening."

Talking about giving to help children was of paramount importance to me. I was healthy, led by God in my life, and was making enormous amounts of money. What help did I need? But my success was the perfect vehicle to guarantee a child being helped somewhere, somehow.

I returned to my table to thunderous applause. My mom was sobbing, dabbing at her eyes valiantly with a tissue. She was not alone. People all over the hall were moved to tears. Countless people approached me afterward saying, "That was beautiful; how did you know what to say?" My response every time was, "I was told to speak from my heart." And the reply typically was, "That is the best advice to follow every time." God had a mission for me way back then. His influence and mentoring was constant. I just happened to pay attention enough to listen and follow.

I knew God had provided me with a successful career, honoring my training and accomplishments, and I certainly wasn't going to apologize for that; I was going to use it to help others. Besides, I enjoyed the blessings being passed around.

⌒ ⌒ ⌒

I had many great experiences with the media, who were intrigued by my combination of youth and athletic ability. While waiting in the green room of the *Good Morning America* show, I met the popular horror and suspense author Stephen King, who also wrote about justice and redemption, and would eventually get critical acclaim for *The Shawshank Redemption* screenplay and many other great works. His short story, "The Mist," was a favorite of mine. Stephen politely responded to every question I had: "So do you get scary nightmares at night? How do you find your material? Does anything scare you?" I was having a total ball.

David Letterman treated me as a special guest on his show. Never once did he talk down to me. In fact, his laughter and humor were so contagious I went away wishing we had more chat time.

I felt I was given an ambassadorship to represent children all around the world. Various celebrities and media representatives asked for instructions on backhands and forehands. My pigtails and braces were beamed across the globe in satellite interviews. After each match, win or lose, I was brought to a press conference area to answer reporters' questions. Unbeknownst to me, God was forging relationships that would prove to be incredibly important in my future children's foundation work.

It would have been easy to get caught up in the privileged life of a professional tennis player, and I had to work hard not to get spoiled by it. All the top players had transportation vehicles that took them to requested addresses. The locker room was full of sponsor gifts. Brand new practice balls were passed out every day. My all-time favorite was hotel room service. I was completely fascinated by the fact that I could pick up the phone and order food at will, and receive it in my room in less than thirty minutes, any time of the day or night.

I was having way too much fun to bother paying attention to the insecurities that some players and classmates had in relation to the attention my tennis talents were receiving. Even when I was defeated easily in my premier professional debut in the first round of the Virginia Slims of Chicago tournament, I had a blast. I dove for balls out of my reach, changed sides as if I was racing to a carnival and enjoyed the full-capacity crowd atmosphere.

The only major adjustment for me was playing featured matches late in the evening. I liked tucking myself in bed at eight or nine with a good book or homework assignment. Now I had to be at my peak performance at eight, nine and sometimes even eleven o'clock at night.

It took me until the second tour event to organize my body clock to perform better at night. Susy, my wise seventeen-year-old sister and travel chaperone, and I headed to the Virginia Slims tournament in Seattle to secure victories and have fun in a new city. My draw was a tough one. Thirty-two of the top players in the world, and I had well-established veterans Rosie Casals, Wendy Turnbull and Sue Barker in my wake. Susy called home to announce my first-round opponent and section in the draw. My parents seemed defeated by the battles before they had begun.

Susy made the collect call after my first match and handed me the phone. My parents gave strict instructions to call regardless of the time. We didn't have to worry about waking them; they were too nervous to sleep. "Hi! It's Andrea. I won tonight."

My parents both said in unison, "You did not. Put Susy on the line." Susy took the phone and the responsibility of convincing my parents that I really did accomplish a win that they thought impossible. They didn't believe her either, at first, but were finally convinced the good news was true. Exchanging the phone back and forth we heard congratulatory remarks at octaves that could shatter glass.

My mom started crying after her shrieks diminished in intensity. "Andrea, we are so proud of you. What did you wear?" My mom was always concerned about my attire.

I said, "Don't worry Mom, I even matched." This was actually beyond a normal parental interest. I had signed large endorsement contracts with Fila clothes and Wilson rackets. It wasn't only playing well that my parents stressed about; I had to look good, too.

My dad came on to discuss the more technical parts of the game and proceeded to give me strategies again on all the players in my section of the draw.

He asked, "Did Rosie Casals crowd the net like I said?"

"Yes, Dad, and I lobbed her like you said."

"Wendy Turnbull is lightning fast," he went on, "so try to keep her on the baseline and remember to pass with that short cross-court angle. And if you lose, it is okay. We are so proud of you already."

"Dad, I know," I told him. "I used your game plan tonight and it worked, just as you said. I will do exactly as you say tomorrow."

I enjoyed the bantering and excitement that my first professional win brought my family. Even the people walking by the arena pay phone were amused by our conversations, offering up their "Well done" remarks, too. This continued for three matches in a row as I beat high-ranking and seeded players. Seeing my family so happy was the best part of winning.

During this particular tour stop, as I was racking up victories, I made my first tour friend. The major dilemma of late-night matches was getting solved, but a new one surfaced: locker-room life. I hated being stuck in such close quarters. It was too hard to hang out in public areas before matches because of safety issues and needing quiet time. Fans approached with autograph requests and questions, and although I enjoyed the rapport, I needed the time to focus on the battles ahead.

Old memories of feeling awkward and shy in front of fellow gym-class students resurfaced. It was traumatizing for me to change in front of people. I used bathroom stalls to dress and undress and refused to shower until safely back in the privacy of my housing or hotel room. Some kids have no problems when it comes to locker-room situations; others do. Unfortunately, I was one of the children who had an awkwardness changing around anyone, even family members.

I usually kept my head down the whole time I was in the locker room, as that helped alleviate some of my anxiety. Fortunately, again, God brought a blessing to me. At my post-match press conference, a reporter commented on how Wendy Turnbull, the player I defeated, commented positively about my abilities. For some time, the players I defeated were not too eager to remark objectively about my chances to make it on the circuit. Wendy, minutes after losing to me, went out of her way to pay homage to my efforts.

I was impressed. I wasn't on a mission to be concerned about what other competitors thought of my game, but it was refreshing to hear someone be respectful and professional. I returned to the locker room dreading the shower and changing ritual. Hiding in my corner, I decided my shyness was going to succeed again. Skipping the shower routine until returning to my hotel, I fled to the bathroom stall to change my shirt. As I sat back in my chair to gather my belongings, I noticed Wendy and a tour press liaison searching for a corkscrew. Wendy evidently decided that losing to a kid called for a drink. The locker room was nearly empty by this time since we were the featured night match.

Wendy showed no animosity and settled in, accepting I was going to be a force to be reckoned with on the circuit. The atmosphere in the locker room was light. Organizing my rackets, I looked up and smiled at the comfort that suddenly came upon me. Wanting to make a gesture to Wendy, I remembered my special black Swiss Army knife that my grandfather had given me. It was secure in my racket bag. With joy greater than my match success provided, I opened the zipper compartment and pulled out the knife. I placed the corkscrew upright, ready to do its job.

I proudly walked over to Wendy and said more words than I ever spoke before in the locker room. "This might help you. It's from my grandfather, and you can use it if you want." I smiled as I handed over my priceless Swiss Army knife, hoping she would be receptive.

The few individuals remaining in the locker room looked at Wendy for her reaction. I sensed that they were hoping she'd snub me. Not everyone was excited about a young upstart making her mark on the pro circuit. Instead of the seasoned pro players making the big headlines, I was featured. I was the flavor of the moment, a refreshing novelty. I suppose it was human nature for people to get jealous.

Wendy seemed to be genuinely kind, and she was the type of person to exhibit true sportsmanship regardless of whether she won or lost. These attributes were in full form that night in the locker room. With a laugh, Wendy asked with her Australian accent, "What are you doing with a corkscrew?" Finally, a question unrelated to tennis.

I answered, "There are all kinds of things on this knife. It was a special gift from my grandfather in Germany."

Wendy showed interest in the items I was eagerly pointing out. In full view for everyone to see, she took the corkscrew from my hand and gave a genuine, drawn-out thank you. With that simple gesture, I knew I had made a friend. God gives all of His children moments like this: immediate acceptance that turns into a protective bond.

Wendy not only became my friend, but also my mentor and protector. She understood her responsibility and honored it until I was safely into adulthood. Throughout my pro career, Wendy watched over me, and I appreciated having her there. Tennis at this level can be a harsh environment, and I was a child breaking records, which certainly didn't endear me to anyone. In fact, there was backlash against Wendy for befriending me. She paid it no mind and stuck by me.

If I couldn't find anyone to practice with, Wendy stepped up, even if it meant hitting the courts at daybreak. When I was without a coach, Wendy stepped in during the transition phase, coaching me to my first tournament win as a professional. At sponsor cocktail parties, in foreign countries and strange environments, Wendy kept a watchful eye over me and filled my sister's shoes when Susy went away to college. Through subtle lessons, she wisely guided and encouraged me, allowing me to feel safe, so my character and personality could develop further.

Life on tour, like life in general, had its ups and downs. My meteoric rise to number two in the world brought both in ample supply. The best parts of the ups were seeing my parents and sponsors well pleased with my victories, and having opportunities open up to help children and other people. The downs were best labeled as important character-building lessons, and so they were never in vain. To say things became a bit peculiar would be an understatement. There were kidnapping attempts—one that took me until I arrived at a New York City tollbooth to figure out that the transportation car was not taking me to the hotel—death threats, scare tactics and wrongful accusations. One time, at the U.S. Open, someone sliced the strings on my rackets, which were in my locker, while I was having lunch on the grounds.

God had me covered on all watch points, quickly coming to my aid whenever a strong lesson needed to be learned. God never deserts a child. I learned this lesson time and time again.

The French Open is a two-week long tournament and is part of the four Grand Slam events that are pinnacle points in a player's career. To advance in the draw takes talent, skill, fortitude and, as I always call it, God's giftings. Despite having excelled on the Paris red clay by winning the mixed doubles crown and getting to the finals once and semifinals in singles twice, while conquering a number-one ranked player in the world in the process, my memory of the French Open goes beyond the tennis courts.

After narrowly going down in the last stages of the tournament, I was confronted with a troubling dilemma. On my birthday, immediately after my last match, my father/coach sprung on me that we were to fly to Germany without delay that evening to conduct free tennis clinics for kids the following day. Since this involved his homeland, I was highly encouraged to join him on the journey.

I rebelled. I didn't feel like racing to pack my bags again, to spend my birthday evening at airports, on a plane and in another foreign hotel. I tried my best to convince my dad that we could make the tennis clinics if we boarded a morning plane, but to no avail. My dad left and, in an act of defiance, I remained. Unfortunately, despite having won thousands of dollars, I was left with no money to buy food.

Normally, that wouldn't be a crisis, because I could order room service. However, I did not have a credit card and in my father's rush he forgot to pay my hotel bill for one more night. I wouldn't be allowed to order food, and someone else would have to pay for my room for the extra night. I scavenged through my tennis bag for some loose francs. I rushed outside, making my way to the local bakery. My relief at finding the shop still open soon turned to dismay when I found I didn't have enough money for one roll or even a cookie for dinner.

Dejected, knowing that my last meal was breakfast, and a light one at that, I hung my head and walked slowly back to the hotel. I didn't want my birthday to be completely miserable, so I reminisced about the times tournament officials planned special birthday cake celebrations for me. I thought about the year I had the honor and privilege of teaming up with Jimmy Arias for the mixed doubles French Open title. I envisioned the cake before me and could almost taste the icing. I had great birthdays in previous years, so I figured I would have to accept that this one might not be so wonderful. These thoughts helped bring me peace, and by the time I reached my hotel I was okay. I wasn't thrilled about going hungry, but I knew there were many people much worse off, and I should be thankful for at least having had breakfast.

I walked in the front door and saw that some of the players were in the lobby. While I was feeling somewhat better, I was still in no mood for conversation. I quickened my pace until I heard my name being called out. "Andrea, what are you doing?" It was Wendy.

My standard reply was, "Nothing."

Her protective questioning didn't cease. "How are you?"

"Fine," I answered automatically. My parents brought me up to be resourceful, and asking for help was considered a weakness in my family. We were certainly not to discuss emotional pain, which worked for me, as I simply thought it was better to experience joy than succumb to trying circumstances. It was easy to detach myself, thus it was simple to resist the temptation to ask for help, because the words were not part of my vocabulary. I glided along the shores of life oblivious to the fact that God was consistently sending me heavenly help and messengers to provide comfort.

Wendy noticed something was amiss. She continued to press me, "Where is your dad?" My hesitation made me immediately feel guilty for not sharing what was really going on. I softly replied the truth, "My dad had to go to Germany." This was a real breakthrough for me. I simply didn't reveal information unless it was to help someone else who might be harmed otherwise by my not speaking up. This was not one of those cases.

The other members in the group seemed bored with the inquisition. I was sure they had no interest in spending their free evening in Paris with a teenager, before heading to the tournaments in England the following day.

Wendy continued talking. "One of my favorite things to do in Paris is to have dinner in the heart of the city and visit a very special place. You are welcome to join me and my friends if you would like. My treat. It's not a huge group, only a few people that I have known for a very long time. We can have a birthday celebration evening in your honor. Make sure you get permission from your mom or dad to go out to dinner with us."

Throughout the two-week event I received birthday cards and gifts from fans all around the world. My birthday landed during the French Open so the French press always announced their well wishes. While it was special to receive such warmth and love from strangers, I was thrilled to get the invitation to spend an evening with someone who knew and cared for me beyond the tennis spectrum. I scrambled up to my room faster than any ball I chased on the court and discussed the situation with my mom on the phone, and from Germany she gave me the okay.

That encounter in the lobby completely changed the course of my evening. I had a night in Paris that I would always remember. My birthday celebration included a festive dinner. I tasted food that I couldn't even pronounce and, surprisingly, I enjoyed it all. Wendy made sure a fancy dessert came for my birthday gala. The gratitude didn't end there. We walked through the artists' district on Montmartre, admiring creative artists' work on display. Following a cobblestone path, we arrived at the famous Basilique du Sacre Coeur. I looked up in total fascination at the brilliant building.

Wendy was responsible for being the first person to ever take me to one of God's special houses in such a sacred fashion, explaining the history and significance of the church before and during our visit. What a church it was. The majesty of the cathedral gave way to the historic backdrop of Paris, the sun setting on its crown. The interior had a celestial presence. An enormous mosaic of Jesus with outstretched arms captivated me and everyone else inside. The sanctuary was filled with love. Each piece of the mosaic represented a blessing waiting to be released.

Our group quietly made a path to the sacred candle-lighting area. Even with my exuberance at wanting to take in the entire sanctuary during this one visit, Wendy protectively made sure I wouldn't get lost in the large crowds. She caught a glimpse of me, smiled at my sheer joy and proceeded to pick up a candle. Before lighting its wick, she paused in thought, as if asking God to present a gift to me. I pushed my hand in my pants pocket and grabbed every coin I had remaining. Mustering with passion the best prayers I could present to God in thanks and appreciation, I lit my candle and placed my coins in His hands. I had the special honor of discovering this vestibule of God on my birthday. It was the best present I could have received, and the remembrance of it will stay with me forever. It was grace that brought Wendy to protect, watch over and care about me in such a way. God brought more than a friend to watch over me; He brought an angel.

Chapter Seven

It is God who arms me with strength,
And makes my way perfect. He makes
my feet like the feet of a deer,
And sets me on my high places.

—Psalms 18:32-33

My continuing relationship with God and tour success became normal to me. I was driven to succeed, be productive, make a difference to those less fortunate than myself and increase my connection and relationship with God. I wouldn't settle for anything less.

The scale I used to judge myself was extreme—downright frightening to some people. While at tour events—more as an opportunity to explore the city I was in than as a way to build endurance—I rose early to get in a morning run of at least five to eight miles. Then I trained for one hour, practicing skills specific for an approaching match. One hour prior to the match, I warmed up on the courts for another half hour. An average match lasted anywhere from one to two hours. Unless I had a doubles match or it was late at night, I usually practiced one more time before retiring to my hotel room.

I would train for big events for weeks and months ahead of time. During those phases, I kept to strict daily training regimens. My morning run was followed by a two-hour practice session without sit-down breaks, as those bored me. The afternoon had simulated match play or another practice session of two hours.

When I trained in the Florida sun, I excitedly upped the ante. I loved being challenged by the elements, and I never became tired or hot. I ran in the morning, as usual, and practiced from nine until eleven thirty. I ate lunch and then had more court time from one until three thirty in the afternoon. I continued with other training in the late afternoon. I began to notice that other lower-ranked players did not have the results I did, because they did not maintain these same high standards for their practice sessions. Every single shot I took had purpose. I didn't like water breaks, chatting while sides were changed or when balls were picked up. I based my work ethic on an almost incomprehensible bar. I couldn't obtain perfection, but working toward it was motivating for me.

The strange thing is, my real goals never had to do with rankings or wins, and yet I trained like I wanted to be number one in the world. I felt my strict regimen had a purpose, but that tennis was not necessarily where the payoff would be.

What brought me the greatest challenge and peace was to quiet my mind from exploring the world and keep it still in prayer. I was in constant motion, and I didn't want any movement without purpose or direction. There were times I couldn't stop my mind from thinking, no matter how I tried. I was always very inquisitive, and my head was filled with ideas and plans for the future. I was also able to see and sense energy patterns. Streams of colors surrounding people, plants, objects and actions appeared to me. Fluctuations in energy hit me like waves rushing to the shore.

Through all these situations I had a hard time placing my mind in stillness, because there was so much I wanted to understand and explore. That is where prayer and listening for God helped me. Both require focus. Prayer has to be given the respect that God so deserves. Listening for God made the need for stillness and tranquility paramount, regardless of what was happening around me. It did me no good to attach to the world if it was at the cost of shunning private time with God. Success had to be oriented toward a higher place that had nothing to do with a ranking sheet.

God released great patience in silencing the noise around me. Always very self-motivated, I thrived in situations that demanded high levels of concentration for hours at a time. Day after day, I maintained an almost robotic focus, methodically acting out all my different roles. I was so absorbed in learning from God that it became more natural than being a normal daughter, student and sister. My quest was to move purposefully toward a common goal, but I couldn't quite grasp the plan. So I let God be my guide and discarded whatever didn't feel right.

My discipline and regimentation had another plus: I was never nervous. In all my years on the professional tennis circuit, I did not play one point of tennis nervous, no matter who I was playing. In my mind, nervousness was a lack of faith and a flaw that I would not permit myself to have. Even when I competed in mixed doubles events with tennis greats Jimmy Connors and John McEnroe, or filmed a commercial with Bjorn Borg, I refused to let nerves dictate my play or enjoyment.

John McEnroe and Jimmy Connors had distinctively different personalities. Jimmy was from my home state of Illinois, and my father used his techniques as a training guide for me. Dad would watch countless matches of his on television so I could learn from a real pro.

Watching John play was like going to the theatre. Captivating, impressionable, devoid of false demeanors, reactive and polished in talent beyond what my era of fans had ever seen, John gave his all and more on the court. Whether fans loved or hated him, he filled stadium seats all around the world.

My introduction to Bjorn Borg came well before we made a watch commercial together. The public saw Bjorn as a player with a steely interior. I had the fortune of seeing his humorous, private side. What a sport he was during our commercial shoot. At the time, his number of Grand Slam victories nearly surpassed my age, and the script had him going down in defeat to me thanks to a net cord winner.

All three of these tennis superstars held their celebrity status for decades. They never let it go to their heads and, when I was a young player on the junior circuit, I was able to see how well they treated their fans. Jimmy, John, Bjorn and I were competing in the Pepsi Grand Slam Cup. They were in the pro division, and I was the up-and-coming star in the junior version of the event. I happened to cross paths with the three competitors and they all treated me like protective, caring, older brothers.

We had great conversations about tennis and life, and they encouraged me by saying, "Have fun, good luck and go get 'em!" We posed for pictures with famous tennis photographers, Art Seitz and Russ Adams, and they never acted like it was a bother.

Eventually, when I achieved enough ranking points to be on the tour as a pro myself, John, Jimmy and Bjorn's support actually increased. Their brotherly ways, especially in John's case, held true and strong throughout my entire tennis career. John was the most outgoing of the trio, and I felt a connection with him immediately. He, especially, has had a daily positive influence on my life and the children's foundation work that I participate in.

The great part about the four Grand Slam events during the calendar year was that both the men and women competed together on the identical site during the same two-week period. Every single male player I encountered was respectful, courteous, inspiring and welcoming. Since I was over a decade younger than most players on the circuit, all the male players treated me like their kid sister. All except for one, that is.

Ilie Nastase's flamboyant antics never ceased, even in the company of women and children. It was a testimony to his truth, which in a strange way I admired. In mixed doubles competition, any other male player would have chosen to hit a winner to the corner, if the shot was available, instead of going full strength at the female player. Not Ilie. He pummeled balls at me with all the force he could muster, all to my sheer enjoyment. It was a challenge to duck out of the way of his missile-like shots. His fear tactics always backfired, and he went down in defeat every time we battled.

Along with my commercial with Bjorn Borg, I was also in a Kentucky Fried Chicken commercial with my mom. It was great fun for us, but the director had his hands full with the Jaeger women. My line was supposed to be, "To be the best in the world. . . ." However, I refused to say "the best in the world" because one, I didn't care about being the best in the world, and two, I wasn't the best in the world, and three, I ate Kentucky Fried Chicken because I liked it, not because I thought it would make me number one in the world. After numerous on-set discussions that held up production, the director agreed to the changes. As with any commercial shoot, the director knew we would be going through several takes, so he told my mother that she could spit out the chicken after the cameras stopped rolling. My mother had her own truth to defend. She refused, not wanting to be disrespectful to the sponsor we were endorsing. One hundred takes later, Mom was so full she could barely take another bite.

∞   ∞   ∞

God provided me with so many blessings while I was a tennis professional. On the tour, I found that the people I had the most in common with were the ball boys and ball girls. The big arenas made great places to play hide-and-seek, tag, football and soccer.

Other than these young companions, Wendy, and the male players I had befriended during Grand Slam events, I was steadily becoming entrenched in the seclusion that my celebrity status brought. In some cases people avoided me because I was a star and they were awestruck. Other people found my introspective nature strange and probably mistook it for arrogance. Some people were so phony, I didn't want to deal with them, and then there were those who only sought my attention for personal or professional gain. For me, at least knowing the categories helped keep things clean and consistent.

It was easy to remove myself emotionally in school or tour settings. I relished the quiet time in my hotel rooms and Lincolnshire bedroom. Since my dad traveled with me the majority of the time as my coach, I always had an excuse that I could use if I didn't want to be around someone.

Throughout my tennis travels around the globe to South Africa, Europe, Japan, Australia and throughout the United States, I frequently came across God's gifts, miracles and blessings. My tennis background became a platform from which I could reach out to children all across the world. During one East Coast tour stop, I had a defining moment that took me a quantum leap in my development.

Quietly sitting in the back seat of the tennis event transporation car on the way back to my accommodations, I looked out the window and saw a large toy store. I asked the driver to take a detour so we could stop at the toy store. This was not for me; I felt God calling me to help sick children and my spur-of-the-moment thought was to purchase a carload of toys and bring them to a local children's hospital. Since I was traveling with a practice partner and not my dad, I was provided a credit card for any personal or professional needs. The driver seemed surprised at my request. I then asked him which children's hospital or pediatric cancer ward was closest to the New Jersey event site I was competing in. He told me that it was the

Helen Hayes Hospital, and he was more than willing to help me get there. He contacted the tournament and explained the lengthy trip he would be taking. In turn, the tournament gladly called the hospital to request that a representative give me a tour of the children's wards.

When in new situations, I typically kept my head down and avoided eye contact with people, not because I was scared, but because I didn't care or need any extra attention because of my tennis accolades. However, as I entered the hospital, I felt different than I had ever felt before. I bounded inside with my large sack of toys, feeling like Santa Claus.

I was welcomed at the door and given a private tour of the hospital. The children's playroom was upstairs. I followed the hospital representative, wishing she would quicken her pace. I never felt nauseous or taken aback at seeing a variety of patients, young and old, with different medical conditions. Instead, the experience was uplifting.

Finally, we reached the playroom. A kind of mystical energy filled the room, like a rush of air—but there were no windows open. I saw three children there, two girls and a boy. They looked up, but they didn't "inspect" me the way so many other people did. I didn't get looked upon as strange because of my tennis talents or gifts from God. I was a guest here and accepted fully. Before I had the chance to start distributing the toys, the boy immediately ran over and challenged me to a video game. "Let's go!" he said enthusiastically. Suddenly, I noticed that he had no hands. The last thing I wanted to do was disappoint a boy in the hospital by beating him in video games. He sensed my hesitation and said, "Come on! Betcha I can beat you." That was all it took. I dashed over and grabbed the controls.

Amazingly, the boy was a video game master. Despite my best efforts, he beat me every single game. We had such a great time and laughed so hard that the previously empty corridor was now filled with people who wanted to see what was so funny. In between the defeats I was taking, I thought about how remarkable this boy was. He was focusing on what he had, not what had been taken away from him. He was making the most of every day before him—pure and simple.

I had a successful professional tennis career because of what I could do with my hands. All the players on the tour did. We had crowds cheering for us because of our manual dexterity. I wondered how many of the people on the tour, including myself, ever experienced the sheer joy for life that this boy was experiencing.

After my video game defeats, the hospital representative handed me my bag of toys. The children were thrilled, and full of surprise and appreciation. They searched for their favorite toys and held them tight. The rest of the gifts would be distributed later to the children who were having treatments.

I visited with the two other children in the room. One adorable little girl was attached to an IV pole. She waltzed across the floor with the cold piece of metal as if it were her dance partner. *What an amazing way to accept her treatment and the bulky apparatus attached to her,* I thought. We chatted about the various presents I brought, and she was pleased to find more than one that wouldn't interfere with her mechanical friend.

Another frail little girl with a delightful smile approached me. She had lost her hair from chemotherapy. She giggled as she touched my long blonde hair, as if my having hair could be considered an inconvenience.

Being in the presence of these children was transformational. So much had been taken away from them, yet they persisted in finding beauty and enjoyment even in this sterile hospital setting. I had walked into the playroom feeling like Santa Claus for what I could give them. I left realizing that the children were the ones passing on to me the most priceless gift of all, and one that would last a lifetime. They had mastered their worlds, finding purpose, love and joy, with a wisdom far beyond what I possessed.

I felt the connection between all of us in that playroom. As I picked up the empty sack, I said to myself, *When I grow up, I am going to help kids who are sick and stuck in the hospital.* As soon as I said those words, I felt that mystical rush of air again. This time it felt familiar. I didn't look around to see what caused it. Now I knew. It was God and His angels in action.

Chapter Eight

"I am the light of the world.
He who follows Me shall not walk in darkness,
but have the light of life."

—Jesus, in John 8:12

I continued with my life as a tennis pro, sometimes visiting children in hospitals or participating in other programs. Even with all the heavenly support I received as a player, it wasn't always fun and games on the tennis circuit. Incredibly, I was often met with hostility because of my focus and other people's lack of interest in helping children. I was surprised at the outbursts I received from disinterested people, but God graced me with enough light to persevere by keeping my energy and spirit moving forward on helping children.

I was in New York City in March 1984 for the Virginia Slims Tennis Tour Championships at Madison Square Garden. Competing at the Garden was always special. The energy from the New York crowds made for victories of unparalleled emotion, captivating the hearts of fans and athletes alike. Many an underdog rose to victory because of fan support. Longtime favorites were applauded whether they won or lost. As a teenager, I felt privileged to be in this storied place, let alone compete there.

Every day at my hotel, I started my morning by reading the *New York Times*. One morning's feature described the shock and fear of citizens in the nearby town of White Plains, where a number of teenaged suicides had taken place. The townspeople were trying to heal from the pain of these tragedies and work out various approaches to avoid copycat deaths. I found the details startling, especially because the kids were teenagers like me—some even younger in age.

I was consumed with getting to White Plains to help. As unsettling as the news was, I felt God securing a place for me to be there to provide help, and assuring me I was being guided. I phoned directory assistance, found the information I needed, and after a few calls, my trip was planned. My tennis notoriety opened the door to help since the first person I spoke to knew my name from past media coverage. My interest was met with great appreciation. I was invited to attend the planned and informal gatherings already scheduled, with the hope that my visit would provide additional support for the high school students, families and community.

Arriving in White Plains in less than two hours, determined to make a difference, I was met by representatives ranging from the high school student council members to parents and caring community individuals. I was filled with ideas for these kids, hoping to help them find a way to voice their fears and struggles before they descended into the kind of dark despair that would bring more tragedy.

My messages of support to the teenagers contained many of the same principles that I had utilized throughout my struggles:

- Pain and suffering are a part of life, but with help they can be experienced and conquered.
- Things can be tough, big and troubling, but God can help you overcome every hurdle.
- Taking one day, one moment, even one breath at a time can

turn things around and bring in a light that makes life a lot
easier to handle.

- Don't give up, because there is always someone out there
  wanting, willing and ready to help.

The tragedy of so many suicides is that afterward people will
say, "I had no idea he was so depressed." "I never thought in a million years she would do such a thing." "There were so many people
who would have loved to have stepped in and helped."

Well aware of how a child's cries for help are often missed and
not heard, I offered up a few thoughts for the adults, many of whom
were parents. "Look, when it has gotten to the point of a teenager
being lost beyond normal adolescent growing pains, it is the adult's
responsibility to pick up the signs. They are always there. Kids
leave a trail of reaching out. It is the adult's job to recognize the
struggles and pain kids are manifesting and provide them a comforting, protective, welcome and receptive environment where they
can release some pain, anger, isolation, suffering and information.
It is the same thing for the adults; don't give up. It doesn't matter if
a teenager refuses to communicate ten times in a row. Try ten more
times in different ways, get ten other people involved, bring in professional support. Just never get frustrated to the point of shutting
the child out worse than he or she already is and feels."

The gathering was beneficial for everyone. The school representatives, students, community members and parents that I met with
gave me heartfelt hugs and thank-yous in appreciation of my visit.
We talked, shared and collaborated together on how to help youngsters who were struggling through emotionally difficult times.

To make room for God to enter and be in my life, I had to work
on allowing His will to command my spirit. There were many times
I felt too tired to say my prayers at night, but I never let myself fall

asleep until I first gave proper thanks to God. Constantly searching myself to live according to His standards came at a price—God's price. God gave up His Son to provide for me in ways I didn't fully understand, but I stepped out in faith toward God's light, always appreciating His efforts.

Helping children lined me up with my purpose. Like a firefighter, police officer, doctor, teacher, parent or anyone whose vocation is to protect and support children, I totally felt that nothing else would work for me. God provided me a watchdog position in His kingdom to help children, and I wanted the post because it fulfilled His purpose and calling for me. It was never about trying to relive my childhood. I loved the childhood God chose for me, but the need to protect and support children was completely ingrained in me, and I would honor it.

Before leaving White Plains and the diverse audience before me, I stated again, "Getting through pain and suffering is always possible. Please hang on to life because God has a plan for you. There is always at least one person in the world who can help you. Keep trying until God reveals to you someone who can pull you out to a place of safety and healing."

The visit took the greater part of the day. I would have stayed even longer if I didn't have to attend the gala event that was part of the championships. My time in White Plains was a universe apart from the celebrity athlete world I left behind at Madison Square Garden. Before drifting off to sleep after what ended up being an eighteen-hour day, I prayed to God to help heal the teenagers and the White Plains community, and to keep sending me wherever He thought I should go.

I didn't expect anyone back in my professional tennis world to be aware of my trip. I never announced to the Women's Tennis Association or any of the players where I was going. Taking my tennis responsibilities seriously was an honor, and I made sure I

Dad, Susy, me and Mom.

Photo credit: Cheryl A. Traendly Photography

Staying focused on the court.
Photo credit: Art Seitz

Representing the United States in team competition.
Photo credit: Russ Adams

Accepting first place trophy.

Photo credit: Russ Adams

Tennis in the early days.

Photo credit: Russ Adams

Keeping my eyes on the ball at Wimbledon.

Photo credit: Russ Adams

First serve at the French Open.

Photo credit: Art Seitz

Not everyone gets to celebrate their sixteenth birthday in Paris at the French Open. Jimmy Arias, Andrea, Roland Jaeger celebrate. Andrea and Jimmy won the French Open mixed doubles title that year.

Photo credit: Art Seitz

Jimmy Arias and Andrea before defeating their opponents to win the French Open Mixed Doubles Championship.

Photo credit: Art Seitz

The Benedict-Forstmann Ranch construction begins.

Fritz and Fabi Benedict, land donors for the ranch.

The Benedict-Forstmann Silver Lining Ranch is officially complete.

visited White Plains on my free time, so as to not shirk any of my tour duties. My dad was in Florida, coaching hopeful youngsters, and he had given me the freedom to take on the week by myself. I had the liberty to go where my spirit called me with no restrictions or explanations.

My interest in going to White Plains to protect teenagers from pursuing copycat roles in the suicides took my focus. It never dawned on me that anyone would react adversely to my visit. Given that, I was enormously surprised the next day when a top player and a tour representative called me to a hotel room to blast me for my visit.

"What do you think you are doing?" I was asked, with eyes glaring at me. I was confused. I rummaged through my memory to come up with something I may have done during the last week to bring about their fury. I thought about my gregarious attempts to convince the chair umpire that calls were made incorrectly. I noted that I would again have to try refraining from questioning line calls.

I thought the discussion was over when a *New York Times* newspaper was thrown at me like a Frisbee. Still perplexed, I looked at the paper after it hit me in the chest to see what all the fuss was about. There was a picture of me talking to the kids in White Plains. I read the caption next to my picture. Apparently, the father of one of the students worked at the *Times*. He was impressed that a teenage professional athlete from out of state wanted to help local New York kids get through painful times. The pieces started falling into place.

I looked up and said, "Oh, yeah, I was in White Plains trying to help the kids."

They immediately pummeled me with a barrage of remarks: "What made you do that? You need to stop it! You are making us look bad." One would attack and then take a break while the other person piled it on. I was mortified.

I took a defensive tactic, hoping to calm them down. Explaining how a few students had already committed suicide at the school, I continued by saying, "Look, the entire community and school were worried about kids copycatting. That was why I went to help: to protect other kids from falling into the same types of choices to harm themselves." My assumption that these malicious people would have to sympathize with the situation was met with further aggression.

"Those kids can't be helped," they said flatly. I gazed dumbfounded and disheartened at both people, whom I had known for years. They presented themselves to the public as caring and compassionate. I was sickened and appalled by their reactions. At that moment, I realized how easily adults could step out of their purpose in protecting and helping children.

I thought about how to deal with these people, or anyone who turns their back on children, especially children in trouble. I still had to travel, compete, interact, share locker rooms, and work with and around these people day in and day out. It was then that I took a stance. As if I represented every child in the world I announced, "Yes, these kids can be protected and helped." I wanted to scream at the top of my lungs, "No one, especially you two, will ever stop me from helping children in trouble." With that I got up.

On my way out the door I thought of turning back to try and change the people's choices of darkness, so that God's love and light could come in. I didn't. They made their choice, and I needed to focus on doing constructive, productive work in protecting and providing for children. Butting heads with them more would have been counterproductive. I took the attack—which only lasted half an hour, but which has stayed with me forever—as a sad reflection of how the industry I worked and lived in could affect people in a dark and destructive manner.

After I left, I took up a chat with God to calm myself down. I thanked Him for allowing me to have the life He gave me. I said, "God, any time you want to send me to help children, I am ready and willing to help, regardless of attacks I may have to endure."

The White Plains visit and the reaction from my fellow competitors was the first incident to prepare me for the backlash that noble and important actions could often bring. In a strange way, I had already felt imprisoned by my tennis talent, because I never felt defeating an opponent was helping to advance the kingdom of God. Now, I had another hurdle to overcome.

In tennis's traditional, at-the-net, post-match handshake, I could barely make eye contact with an opponent I recently defeated. I felt rather crummy, instead of excited about winning. Seeing disappointment registered on a player's face brought me little satisfaction as far as serving God was concerned. The fact that my family, sponsors and fans were pleased when I won enabled me to be a top-three ranked player for the majority of my career.

Fortunately for my tennis career, on most occasions my competitive nature usually rose to the challenge. I truly loved trying my hardest for each shot, even if it meant at times diving for balls out of my reach. If I could have given 100 percent and had the score be tied at the end, that would have brought me a truer feeling that God was happy with my result.

Reactions from my opponents ran the gamut of emotions. One player cried during a match. On the changeovers, I wanted to sit down with her and provide comfort. Maybe something else was going on in her life. I wanted to ask her during the match what was so important that she had to cry. I won the match 6–1, 6–0, losing only one game the entire match. I really wanted to give away the match, hoping it would change her demeanor, but I knew my dad was watching. He would reprimand me if he knew I had such a soft spot, which in his eyes, and all the other coaches' eyes that I knew, is not what makes a champion.

If players were nice to me, they had a better chance of winning than if they were jerks. At Madison Square Garden, one of my opponents, who was German, called me an asshole in her native tongue as we changed sides after I broke her serve to go up 5–4 in the first set. I knew enough German to clearly translate the remark.

As tempting as it was, I refused to answer the player back in German or English. The incredible part was that her ridiculous attempt to psyche me out had the completely opposite effect. Of course there was no way I could let her win the match after that. She didn't. Her comment didn't upset me; it motivated me to win and only clouded her with darkness.

Several players tried gamesmanship on the court with me, never realizing it was the worst possible strategy. Their shortsightedness provided for amusing and entertaining moments.

In my hometown of Chicago, the biggest tournament to hit the Windy City arrived. The tour knew I was still attending my regular public high school. There was no point in wasting my entire day sitting around waiting to play a night match if I could keep up with my classes and course work. Due to an abrupt change in the match schedule, I was called to immediately leave my class and rush to the arena to play my match. The traffic flow was in our favor, but I lost out on a normal prematch warm-up routine.

My opponent looked upset that I showed up at all. During the designated five-minute warm-up in the match, she rudely hit balls everywhere but to me. I scrambled, rarely making contact as spectators sat surprised at my opponent's unsportsmanlike behavior. This player was well aware I received the match schedule change late, therefore making it impossible for me to get a standard hit before the match. Her unfair attitude had the reverse effect on me. Instead of getting rattled, I became determined; I refused to lose, and unleashed some of my best tennis. For the rest of my career, I refused to ever lose to that player.

There were many dark episodes like this, but they were offset by countless special tennis victories that kept my heart filled with light about how much I truly loved the sport. Beating Chris Evert on the red clay in Paris in the semifinals of the French Open was important to me. Overhearing a conversation in the locker room about how I wouldn't be able to stop Chris's long match streak worked in my favor. I was energized by the challenge. I took it on with ferocity and won that contest easily, 6–0, 6–3.

Winning the French Open mixed title with Jimmy Arias was a fairytale experience. I was hoping just to convince him to have breakfast with me one day, and we ended up partnering up on the court and enjoying off-court time, too. Jimmy and I grew up in juniors together and it was fun to see a friendly face.

Jimmy's heart was golden. He had an engaging personality, a lethal forehand, a captivating smile and the crowd's support everywhere he played. As teenagers, we swept the field, creating a new record for the youngest mixed-doubles champions. More importantly, the time spent with Jimmy always brought fun and laughter.

In 1983, I took part in a historic semifinal match with Billie Jean King on center court at Wimbledon. Her grit, intensity and determination on and off the court were legendary. The pinnacles Billie Jean King achieved in her already illustrious career were platforms I would never come close to in ten lifetimes. Every athlete, both professional and recreational, should give thanks for the battles Billie Jean King fought in order for girls and women to have athletic opportunities in life. She was a pioneer who delighted in helping other people.

It was a distinct honor to walk on the perfectly manicured grass at center court for our Wimbledon match. There was talk that Billie Jean, who was contemplating retirement, was pulling out every shot in her repertoire to win one more Wimbledon title. She was only two matches away from reaching that goal.

As much as I applauded all of her sacrifices, I couldn't let her win. Billie Jean beat my friend Wendy in a previous round, and I felt it was my duty to stop her victorious run. I won the match decisively, 6–1, 6–1, and in a strange way I felt that nothing else I ever did at a tournament would surpass that victory. I ended up coming in second that year at Wimbledon, but in the heart of what mattered to me, I came in first.

Avenging the loss of my friend and defeating the very person who was the catalyst for me to become a professional was an amazing accomplishment set in an arena rich in tradition. Perhaps that is why God chose the timing of my injury soon after, so that I would never again play another Wimbledon tournament. He gave me a great present, and then He moved me to a field where my gifts of the heart and spirit had more value.

Success in an individual sport requires sacrifice or selfishness, many times both, to get and stay on top. I wanted to preserve the rare acts of friendships I experienced, not see them destroyed because of my talent. If I had chosen to fire on all cylinders with a ruthless killer instinct, I probably would have had even greater results and possibly played professionally for twenty years. God didn't design it that way, and I, thankfully, chose His path for me. He gave me the number-two ranking and a professional career that spanned five years, from age fourteen to nineteen, and then I became fatefully injured—all for a reason.

Chapter Nine

In Him also we have obtained an inheritance,
being predestined according to the
purpose of Him who works all things
according to the counsel of His will.

—Ephesians 1:11

In May 1984, my life changed in ways I could never have imagined. It was the first round of the French Open. I was on familiar turf—center court on the red clay—smacking winners and outplaying my lower ranked opponent. It was a crisp, cool day in Paris, and I longed to skip sitting on the odd changeovers so as to speed up the tempo of the match. Having been continuously told over the years that changeovers were not only for players' rest time, but also for television's advertising time, I sat for the last time, healthy, during the match at 5–0.

I usually occupied my time in-between games and points with thoughts of very basic match strategy. My focus was intense and concentration came naturally, so I never lost my leverage mentally unless I wanted to. Usually my inner conversations went like this: *Get your first serve in, win the first two points of every game, and*

before you attempt anything new, try to run the player side to side,
while always hitting down the line before them.

I played with my racket strings, tied my shoes, made up constant activity games—did anything to keep busy while waiting for an opponent to get ready. This match was going at the usual pace to victory. God's interruption actually removed me from the performance arena in which I was so gifted, all for a greater purpose.

I usually followed through on all my ground strokes fluidly and with great ease. Unfortunately, this was not to occur on a fateful backhand after forging ahead 5–0 in the first set. On one particular backhand groundstroke, when I finished my swing, I heard a popping noise that sounded to me as if a gun had gone off. At the same time, I felt as if a shark had ripped my shoulder out of its socket. It was the eeriest, most painful noise and feeling I had ever experienced. I immediately felt lame, as if my right shoulder, arm and hand were never going to function the same again. I labored through a few points and games before I approached the chair umpire to announce my default. I knew this wasn't one of those bothersome nuisances that come up in the body and can be played through. I honestly thought this might be one of those career-ending moments that sports documentaries describe as "the final shot of an illustrious career."

The tennis world was taken aback, because I was so young and my talent had yet to peak. One sportswriter had commented about me before my injury, "In her sport, Andrea Jaeger may someday be Borg." My right arm dangled at my side as if it wasn't even my own, leaving my headband as the only thing resembling Bjorn Borg.

As the tennis media descended on the news of my injury, I was on a plane from Paris to San Francisco. Susy was graduating from Stanford and now I would be able to attend the ceremony. Even though no one at the time knew the severity of my injury, I felt it was a blessing in disguise for a variety of reasons.

Our family's happiness at Susy's graduation from such an esteemed place of higher education was somewhat clouded with tension by the doctor's visits and physical therapy sessions I needed.

Instead of Susy getting her full glory, my parents and I fielded questions from curious onlookers in the ceremony stands as to why I wasn't playing at the French Open. It was strange how honoring the achievement of my sister's most important goal—graduating from a top university, which she had attended while on a full tennis scholarship—became less of an accomplishment in people's eyes because focus was placed on me and my injury.

Susy and I were used to avoiding the obvious. When Susy won an award her senior year of high school that included receiving college financial support, the Chicago sponsor of the prize pulled the honor saying, "Why should Susy get it? Let Andrea pay for her college with her tennis earnings." Even more devastating was that the adults in charge asked Susy, and especially me, to attend the dinner to accept the trophy without the check.

There were many disturbing moments of Susy being treated like a second-class citizen, but this one was especially hurtful. I had to bite my tongue as we watched all the other award recipients receive their checks and trophies while Susy was denied her due reward. The only thing that helped soothe these types of wounds was that Susy forged on, never letting anyone steal away her dreams or prevent her from reaching her goals.

I was so proud of Susy. She was always there for me, and now I could return the favor. I clapped enthusiastically as she walked across the Stanford University stage to receive her diploma, not caring that even this mere motion sent a searing pain up and down the right side of my arm, shoulder, scapula and neck. It was all worth it and no one was going to rain on this parade.

With the celebrations concluded, I returned to Florida with my parents to our training headquarters. I had graduated early from high school, prior to Susy's graduation, choosing to miss my own ceremony to move from Chicago to Largo, Florida, a more favorable environment for year-round tennis training. My dad had settled into full-time tennis coaching. Dad had taken his coaching skills to a new level by working at one of the best, if not *the* best, training programs in the world: Harry Hopman's International Tennis Camp.

With my injury, however, everything was off-kilter. I was the part that held this machine together and the reason we were in Florida in the first place—and I was on the treatment table, injured. Susy stayed in California. With her diploma came a new life. She had recently married, and she loved the California lifestyle. The rest of the Jaegers were left trying to adjust to a new schedule that left everyone at home during the peak of the summer tennis season.

At dinner one night, I looked across the table at my parents, who suddenly looked like total strangers. We weren't sure where to begin or end a conversation for fear of treading on turbulent waters. I thought to myself, *Did that much time go by that I don't even know how to converse with them as their daughter?* To say the least, they were not thrilled with the extent of my shoulder problems and inactive lifestyle.

We lived in a surreal environment. Our home was beautiful, with a pool in the backyard and two Mercedes-Benzes in the driveway. The Florida sunshine shone all around. It was disappointing to see how my injury sapped joy from our home.

I tried my best to communicate with my parents but we could only talk about the weather for so long. "Well, Dad, it looked like it dipped from 100 degrees to 99 today. How about that?" He disgustedly left the table.

Trying to be helpful, I once asked, "Mom, want any company grocery shopping tomorrow?"

She mumbled, "Like you aren't getting fat enough without playing."

I suppose I could have been hurt by my parents' reactions, but I really felt for them. The phone that used to ring constantly with offers and media requests for interviews and appearances now sat silent most of the time. Other players and tour associates started giving interviews about my injury as if they knew what was going on. They were neither truthful nor positive, and reading and hearing these remarks did nothing but add to the heaviness that was sinking my parents' spirits. Through all this, I knew I didn't fail myself. In my heart, I believed my shoulder injury was a package from God and it was time to open it up, but my parents were distraught. They had sacrificed their lives for me to achieve tennis goals, and they felt I had failed in obtaining what they had in mind for me. They wanted me to be rewarded for all my hard work and training efforts. All the sunshine in the world could not bring light to the dark days shadowing their hearts.

We all wanted out of this misery, which was getting worse by the day, but we didn't know which way to go. Even though I stood up more for others in need than for myself, I did have a confrontational side to my personality when I was pushed to the extreme. I also had the tendency to go enormous lengths of time without talking at all if I felt unwelcome. I retreated into a shell—and a weak one at that. My parents vented their frustrations out on each other and me in an attempt to resolve the unwanted tension.

Since we could barely talk about the most mundane things, I didn't feel my parents could handle, "God has a great plan for me. Look, I can serve God and come out as a bigger winner than a tennis match victory could ever bring." For every disappointment others had in me, I had ten reasons that I was excited about my future—and they all had to do with God. The more I seemed at peace with having to leave tennis because of my injury, the more it frustrated others, so naturally I contained all my enthusiasm.

Susy, ever the family mediator, realized we were going through turmoil and raced to Tampa to try to help us reach some kind of balance. Susy settled down our emotions and asked all of us to try and understand we were in a difficult transitional phase that would eventually work its way out.

Between doctor appointments and physical therapy, finding some purposeful activity for my free time became paramount for my mindset. Several times a week, I drove an hour each way volunteering at an abuse shelter for children. Every day I researched how to provide support for children in foster care and abuse shelters. This was something I could not have done on my previous tennis schedule, because of the responsibilities and time commitments I had to honor. After taking training classes at the abuse shelter, I could eventually attend family crisis counselor meetings as long as I didn't say anything until I completed my next set of training classes. I was ready and willing to make a difference. I was also fairly young and definitely naïve in certain ways of the world. I sat in bewilderment, listening to hair-raising stories from frightened youngsters. The sheer terror these kids lived under was appalling. I drove home in shock after every evening visit. Now my lifetime vow of helping children in need grew in scope. It wasn't only children who were hospitalized that I wanted to make a difference for; it was all children in trouble.

Reporters checked in periodically to see if I was ready to return to the circuit. My replies and style were to look on the bright side: "My shoulder still hurts. No release or relief yet from physical therapy treatments, but tomorrow is a new day that can bring better results." The reality was that I could barely get dressed by myself, let alone return to professional tennis. The doctors had no quick remedies, and this was becoming a slow, torture-filled lesson on the myth of indestructibility.

�✆   ✆   ✆

My old world of the tour and familiar surroundings were onboard a plane going full speed ahead—without me. I can't say it was easy watching it leave, because being healthy and pain-free was a plus. I loved playing tennis, though I did feel relieved to be removed from certain people. I discovered through this experience what Fleetwood Mac meant when they sang, "People only love you when you're playing." The disappointment of this reality collided with another part of me that often enjoyed and even thrived on not needing people. The latter was a creation of being tired of dealing with people's hidden agendas that were so obvious to see. It was a survival technique that became a permanent part of my personality, especially since God was in my life, so consistent, protective, loving and comforting.

I did search for a doctor who could repair my shoulder, even though I was growing weary of talking about the constant stabbing pain deep in my scapula and the nearly total lack of mobility in my shoulder. Still, every step I took away from tennis appeared to people as some hideous form of defiance to my parents and the tennis industry I had joyfully lived, played and worked in. In a move to give everyone else what they wanted—a subject on which I had become an expert—I headed back to the tennis courts, ashamed of what my professional world had become.

At first the tennis world was abuzz about my return, then it became embarrassingly obvious to everyone that my form was only a shadow of its former self. Apart from doing anything right-handed, which included pretty much everything from brushing my hair and teeth to driving and moving my arm in any direction, my shoulder was great. I was stellar on the traditional tennis-match coin toss by the umpire, where I either watched or called heads or tails myself. I didn't play my last match until 1987, but I secretly knew, much earlier, that God thought it was time for me to be doing something else besides tennis. Before I left the circuit for good, He had a few lessons still in store for me as a tennis player.

The ultimate honor in sports, at least in my mind, is to compete in honor of one's country. I had had this opportunity many times before, and I had always jumped at the invitations. Now, during my most injured period, however, a never-before-received Olympic invitation came my way.

The United States Olympic Committee had decided to reintroduce tennis to the Olympic Games starting in Los Angeles in 1984. I was ecstatic on hearing the news. Like so many kids, I grew up watching the summer and winter Olympics and marveled at the fact that athletes would train their entire lives for an opportunity, once every four years, where the difference between victory and defeat could be defined by a thousandth of a second or a mere point. Watching the champions compete and stand on the medal platform, singing national anthems as they represented their countries, was always an emotional experience, and one of the finer moments in sports.

I skipped Wimbledon, hoping the time off would help speed up my recovery in time to play for the Olympics. The pre-summer team selection process was based upon my solid ranking of number three in the world. Both players ranked above me, Chris Evert and Martina Navratilova, chose to skip the Olympic competition, so I would be representing the United States as the number-one player and seed in the Olympic tournament. As grand a platform as the Olympics represented for me, I was in utter turmoil. If I couldn't complete the tournament, I didn't want to secure my spot on the team, taking the place away from a talented, healthy player.

Every night for the few months before the Olympics, I pleaded with God to give the prestigious position on the team to the player worthy of its honor, whether it was me or not. When it was time for me to begin the athlete check-in procedure, I had still not heard from God whether my spot was to be relinquished, so I moved forward. I failed my medical examination. Perhaps my awkwardness in trying to remove my warm-up jacket due to my shoulder pain signaled the doctors that something was amiss.

The best doctors in the world examined my atrophied right shoulder. It would later be discovered that I had posterior and anterior subluxation (dislocations of the joint in a variety of directions). The Olympic doctors were surprised I could endure the pain I had been experiencing for months.

Although I failed my medical exam, I was cleared to play and be a member of the team. Surprised at the confirmation to play, I noticed a glint in one of the doctor's eyes. There was an unmistakable light sparkling at me. When I looked closer, the doctor smiled as if he was there for the sole purpose of allowing me to play. God was setting me up for something.

I checked into my assigned dorm room in the athletes' village. This was a far cry from the peace and quiet of the private accommodations to which I had become accustomed as a player on the pro tennis circuit. Here, the noise was constant. Everywhere I looked, athletes laughed and played together in a spirit of genuine camaraderie. Before the competition had even started, my expectations of a personal Olympic experience already soared beyond what I thought possible. The bond, connection, love and respect the athletes shared together is something the television cameras never captured fully. In my mind, this sharing far surpassed even the grandeur of the medal ceremonies. Now I knew why God cleared my medical examination.

For me, the actual tennis competition was a disappointment. I won my first round, but the extent of my shoulder injury soon became apparent and I had no other choice than to default. The Olympic rewards God had destined for me were about blessings off the court and medal ceremony platform, not on. Still, I was dejected, not necessarily because I missed my Olympic moment, but because I had taken away a healthy player's opportunity to enjoy the experience.

Minutes after this realization, a knock came at my door. Bounding in came Gayle Godwin, the United States Olympic tennis coach, and Gretchen Rush (now Gretchen Magers), fellow pro tennis tour player and Olympic teammate. These two women represented what was the best part of sport and life—the heart—and I was happy to see them.

Gretchen's kind ways, Christian roots and manner, won her sportsmanship awards throughout her career, but never any Grand Slam singles titles. Gretchen didn't get frazzled over incorrect line calls, getting shortchanged in team competitions, receiving lesser practice situations or double faulting in crucial match situations. Top players, myself included, viewed her faith and sweet demeanor as a weakness, one that could be taken advantage of on a tennis court.

Gretchen started and finished her day with the sign of the cross. Her level of success could not be measured on a piece of paper or calculated in a computer ranking. Her joy came from above, and she shared that with everyone she met. I would eventually discover that her way of life, serving God first and tennis second, was far more advanced than what I was experiencing, despite all my high-ranking tennis results.

Gayle was a coach who was one in a million. She had been a mentor to UCLA students for years. I first met Gayle during Susy's college recruiting days. She left an impression even then, exemplifying how women, without being ruthless, could coach as well as men. I was afraid to look Gayle in the eye after realizing my arm was too injured to continue. I didn't know if I could bear the disappointment. If Gayle coached a player to a gold medal victory, *her* platform and opportunities in the sport would be raised. I was her best chance and now I was scratched from the event. I changed her future, and I felt it was not necessarily for the better.

Gayle had more important things to worry about. One of her team members was hurt. Her display of compassion was an act to be treasured and a far cry from the typical top-ranked athletes' behavior: smug and self-centered, always looking to secure a competitive edge and be number one. For instance, when I was planning a trip to visit my old doubles partner in Czechoslovakia, who had been put in prison because of a car accident she was involved in, the only response certain players passed along was, "Good, now I will move one place ahead in the rankings." Great players often sacrificed a large part of their souls, thinking it would advance their worth. It never did.

Gayle cared before, during and after competing. Her coaching was about enriching the person and humanity, not only the sport. Putting her self-interests aside, she chose to sit in my dorm room to try and lift my spirits.

Knowing the morning would bring the default confirmation, I took a place on the floor, not even feeling worthy to sit in a chair. The laughter of athletes filled the halls. I sulked, burying my misery in the pizza-sized chocolate chip cookie they both brought. Gayle and Gretchen refused to allow me to feel as if I had disappointed the team. We laughed, cried, ate and shared. This would be my Olympic moment, a reflection of far greater things in life. These amazing women draped me in full Olympic glory as a member of the United States Olympic team. Injured and medal-less, I was instead bestowed with the true spirit of the Olympics—humanity, compassion, love and integrity that transcends sports.

When news of my second-round default went public, the national television media covering the Olympics requested an interview. Arthur Ashe conducted it in his respectful and engaging way. I answered the standard questions, polished from my years of press conferences. I was surprisingly taken aback by one of his last remarks. Arthur commented, "For having to default as the number-one seed in the return of tennis to the Olympics, you don't appear very disappointed."

On national television, with the most haunting, traumatic encounter I ever had to deal with in my tennis career and the fact of my defaulting just a short time behind me, I smiled. Even I couldn't believe it. A normal person probably would have broken down, showing their devastation and disappointment in tears that all the world could see. I smiled. I couldn't help it.

Arthur looked surprised. I answered his question, high atop the commentary booth, saying, "Well, you should have seen me last night. It is hard to explain what has happened here, but the default had an effect on me in more ways than you can imagine."

Gayle and Gretchen—who sat in my room throughout the previous night, assuring me they were proud I was on their team even if I didn't bring home the gold medal—were the reason I was smiling. God's angelic messengers don't take breaks, even at night. I had the brightest smile of all during that interview because, again, the grace of God washed away defeat with a very special victory.

Part of God's grace is that He swoops in during our most vulnerable moments. His miracles can happen in a blink of an eye. The more I started understanding my responsibility to give, the further I recognized God's hand directing my life to receive.

After my Olympics experience, a big box arrived at my front door in Florida. I signed for the package and proceeded to open it immediately. A short note was delicately placed on top. The note from Gayle said, "For you." Underneath was a United States flag that had flown at the Olympics.

Chapter Ten

Giving thanks to the Father who has
qualified us to be partakers of
the inheritance of the saints in the light.

—Colossians 1:12

While I was still in a state of limbo, living at home with my lame shoulder, God decided it was time for further grooming. My heart and spirit were tuned in to His miraculous ways; I believed without seeing. Now I was approaching a critical juncture at which my faith would either grow or succumb to the weight of the forces outside me.

I was still on the merry-go-round of constant medical appointments for my shoulder. The treatment for this joint was not as advanced as other sports-related injury procedures, such as those for knee injuries. I was diagnosed initially with a pinched nerve in my neck, rotator cuff problems and a few other muscle problems that I never learned how to pronounce.

The main problem was the continuing subluxation issues which caused other surrounding ailments, challenging even my pain threshold and the doctors' knowledge. I still had trouble doing basic things like getting dressed, reaching in a cupboard, writing and opening a car door. Driving a stick shift was out of the question. My left-handed writing skills improved at a slow pace, and with great work I was training my nondominant side to take over.

Happily, I continued to be drawn to my calling of helping children, knowing it would eventually be the full focal point of my life. My shoulder problems and practically nonexistent tournament schedule gave me ample time to research children's programs. Realizing that I would need to raise a lot of money to help make God's calling for me come to fruition, I decided it was time to put more value on two of my largest and most expensive possessions.

Part of the earnings for my watch commercial endorsement was a solid gold timepiece worth more than $18,000 from the Concord Watch Company, a reward for the hard work, true grit, determination and success I brought to the game. I wore it on many occasions and it held many great memories for me. I surveyed the watch and its fine details. If I sold it, I could buy a lot of toys for children at a hospital. The idea appeared so logical to me that I never bothered to consult anyone, and off I went to the largest pawnshop I could find. The watch became more than an $18,000 piece of beautiful jewelry; it took on a calling of its own.

I located the nearest hospitals and dropped off sacks of toys and gifts that I had purchased with the proceeds from the watch. Barbie dolls, Matchbox cars, Tonka trucks, video games, books, board games, electronic toys—the list and sacks went on and on. I did everything anonymously. At the last drop-off area, a children's hospital in St. Petersburg, Florida, I hid behind a wall, peeking every so often to watch the reactions from children, their families and hospital representatives. All around there were big smiles, laughter and appreciation of the presents. Children would grab toys and race down the hall with joy.

Having felt such euphoria at making a difference with my watch effort, I decided to trade in something with an even bigger price tag: my sporty Mercedes-Benz. When I walked in my house with the license plate under my arm, I thought my parents were going to have heart attacks. It took them a full year to realize I really did sell my car. The thrill in dispersing the proceeds from those funds was priceless as well.

I was hooked. God was showing me how blessings are released from the pure intentions of giving. I had always strived to be generous, giving from my heart, but this took on a life of its own. There was a higher purpose behind my philanthropy. I wasn't looking for a thank-you or reward for my efforts in helping children, but God brought them.

God decided it was time to take me in a new direction, a path I could not have even have dreamed of finding on my own. I heard God call me to move from my house in Largo to Wesley Chapel, Florida, leaving behind the security of my family environment.

This was not an easy transition. My parents longed for me to stay home, worried that I wouldn't find my way. I left in a battered rental car, watching my parents in the rearview mirror, pleading and crying for me to stay. I never saw my dad cry before and it upset me. Even though I felt this incredible sense of freedom and excitement about fully engaging in my intended purpose, the image of my parents' sadness at my departure pierced my heart. They didn't need any more heartache and there I went, adding to it again.

Every penny I had, besides what I needed to live on, was going to help others, so I searched for the cheapest housing and car I could find. An old tennis instructor friend gave me a wonderful opportunity. On the other side of Tampa, the famous Harry Hopman International Tennis Camp had moved to Saddlebrook Resort, an exclusive residential community with incredible tennis facilities. My dad had become a stable supporter of the program by lending his tennis expertise to students eager to hone their skills. I could train at the facility, see whether my shoulder would fall in place, and support my cause of helping children by assisting with the establishment. There would be no assurance of living arrangements, other than moving from one room or unit to another as they were vacated by the tennis professionals who made monthly visits. I was told I could perhaps patch together a few weeks or months, and that the Days Inn down the road had cheap rooms, too. Still, I was excited about the prospect, and I cruised down the causeway to my new life.

God was leading me to my calling. I had to be accountable to Him, regardless of how it would change my immediate circumstances and the surroundings and trappings of success to which I had become accustomed. Stepping out in faith required more than hearing God and His Word—it involved doing what He called me to do. I was still concerned about pleasing others, and I had other ingrained patterns that made guilt-free decisions nonexistent, but I knew that the journey God put me on could be taken one step at a time.

That is how I ventured forward, one step at a time, totally unaware that God was about to release an angel to me that would provide tremendous long-term wisdom, guidance and support for the children's programs to come. Approaching the lushly landscaped Saddlebrook Resort guardhouse, I immediately felt an enormous, protective presence. I followed the winding road to a tiny room where I would set up camp.

It was definitely not what you would expect from resort living. The carpet smelled musty, paint was chipping off the walls, the furniture was worn and the television only worked sporadically. Due for remodeling long before my visit, the unit had been taken off the computer reservation for guest use. Still, I had a place—for free—for at least a month. God secured the roof over my head.

The year-round Harry Hopman International Tennis Camp was world-renowned. Eager youngsters from ten to eighteen years of age, as well as adults, came from the four corners of the globe to fine-tune their tennis skills. The camp also included a makeshift academic program that provided for curriculum credits and high school diplomas. Parents spared no expense in getting their children the best possible tennis training.

At the same time I started living at the camp, my incredible pain threshold, which had held up so magnificently for me over the years, began slipping. My shoulder quit functioning on normal activities no matter how hard I tried to block out the pain. The injury now started to affect my life on a much bigger scale. Sleeping, walking, eating—any movement whatsoever—elicited searing pain in my scapula area. Pain pills were of limited value because they made me sick. I had the choice of either excruciating pain or wrenching nausea.

To say the least, I wasn't operating at my peak. Sleep deprivation, vomiting and the constant pain left me with dark circles under my eyes and a pale complexion that made me look as bad as I felt.

Despite my physical challenges, I still bounded about enthusiastically. The kids at the complex brought out my protective instincts. Becoming part of the year-round students' support system was never my intention, but as each day passed I became absorbed in their world.

I had long given up my rental car and, not having replaced it with a vehicle of my own, I walked everywhere—which is not easy in Florida, where everything is so spread out. Susy came to my rescue. She and her husband, a professional tennis player, had moved to Tampa to be closer to training partners and so Susy could be nearer to our family. Since she and her husband were often on the road, she insisted on allowing me to use their car while they were out of town. With Susy's styling wheels, I became the driver's ed instructor for camp teenagers who already possessed a learner's permit.

I was also recruited to the school faculty, teaching an English class for the few foreign students who were not adept at the language. A resident assistant departed suddenly, leaving a void to be filled immediately, and that is where I stepped in. The positions came with free accommodations on the property, free meals and a monthly stipend. Things were really falling into place.

God was busy with me. It seemed like every week a new assignment with additional responsibilities to help children was placed before me. I took every opportunity with keen interest and great excitement. In response, the blessings and rewards kept flowing. I didn't know I was sowing seeds and reaping the harvest; all I knew was that I was having a ball.

Working His ways, God kept guiding me. I never faltered in my faith, regardless of my circumstances, and the results were blessings in every area of need. I was gaining in experience in a wide range of activities. I had the responsibilities of cooking, cleaning and caring for children and teenagers. It was always an adventure. The teenagers, with their enthusiasm and budding sense of independence, constantly challenged me in many ways. It was consistent entertainment that kept my medical problems far back in my mind.

The meals I prepared for the group I was in charge of definitely weren't gourmet. But every appetizer, main plate and dessert was made with love. My days started at 6:00 A.M. and ended late at night, when I had to frequently check to make sure the teenagers weren't sneaking out of their rooms.

School started early, so my lesson plans had to be prepared the previous night. Tennis training was sandwiched between, followed by more class time, meals and the student's free-time supervision. I had the luxury of assisting in leisure activity selections during weekends, holidays and daily open times. I emphasized the finer points of having fun as a child and teen. I wanted the kids to have a balanced life, showing them the value of play as well as hard work.

I was grateful for the way God had set me up so perfectly, but the biggest miracle was still to come.

Chapter Eleven

"For where two or three are gathered together in My name, I am there in the midst of them."

—Jesus, in Matthew 18:20

L ife was moving along at a brisk and enjoyable pace. I felt fulfilled and was having a grand time. Then things took a dramatic shift. Every step had purpose, and God was about to bring me unparalleled blessings.

At the courts, my students asked why some American kids toilet-paper places on the night before Halloween. I didn't know why, other than that kids did it in my old Lincolnshire neighborhood for fun. Unfortunately, I didn't discourage the teenagers from the activity. I told them it was the least harmful of the things on the list they were looking to do. At twenty-one years of age, I had enough of my own wonderful Halloween memories to know that a little harmless merrymaking was a great equalizer, especially when kids are far from home.

The end result was disastrous. I didn't realize the green clay courts would be watered at night. The following morning I saw a resort executive, a confident blonde woman wearing a polo shirt and matching skirt, and a group of her employees inspecting the premises. She didn't look pleased at the white, wet tissue draped on and across the tennis courts. The morning practice session would have to be called off. The grounds crew would have to hand pick individual pieces of the soggy paper off the granule clay courts, which amounted to countless overtime hours for the staff.

Saddlebrook Resort had never experienced a toilet-papering incident. The resort was fairly rigid and certainly not built with teenagers in mind. It was a beautiful, upscale community developed for professionals, golfers, retirees and soon-to-be retirees. Security and tranquility were two big reasons why people flocked to buy homes there. This certainly didn't do much for improving relations between the homeowners and the kids—not to mention the grounds crew.

The kids sat back waiting to see what their punishment would be. I was prepared to take full responsibility. We were all shocked and relieved when no reprimand was given. The executive walked in front of us that Halloween morning and gave a look that said no real harm was done. Perhaps she knew what it was like to be young and living in a foreign country with different rules and customs. Many of the youngsters attending were away from home for years at a time, over all the holidays. If this was the worst of their pranks, perhaps she was going to smile and let it slip. Besides, she seemed to know who the guilty party was and waited to see if anyone would step forward and assume the responsibility. That would certainly be easier than punishing everyone.

I didn't fess up to my involvement, but I did volunteer to help in the clean-up, spending the morning removing the prank's evidence. From there on out, I made sure all the students knew that toilet-papering was not an appropriate activity. While the kids escaped punishment, I gladly did not.

On occasions when my sister was in town and needed her car, she lent me her moped. One day, I whipped around on the bike to attend to some of my responsibilities on the other side of the complex.

I always kept to the low speed limit on resort property, but strangely enough, for a reason I was to discover later, I used a new route that took me through a pool area. I cut the corner a bit close, which would not have been a problem if the concrete was dry. It wasn't. I drove the moped around the wet pool deck, feeling the wheel sliding out, but managed to gain enough control to not take out any pool chairs or the sunbathers in them. I skidded a few feet before I crashed. Calmly, and with a large laugh, I disentangled myself and proceeded to drive to my destination.

No one was hurt, but a few of the older resort residents were appalled at my transportation choice in such close proximity to the pool. They had a reason to be annoyed. I shouldn't have been hurrying through there. I promised myself that I wouldn't do it again and, in hindsight, wondered why I had made this choice.

The high-ranking executive who had let our toilet-papering prank slide was summoned to attend to this serious matter. The uniformed security guards balked at removing my only mode of transportation. The executive took the initiative explaining, "I will handle it."

This confrontation would be my first one-on-one meeting with the very person God was divinely lining up with me to help children with cancer. The executive approached me and stated, "My name is Heidi Bookout and I work here. Security asked me to talk to you about the moped. You can no longer ride it on resort property."

The tone of the reprimand was light. I replied, "So, why aren't they here?"

Heidi calmly stated, "They were afraid to talk to you. No one wants you to get mad and leave the resort." I admired her honesty. I was tired of the usual absurd reactions from people when a situation involved professional athletes: Give them whatever they request, regardless of the moral implications; or hide the truth, because a happy athlete is a better athlete. I always felt these approaches devalued the entire system by absolving an individual from taking responsibility for his or her own actions.

As much as I would miss the moped excursions, it was refreshing to find a person who wasn't afraid of being honest with me. Knowing that the truth was a better road to progress than skirting fault and laying false blame, I promised to immediately take the moped over to the front security gate. I then added, "Do you remember that toilet-paper mess on the tennis courts?"

Heidi's eyebrows rose as she said, "Yes."

"Well, that was me," I admitted. There I was, waiting for the hammer of justice to come down on me.

She replied, "I have plenty of courts for you to clean." Heidi proceeded to give me the entire clay court watering and sweeping schedule. I had no idea someone was there at 6:00 A.M. making sure everything was ready for tennis camp. With this turn of events, I realized my life was changing.

My antics gave me a crash course in how truth and honesty from strangers can build a permanent level of trust, and how taking responsibility for one's conduct acknowledges that every action has a ripple effect in a way God has designed.

God was not finished in bringing together His designated team. Two of the more popular teaching pros were taking in a tennis workout of their own at the end of the day. I had some free time before the evening academic classes and wanted to put the time to good use. I went over to the court where Linda "Beene" Bookout, Heidi's sister, and Kate Finneran were playing. Heidi was there also. I asked, "Would it be okay if I joined you?"

Beene and Kate were two of the most welcoming, accepting people I knew. They truly cared for people, always acknowledging their strengths and never harping about their flaws. They helped people in many ways, both on and off the court.

Most people would be ecstatic to hit balls with a former world-ranked Grand Slam champion. Heidi couldn't have cared less. Unimpressed with my tennis accolades, she continued exchanging volleys with her sister Beene. Her only change of pace was to spar with Beene on ground strokes. For the entire thirty-minute practice session, Heidi refused to change her demeanor. It was so refreshing to be looked at simply as a person. Heidi wasn't snubbing me; she wanted to spend time with her younger sister instead of a stranger.

Again, I was excited with the reception. No one wanted or expected anything from me and it was uplifting. There were no hidden agendas and the attitude on the court was genuine, not contrived. I didn't have to hide, cower or flee from overbearing, needy, attention-seeking individuals.

Another large confirmation that Heidi was a miracle gift from above came in an incredibly orchestrated act by God. The tennis instructor who invited me to the resort was worried about my lack of interaction with adults. I had turned down many invitations to socialize but he hadn't yet given up on trying to get me with people closer to my own age. While I was babysitting his three children one evening, he was at a local hangout and begged Heidi, Beene and Kate to take me to dinner. They kindly obliged to do the favor.

That night as the trio was returning to their condos, they saw me, post-babysitting, riding bicycles with the kids I was in charge of during various times of the day and night. They poked their heads out of the black BMW and invited me to dinner the following evening, which I gladly accepted.

The following evening I stood on the curb waiting to be picked up. Heidi, Beene and Kate represented a grown-up version of the cool club at the resort. In addition, their hearts were golden and pure. The entire time I lived at the resort, I never heard one bad word about or from them. They had no pretensions or malicious agendas. They were great-natured people making their way through the world. The dinner conversation was not superficial, but rather centered on making me feel comfortable and welcome in my new peer-group surroundings.

When the bill arrived, another one of those God-is-in-charge moments arrived. I went to grab the check. With rifle-like accuracy and quick motion, Heidi snatched the bill. That was a first for me. Ever since I was fourteen years old, people expected me to pay for everything. When my prize money and endorsement deals went over the million-dollar mark, individuals not only didn't try to offer to pay, they literally forgot their wallets.

I wasn't used to this and watched curiously as Heidi, Beene and Kate calculated how much tip to add and how to divvy up the check.

I asked, "How much is mine?" Heidi, the obvious leader of the group, replied, "You are injured, right?"

I was taken aback with the question, wondering what that could possibly have to do with anything. As I soon found out, it had everything to do with the subject. I replied, "Yes, I am injured."

"So currently you lost your regular paying job?" she continued.

Still perplexed, I answered, "That would be correct."

"Well, we have our steady jobs. We are taking you to dinner. When you get back on your feet with a regular job, then you can take us to dinner if you want. Until then, we will pay," she said, matter-of-factly. That is what they did. Even though I had more money in the bank than they did, every time I participated in a girls' night out, reaching for my wallet was not allowed. It was such a wonderful act of generosity. Heidi was ten years older than me, and Beene and Kate were both four years my senior. Despite the age difference, we were like four peas in a pod.

Every week, Heidi made dinner at her condo and invited people over. Despite my worldly travels, socializing, particularly at meals, was not my strong suit. Artichokes baffled me. Pizza and ice cream night triggered a fasting mechanism in me. One night,

Heidi was wandering through the crowd and asked why I wasn't eating. "I really shouldn't eat pizza and ice cream," I replied.

I had heard countless times from past coaches about restricting my diet to get a competitive edge. This meant pizza and ice cream were forbidden. Slowly coming to understand my numerous quirky ways, Heidi continued, "And why would that be, Andrea?"

I answered matter-of-factly, "I could get in trouble, because they are so fattening."

Heidi had a nurturing quality that always put me at ease. Without telling me what to do, she could gracefully turn a conversation into a learning experience that made my previous logic antiquated. I couldn't place my finger on it exactly, but Heidi had a presence about her that made me take notice, and I sensed that she was destined to pursue a larger purpose for God. Her spirit lit up a room and she shined in ways that practically brought a glow to the path before her.

Heidi had a mission-based mindset, combined with the fortitude to stay true to her values, morals and principles. She was altruistic yet fun, with a quick wit and a wonderful sense of humor. These personality traits and her degree in psychology made her a terrific resource to help me break my old destructive patterns, ingrained in me after years of living the strange life of a child tennis phenomenon. Around Heidi, I always seemed to be laughing, thinking or learning.

"Okay, Andrea, who here in this room is going to get you in trouble for eating a piece of pizza?" Put that way, the mere thought seemed ridiculous. I smiled and grabbed a piece of pizza, savoring every bite.

Later in the evening, Heidi asked, "Did you enjoy dinner?"

I answered, "Oh, yes! My one piece of pizza was great."

"Are you still hungry?" she said.

"Yes, but that's okay," I replied. "I am supposed to be."

"And why are you supposed to be?" she asked back, making me think about why I answered the way I did.

The evenings often went on like that. I was learning to develop new thought patterns based upon what I required, not what boxes other people placed me in. Ordinary things like eating and social conversation were areas I had yet to experience in normal development patterns. Even the simple idea of what to eat three times a day threw me off.

Unless I had a purpose of helping someone, I was disoriented. Kate would discuss music, the latest articles in *People* magazine or other entertaining news to be nice and include me in conversations, not realizing that unless topics had some long-range purpose I detached myself and looked bewildered.

Mary, an elementary school teacher and Heidi and Beene's other sister, often joined our evening events. Her stories about kids at her school constantly fascinated me. But more often than not, socializing required work on my behalf. I know all the girls must have shaken their heads in confusion when I'd ask, "So, that matters because . . . ?" Or my favorite word, "Why?"

As much fun as I was having with my new friends, I absolutely did not want to enlarge my circle of adult companions. From past experience, I realized one true friend was a blessing and miracle, now I had four friends who acted as one unit. Having come from a distrustful place where people were concerned, I didn't want to push my chances. Quite frankly, I couldn't have handled any other adult friends coming into my life at that time.

Without any of us realizing it, Heidi became my personal gate-keeper. I instinctively felt safe around Heidi, Beene, Kate and Mary. Heidi gained my trust in so many ways and on a variety of different levels, which was critical in our forming a lifetime partnership to help children with cancer.

The talk of the resort was the exciting upcoming ski trip Heidi,

Beene and Kate were taking to Aspen, Colorado. Months of the hot, humid Florida climate made everyone long for snowcapped mountains and a winter wonderland. Heidi called on me to discuss the trip. I was brimming with excitement. I had never visited Aspen. The last time I was even remotely close was as a teenager, visiting Denver to play in a charity exhibition match against Pam Shriver.

On the short walk to Heidi's condo, I envisioned purchasing my ticket and snowsuit because I was sure I would be included on the journey. Walking up the wooden steps in full pride over my complete acceptance, I joyfully knocked on the door.

Heidi answered and immediately went into a brilliant and profound conversation about how much she trusted me. I drifted off, wondering whether to buy gloves or mittens. As I decided on gloves, I heard, "Would you feed my fish while I am in Aspen?" Perhaps the snow-covered mountains clouded my head. I stammered out, "Excuse me?"

"The fish need to be fed while I am on my Aspen ski trip," she said, oblivious to my expression. "Of course you have noticed my salt-water tank before, right? I would like you to have a key to my condo to feed my fish."

I almost fell down from the impact of the statement. Deflated, I began to evaluate what happened. Then the truth of the situation revealed itself. I was not being rejected. Heidi trusted me enough to hand over her condo key and the responsibility of caring for her fish. My despondence melted and evaporated like ice in the hot Florida sun. Snowballs and snow angels would have to wait. I was given the gift of trust and I needed to appreciate its significance.

I replied, "I would love to take care of your fish." This was the beginning of a great friendship and, more importantly, God was laying the foundation for people to come together in His name, majesty and glory—forming the structure that would carry out His work in completion of our calling and purpose.

Chapter Twelve

He who dwells in the secret place of
the Most High Shall abide under
the shadow of the Almighty. I will say
of the Lord, "He is my refuge and my fortress;
My God, in Him I will trust."

—Psalms 91:1–2

As the months passed, it became obvious that no amount of physical therapy or rest was going to heal my shoulder. Surgery was offered as an option, and I was referred to a pioneer in the orthopedic field, Dr. Jim Andrews, in Birmingham, Alabama. I was excited that full range of motion and freedom from pain could be an operation away. The surgery was successful in fixing a tear in my rotator cuff, but the undiagnosed subluxations problems and the stabbing pain in my scapula seemed to sear with increased intensity.

I now had concerns much bigger than whether or not I would be able to play professional tennis again; the more important question was whether or not I'd be able to use my shoulder for normal activities. It was also unclear if the pain I felt would be my constant companion. I retired before the start of the 1987 summer Grand Slam season. God didn't waste any time showing me where He was in my life and where He would stay.

Settled back in Tampa after my out-of-state hospital stay, I had a most incredible dream. The vivid accounts of what God was revealing were future blueprints of my life. The dream gave instructions about what to do when any trouble and danger arrive: Go to God for protection and safety.

I was in a wide-open field. Groups of people were gathered around calmly conversing. As I walked away, the field became narrower. My stepping away from the crowd caused people to react with disapproval. This continued and I grew uneasy. I picked up my pace, wanting to get more distance between me and the crowd.

To my dismay, several people decided to chase after me to stop the progress I was making in the direction I felt compelled to take. When I glanced back and saw that the crowd was looking to harm me, I started to run. I recognized many faces; a few were from my tennis past. Seeing a mountain in the distance I ran toward it as fast as my legs would carry me. The group of people following me had weapons, bats and clubs. Their facial features were distorted and their menacing looks and screams of horror frightened me. It was all very real and disturbing.

Strangers joined the angry crowd. I had no idea why they were so intent on harming me. The strangest part was, as I was fleeing, my path kept getting narrower and more directed to the mountain. If I swayed to the right or the left I would go off course. In my heart, I knew that if I could get to the mountain, I would be safe. There were no buildings around, no cars—only the large grass field and an enormous mountain. As my legs finally brought me nearer to the peak, I realized that the face of Jesus was in the mountain. I was sprinting to Jesus.

It was beautiful. I was amazed at the meticulous depiction of Jesus.

There was certainly no mistaking His existence. His eyes were pools of warmth and love. His face reflected strength and power within a comforting, calming and safe presence. His lips, ever so slightly and gently curved upwards, welcomed me with His loving kindness.

When I arrived at the base of the mountain, I was so awestruck by Jesus' face that I stopped all forward progress. To have any hope of safety from the mob following me I would need to climb the mountain. I didn't want to show disrespect to Jesus by climbing on Him. I was more worried about damaging Him than I was about being bludgeoned to death by the growing crowd. I remained motionless, keeping my eyes focused on Jesus.

Jesus looked at me and said, "Climb upon Me. I will protect you. I will save you." This miraculous appearance looked similar to the detail of the presidential figures on Mount Rushmore. However, in my dream, Jesus was much larger than Mount Rushmore, and green grass was the backdrop for the figure, rather than stone.

The violent crowd was getting closer. I looked back at the group of people, taking special note of the faces I recognized, to try and understand what could possibly be in their hearts to want to cause me—or anyone—such pain and suffering. It was only a matter of seconds before they would reach me. I looked up again at the face of Jesus and before I could even ask, "Are You sure I can climb on You for help?" Jesus said, "Come. You will be safe with Me."

Trusting His words, I started the climb. The movements came naturally even though I had no climbing experience. After a few steps, I looked back again. The entire group of people, every last one of them, had stopped at the base of the mountain of Jesus. They appeared frozen, unable to speak or move. I clung tightly to Jesus. Suddenly, the crowd started to disperse. People dropped their weapons, turned and walked away in defeat.

I was able to breathe normally now. I decided to climb a few feet farther up, eventually resting right before reaching Jesus' eyes. At that point, I stopped. Relieved to be in such sheltered surroundings, I sat back and let out a long sigh. I was embraced by the love and protection of Jesus. He provided an escape route that was victorious over evils of the world. Peace came over my body. Right at that point, I woke up.

Immediately after waking up, I remembered each moment of the dream with intricate detail. I debated between trying to go back to sleep to see if God would reveal more to me, or grabbing my pen and journal to capture the incredible dream in full color. I chose to write down the experience, knowing full well God woke me up at the appropriate time.

I raced to find Heidi to share the story. She was used to my energy and enthusiasm. Heidi listened intently as I described the dream, waving my arms. As I finished, I felt even more aglow with the light of God than when I woke up.

Heidi smiled, as if she was destined all along to deliver this line to me, and said, "It looks like God is reaching out to you. If you want, I can share some spiritual encounters I have had. They reflect the faith that helped solidify my knowing that God is real, and that He is the God of miracles and protection."

I know God was pleased with the results of Heidi and me as partners in His mighty name. We were excited to have a trusted ally in sharing God's supernatural ways of embracing our lives. Little did we know these small beginnings of sacred bondings would lead to incredible manifestations of blessings and miracles. God knew. He had the blueprint all along. Since we were aligning ourselves with Him, He was positioning us to be in the right places and times for incredible gifts to be released.

God knew I needed saving and protection. He sent one of his very best angels, manifested in Heidi, to help me lose the things I would no longer need, and find the things I would have to hold on to and develop. God was gearing me up to be saved. I didn't know I needed saving, but as time would progress, it started becoming more apparent that His presence increased as Heidi and I came together to help children with cancer.

During my research phases of the children's programs, Heidi agreed to chauffeur me to and from the University of South Florida library, so I could continue finding necessary information on children's nonprofit organizations and hospital-care programs. With my arm draped in various medical contraptions, I bundled together my notepads and set my focus. Regardless of the countless disappointing medical reports and sobering news in getting pain relief, my life was in full swing, exploring the love and joy of God.

Eventually, I decided I needed to develop my business skills. For my future work at a children's foundation, I needed to acquire work skills beyond the tennis court.

One night Heidi, Beene and Kate told me that Time, Inc., was moving their customer service division from Chicago to Tampa. They suggested I apply there. Understanding I'd need my own car if I acquired a job, I had Heidi help me negotiate a deal on a Volkswagen, then I applied for the only office position I qualified for at Time's Customer Service, Inc.: the building receptionist.

Since I had used hotel phones with more than one button, I assumed I had the skills to run a corporate switchboard. The media giant, which published *People, Time, Life* and *Sports Illustrated* magazines, would certainly have a highly sophisticated phone system, but I thought I was ready for it. I proudly entered the building in my new corporate wardrobe—business top, skirt, pantyhose and fancy shoes. I practiced my delivery: "Good morning, Time Customer Service. How may I help you?"

The first day was a hoot as I pretty much disconnected all the callers. Not once or twice, but usually several times I hit the completely wrong button. Mr. John Hughes, the head honcho, who was in charge of making sure all the Time personnel made smooth transitions to the Sunshine State, ended up racking up the most disconnects before I had a handle on things. Instead of being upset, Mr. Hughes gave me a friendly pep talk that made me feel welcome and more determined to be an asset to the company.

I practiced hard, laughed a lot and walked around on breaks trying to learn the intricacies of this new business. In a short time, I was promoted from the building receptionist position to personnel assistant. Then I was recruited and promoted within the company to a methods analyst position.

The career moves I made to gain experience in the corporate business world were very different from my job as a professional tennis player. As a trained methods analyst, I could make my hours as early as I wanted. I usually arrived at work at 6:00 A.M. I enjoyed the quiet time and it allowed me to concentrate, working with my newly acquired skills.

Every day seemed to bring a new blessing. The honor of being part of the Bookout's close-knit family was a gift that kept on giving. My children's program research was in full throttle. I was having the time of my life: I volunteered in the pediatric ward at the Moffitt Cancer Center, had a challenging business career, still checked in on the kids at Saddlebrook Resort, enjoyed my fun, new friends—and was loved, embraced and protected by God. All the voids I wanted filled were full. Things were absolutely great.

On November 4, 1988, God decided to intervene in my life again in a bold way. He knew the big picture of my blessings to come, but instead of giving me free access to them, I was tested to see what that experience would do to my faith in God.

I was merrily driving home from an early dinner with Heidi and Mary. It was a pleasant autumn evening and dusk was settling in. I approached the busy intersection, slowing down to stop at the red light. I watched the cars in front of me as I waited for the green light to appear.

God's angels must have prompted me to look in my rearview mirror, since all the action was in front of me—or so I thought. Instead, I looked behind to see a large, black fast-moving object seconds away from smashing into my red Volkswagen. It was too late to react, even to scream. The incredible impact and sound of grating metal made me feel that the speeding vehicle was going to go right through us. The only flicker of thought I had was that our chances of survival would be slim at best.

It was over in a matter of seconds. I saw that Heidi and Mary were okay. I thanked God. I was alive. I thanked God again. I was totally shocked that an impact of that magnitude didn't kill us. Then the light turned green. I found that ironic, as there was no chance of me going anywhere now. With my sudden appreciation for being alive intact, I was determined to see what kind of driver almost killed us while we were stopped at an obvious red light.

I opened the door handle with my left hand and stepped out of the car. Immediately I felt a huge shock go up my spine. I screamed in agony and sat back in the car. I looked forward and kept my focus on breathing through the pain. The police arrived and asked both of the drivers of the damaged cars to move to the safety of the corner gas station parking lot. I wasn't sure we would make it with all the clunking, clanking and damage, but we did.

The driver who hit us was a teenager with no license, insurance, shoes, shirt or sense. He tried to come over and apologize. He fell three times—but not from injuries sustained in the accident. He had consumed enough liquor, and what looked like drugs as well, to totally impair his ability to walk. Dragging himself off the ground numerous times, he eventually made his way to my car window. His breath smelled like a refinery and his eyes were glassy. He tried to say "Sorry" but he was so wasted he couldn't manage to get the "S" out. The police officer took him away and later gave me the obvious news that the driver had been drinking. From the black streak marks left on the street, the officer estimated that he probably hit us going at least forty-five and maybe as much as fifty-five miles per hour.

I had my fill of doctors poking and prodding me after my tennis injury, so I decided to wait until morning to submit to a medical examination. I had no desire to spend the night in the hospital, and my neck and spine hurt so much that I couldn't bear the thought of anyone touching me. I crawled into bed, trying unsuccessfully to find a position that didn't ache. I mumbled my prayers of thanks, knowing full well that the only reason we all survived, us and the other driver, was because of a miracle. There was no other logical explanation. God kept us safe because it wasn't our time. We all had work to do in His name, for His glory.

The morning brought additional pain. I had a pulsating migraine. My neck hurt so much that my head did not feel like it was part of my body. Taking a breath set my spine on fire. The greatest relief was that Heidi and Mary were fine. My side of the car bore the brunt of the impact. It was a great blessing that no one was seated behind me. Heidi took the day off work to drive me to medical appointments. X-rays revealed that I had a spine fracture. There was other damage: A piece of bone from my spine had broken and flown off, and was now putting pressure on a nerve. A few centimeters over and things would have been tragically much different.

Surgery was too risky an option. Even if it were not, the body cast I would have to wear would cause me greater shoulder problems and possible lung difficulties as well.

I sat on the doctor's table in my thin, paper gown hoping for another alternative. My best option was also the most unpalatable to me. I was to move as little as possible for the next six months to a year and hope that, in due time, the spinal fracture would repair itself. I thought, *Due time? Due time is getting to the McDonald's drive-through line before the lunch hour rush.*

In a blink of an eye, my life had changed dramatically—again.

Calling my office with the somber news was demoralizing. I had worked and trained hard in my position.

Reading, researching and studying for the children's foundation during this painful recovery stage took creativity and ingenuity. I used savings from my job at Time and a majority of my tennis earnings to keep the research and gift-giving programs running, but getting the work completed was painstaking.

I could only stand, sit or lie down for very short periods of time, five to ten minutes at the most, because my back throbbed. If I tried to go any longer without switching positions, my breathing patterns would get interrupted and my spine would feel like it was collapsing. I never prayed to God to ease my pain, because I wrongly assumed that all of us surviving the accident used up our quota of blessings. God, of course, doesn't give us a limited supply of love or blessings. All I had to do was come in faith, and He would release countless blessings and miracles.

When I was at the Moffitt Cancer Center, I delivered mail to the young oncology patients. The clunking of the hospital elevator when it stopped at a floor was too much on my sensitive spine. I had to walk and sometimes crawl up and down the stairs to deliver the mail. Seeing the happy faces as children discovered a package or card had arrived for them was priceless and worth the effort.

One particular time, as I was hanging on to the stair banister for support, and gutting out every step, a member of the medical staff asked me if I needed help back to my room. When I turned to answer, showing my white volunteer robe and name tag, he apologized.

It was at this juncture that I discovered "due time" for recovery could mean years and years. I could understand why my shoulder popped at the French Open in 1984, therefore catapulting me closer to my bigger intended purposes and calling. The car accident was harder to place. I had to let go of worrying about the effects and changes the accident brought and feel secure that God had me under His watchful eyes and in His protective arms.

I gave it up to God that He knew the bigger picture, and I ventured forward in the best ways I knew how. At the end of 1988, Heidi decided she would follow Beene and Kate to Aspen, where they were visiting for the winter. Heidi was taking her venture one step further; she decided to move there. Now, I was not only looking at my spine being shattered, but also my circle of friends.

Coming back from an excruciating medical appointment, where attempts were made to break up the scar tissue, and truly test my pain threshold, I passed countless vacant tennis courts; the Time building where I used to design computer programs; Chili's, the very first restaurant where Heidi, Beene and Kate took me to dinner; and the Moffitt Cancer Center.

As Heidi drove on, she explained, "Ever since I graduated college in Boulder, Colorado, I knew I would head back to the West to live. Beene and Kate love Aspen, and I am heading out, too. You are more than welcome to come."

It wasn't a hard decision. I certainly could use a new environment. I fully realized my life in Tampa was now behind me. I knew nothing about living in Aspen, but as soon as the car stopped, I was going to accept the generous offer to try out living in the Rocky Mountains of Colorado.

God's purpose for Heidi and me was coming together without us even realizing it. We were being protected by our faith in a secret place in which God dwelled. Trusting in God with all things made it easier to step out in faith. Since I was a child, the West had called to me. The mountains beckoned in ways I didn't quite understand, but I followed anyway. God gifted Heidi with the breakthroughs. She unknowingly signed on for a duty that she would never leave in all her waking breaths. Thankfully, God made sure I was under His protective covering and Heidi's shielding ways.

Chapter Thirteen

"What I am doing you do not understand now,
but you will know after this."

—Jesus, in John 13:7

Talk about living in the unknown and resting everything on God. The doctor had not yet released me for airline travel so I would have to make the journey from Tampa to Aspen by car in the coldest month of the year, January. Unless I wanted to commit to a complicated plane ambulatory care system, as the doctor explained to me, I needed to stay in Tampa until more healing occurred, or try the drive with the passenger seat in a lie-back position at a certain angle so no more damage would occur to my back and neck. The shoulder injury was a moot point since its degree of pain was far surpassed by my more recent injuries from the car accident.

Fortunately, Heidi was not getting impatient with the supportive medical role she was playing. Beene and Kate were already nestled in the picturesque mountain region in order to take full advantage of the ski season. My parents had taken up residence in a home at Saddlebrook Resort, and their life's balance was being restored. Heidi swapped her black BMW for a four-wheel drive vehicle. It was filled to capacity for the trip that would take us cross country.

A model passenger I was not. I only had a few of my seven shoulder surgeries behind me, so I was yet to discover how allergic to pain pills I really was. Besides being carsick from Florida to Texas, I was getting restless in my awkward travel position. The trip also provided ample time to reflect on people's comments about my abrupt change of locations: "You are crazy. What are you going to do there?" "You don't even know how to ski, let alone the doctors won't allow you." "Is Aspen even open in the summer?"

They were all valid questions. I didn't even understand what was going on. I felt led to Aspen. It helped that I had no ambition to learn how to ski, as I was certainly in no medical condition to try. I had made enough money to never work again, but that didn't concern me. I had been investing heavily in researching the children's programs and that was vital to my work interests. The possibilities seemed endless in my spirit, even though I had no idea what was before me.

I had God's guidance and was in great company, so anxiety never had a chance to enter the picture. Ironically, the tape and song that Heidi and I played over and over in the car driving across country was *New World* by Karla Bonoff. We crossed the border into Colorado and were surprised to discover that we were two days ahead of the movers. Unless I wanted to sleep on the floor for a few days, which was out of the question with my back, we had to slow down our pace. Colorado Springs and the scenic attractions would welcome us during our free time. I breathed in the crisp mountain air at our first Colorado stop. There was something extremely permanent that kept playing on my spirit, rooting me to the land and a presence I had yet to discover.

I still had no idea what to expect about my new Rocky Mountain life, but it was like everything else God brought into my life—joyful, comforting and peaceful for my heart, spirit and soul. The Garden of the Gods rock formation park and the Cheyenne

Mountain Zoo proved to be perfect escapes blossoming with Colorado flavor. God was doing well in watching over us because in the middle of winter, we had some of the balmiest weather Colorado had seen. We didn't have one snowflake fall until after we arrived safely at our Aspen destination. What a night to arrive! January 21, 1989, the exact evening we drove into the town I would call home, the Winterskol festival was at its peak. Not being a seasoned Aspen veteran, it would take me some time to learn that Winterskol was a historic annual winter carnival that displayed the specialties of a small, tight-knit town combined with the trademark of a renowned resort community.

Fireworks went off in splendid fashion, triggering a celebration in my spirit to soar with each explosion in the sky. Of all the days we could have arrived in Aspen, this one was the most spectacular. The black night sky lit up like daytime. The backdrop of the snow-capped mountains illuminated the reds, blues and silver hues of the fireworks display magnificently. God didn't only give me a new home, He arranged a welcoming party to boot.

Before departing to take up residency in Aspen, I had seven candidates that wanted to go in on purchasing a property. A few wanted the opportunity purely as an investment, and the others were looking for both a residence and a financial investment. In the end, God made the choice. Heidi and I divided responsibilities and she sunk part of her trust fund and savings into a great fixer-upper.

The roof had been designed to be solar paneled, but never made it to completion. It sagged, leaked and needed replacement. The carpet was burnt orange and ratted and despite demands in the contract to have the carpet, walls and contents cleaned, we walked into pet feces and hair imbedded in the carpet, children's markings of no specific design on the white walls and garbage scattered throughout the two-bedroom, two-bath abode.

The heat generally needed to come from a small wood stove, and dozens of buckets would be needed to catch the leaks on rainy days. The kitchen had warped floorboards and counters, and the nook adjacent to it used for the business office had a slanted roof so extreme you had to duck to get near the desk. The retaining wall had fallen into the driveway, and the garage was open for anyone to drive in since it was missing its door. The yard had no trees, and the wood framing splintered in all directions. Even in the house's dilapidated state, Heidi and I could see its potential.

I felt a little like the house. God loved me despite all of my short-comings because He saw the pilot light and potential inside of me desperately wanting to get aflame on my calling. Heidi and I envisioned the results the house would become; in similar ways, we glimpsed the permanent facility we were to build one day for children with cancer.

I knew from my first night in Aspen that the best therapeutic, majestic and healing surroundings for the children's cancer programs had been found. Aspen would not only be my home, but the home for children who have spent countless days and nights in the hospital fretting about if they would ever get a chance at having a tomorrow. The following Monday, I contacted my Chicago-based lawyer, who I had known since the age of fourteen, and gave him the address for the children's foundation. His reply of, "That's great Andrea, but you still need a vice president," made an impact. Hanging up the phone, it dawned on me who I needed to get to commit to the program. "Heidi, I need a vice president. Would you be the vice president?"

Heidi was familiar with my aspirations to help children. Without looking up from her magazine on Aspen, she said, "Sure." It was uncanny how things were falling into place. I looked out the picture window facing Aspen Mountain. I couldn't help but wonder why it looked so familiar. I pressed my face against the glass as if the additional inches gained would disclose the information. It didn't. Still, I was drawn to the mountain and it bugged me why it was so familiar. It suddenly occurred to me that this was the Jesus Mountain I had seen in my dream. Again God was showing me the way.

ℂ   ℂ   ℂ

The Aspen seasons changed with the brilliance I had been so accustomed to seeing in Chicago. The difference in why Aspen was a premier destination resort was uncovered in a variety of ways. The white splendor of winter greeted the spring birthing of four shades of green, covering a plethora of mountains. Aspen Mountain was closely located to other showcase mountains—Highlands, Buttermilk, Snowmass and Tiehack.

The elegant Aspen tree, the largest living organism in the world, found its home in Colorado. The trees' white trunks and graceful leaves dotted the landscape. Flowers with vibrant colors came blooming out with great luster. Summer gave way to fall as if bowing to its famous golden hues, orange and red shades jumping out in complete exhibition. Every view, from any angle, was a picture postcard.

The financial investment I was making during the children's program research phase, and the funds I would need to give for the foundation to stay afloat, felt like a natural act, a given. What I did have to address was the emotional and spiritual commitment needed. Before signing the final pile of papers to be sent off to establish the nonprofit and tax-exempt foundation, I firmly asked myself one question, *Can you help children for the rest of your life?* I followed with, *Don't start this if you can't commit to it for life.*

They were the same types of concerns I would have had in having children of my own. Children aren't meant to be playthings for adults to engage with for a few years, only later to get bored with or frustrated at the responsibilities. Children can't be tossed away when things get difficult or draining. Protecting and equipping children had to be of paramount importance. The foundation was like my child. I felt I was giving birth to something extremely sacred and special. It was my responsibility to see the programs come to fruition in helping children and to be involved in all aspects of its growth, development and maintenance until my last breath, and even thereafter if God so obliged.

Creating a long-term support program for children with cancer and other life-threatening diseases was a terrific concept that I wanted to take on. I knew it would take an annual budget in the millions to fund the programs. The depth and magnitude of the commitment I was taking on did not go unnoticed or without its own research on the advantages and pitfalls. The leadership needed to be passionate, consistent, courageous, wise, faith-driven and oriented, and determined.

The last kind of program leadership the children needed were people who said, "Sure, we will be around for a few years to help," and then, after a few months or years, because the leaders felt like making a career change, the program fell apart or disbanded. I answered the question defiantly, looking above to make it perfectly clear that I was not only answering myself but also declaring to God my level of pursuing my purpose in life. "Yes, I can do this for the rest of my life, and I gladly *will* do it forever." I took the leap of faith knowing full well that I was prepared to help children forever. It was my calling from God and I was not going to toss it aside on a whim.

God installed the freedom of choice mechanism for me, just like He did for everyone born before me and does for everyone born after me. Mine made a lifetime declaration of faith to serve God and to help children. The children's research programs had already brought great support to children and knowledge to prepare Heidi and me on what was to come. The IRS and corporation papers were signed, sealed and delivered, and I waited for the approval news with keen anticipation.

Meanwhile, programs continued being run from my personal accounts with no tax benefits. Heidi covered the house remodeling and daily bills. We had full faith the tax-exempt status would come one day, and we kept our focus on distributing educational materials, clothing, toys and supplies to children in hospitals all around the world.

My lawyer was extremely patient with my persistent calls, "Is it in yet? Did the IRS send a nonprofit confirmation letter yet? Do we have our 501c3 status?"

Every call I made received the same reply, "Andrea, this takes time, months and months, upwards sometime to a year or years. Be patient. I will call you when I receive any news."

I would hang up the phone as impatient as when I picked it up. The weeks did turn into months and the year changed before my eyes and still no response from the IRS. Heidi and I were not deterred. We kept plugging along. I attended physical therapy appointments between our children's program work and eventually purchased a puppy. The seasons kept changing and my impatience never became easier to handle. I was like an expectant parent pacing back and forth.

The phone rang on a clear summer morning and I answered in my usual perky way. "Andrea?" the voice asked. "Yes. Oh, hi Drake." My lawyer was calling.

"Well, you have someone watching over you because how is this for a birthday present?! The IRS granted your nonprofit status and the Foundation papers received their stamped approval on your birthday, June 4, 1990."

I started screaming. Heidi raced over with great anticipation of the news. No, we didn't understand a lot of the logic leading up to moving to Aspen, but now answers were being revealed to questions we hadn't even discovered yet. It was apparent God partnered us up together and sent us to Aspen for a purpose. The acceptance and approval of Heidi and me being where we were supposed to be, doing what we were called to do, all had a Divine purpose and connection.

We followed in faith and the validation arrived. The essential registered approval was significant since it meant that anyone kind enough to donate would receive tax benefits. My lawyer promised to FedEx the letter, as we were keeping costs down so much we hadn't invested in any type of equipment such as a fax machine.

The following afternoon, I read my lawyer's letter noting the extraordinary event. He was even amazed that of all days in the year, the one selected to be stamped for the birthing of the Foundation would be my very own birth date.

It was a wonderful birthday present. God was announcing to me, in His incredible ways, "You may not have understood how or why your travels, trials and tribulations, and adventures brought you here, but now the blessings and purpose you have been given may be clearer for you to understand." I didn't have a "purpose telescope" to automatically tell me which direction to go and with whom to tag along. I leapt out in faith, believing that our choices, the actions Heidi and I were making, secured our God-ordained path, which in turn lined us up with God and our callings.

With God's blessing permanently recorded in the IRS nonprofit organization department, Heidi and I ventured forward with increased exuberance and commitment. We realized we were chosen for the work of helping children with cancer and other life-threatening diseases and hardships, and we were going to make the most of it.

Beyond the horizon, where the naked eye could not see, what we were soon to discover was that God was preparing us for another step, this one an even bigger miracle than we had ever experienced.

Chapter Fourteen

For His eyes are on the ways of man,
And He sees all his steps.

—Job 34:21

The establishment of the foundation in Aspen secured my permanent residency in the mountain town. Now I was determined to give my faith a home, as well, beyond the outskirts of my spirit. I knew faith relied on a relationship with God and not walls, but I wanted fellowship in God's house, too, for the spiritual growth it provided.

It was time to figure out what church I would attend and what religion I would follow. I went to the town library to do some research. Fitting into a denomination's religious principles was harder than I thought. Talking to God and having a close bond with Him was much easier than looking for a manmade structure to walk in and worship at.

After hours of research, I checked out as many books as the library would allow me and headed up to the foundation office, located in the house, to read some more. The Catholic faith, steeped in tradition, appealed to me. As a child I secretly thought about being a nun, and working in a convent sounded like a lot of fun.

This desire was further fueled by Julie Andrews' unforgettable portrayal of the nun, Maria, in *The Sound of Music*. When my parents first took me to the film, I took it beyond the entertainment value; I took it to heart.

Along with followers of the Catholic faith, I certainly believed that Jesus was the Son of God, that He died on the cross for my sins, was buried, rose again and was now seated at the right-hand side of God in heaven. However, I was not resolved to allow a church, and not a woman, be the determining factor in deciding if abortion should be legal. My viewpoint on the subject had always been that women should have the right to choose whether or not to have an abortion. I based that strong premise on the fact that if a woman was raped and conception occurred, that woman, not the church, should have the right to choose to keep the baby or not.

I discovered books on religions where the main beliefs ignored Jesus being the Son of God and God being the creator of the universe. I didn't want to be brainwashed away from my faith in God's existence, so I continued reviewing other religions, denominations and church programs.

I tried a variety of church services. One church I attended had holy water, one didn't. At one service, people kneeled a lot during the service, and at a different church no one kneeled. The body and blood of Christ would be represented with a wafer and wine at the end of some services and never at others. It was a whirlwind. I came across people who worshipped, prayed and looked toward other gods, and I certainly wanted to avoid those false doctrines. A few times, I could barely stay awake at certain services. Then there were the constant pleas for money that made me feel pushed and persuaded to give—rather than joyfully share. I was becoming frustrated. I wanted to be closer to God, but I kept hitting blank spots. The voids I needed filled stayed empty. The answers I longed to hear stayed distances away.

I approached Heidi with my dilemma. She was raised in a strict Catholic environment and attended parochial schools. Every Sunday her family loaded up the car and made their way to Mass. Of course, I thought Heidi would tell me what religion I belonged to. However, I was sent back to the drawing board before I could even finish the question. In my lengthy explanation of disappointment in finding a church and religion, Heidi interrupted. "Have you asked God where He wants you? Is it more important to have a relationship with Him or with four walls in a church? Ask Him for advice."

It appeared so simple. The answer was there all along. If I could find God in my heart and spirit, actions and in the Bible, amongst other things, then I could go to Him and ask for further direction. I came to understand that church services, regardless of where I went, were not to be used as replacements for my time spent with God; they were to be used in addition to it. That concept, once released, gave me the freedom to continue my current relationship with God while exploring other opportunities for fellowship and worship.

As time passed, the remainder of my tennis prize money and endorsement proceeds were getting used up quickly by the transition of children's research programs to supportive children's programs. I traveled and gave money, gifts and time to other organizations and programs—not only to provide support, but to gain information on how to best run my own programs.

The dream my parents worked so hard to obtain, that I could live the good life off my earnings and never have to work another day in my life, was dwindling away as I tapped into my retirement funds. The question of where do we get the money to help the children was always answered initially by my money. My vision of helping children with cancer was vast and detailed. It involved land, buildings, vehicles and things that required financially more than one thousand times what my tennis earnings could provide.

The development of Kids' Stuff Foundation, which was eventually renamed the Silver Lining Foundation, was quite incredible. I worked hard on being obedient to God because I knew He was making the impossible possible, the improbable definitely probable, and the unobtainable certainly achievable. I trusted that He would help us fund this grand plan.

Heidi and I were the only year-round staff for the foundation. Beene and Kate stepped in to help when they could, initially on a limited basis. Besides running the foundation, I studied management, fund-raising, administration and any relevant business materials I could get my hands on. I surveyed a business plan that numerous charities have followed successfully. It involved the following:

❑ Raise money for a staff
❑ Staff acquired
❑ Raise money for land
❑ Land acquired
❑ Raise money for buildings
❑ Buildings acquired
❑ Raise money for children's programs
❑ Children's programs go into full operation

I looked at that business plan and said, "No way! That will take way too long! If we do it *that* way, too many kids will have died and too many spirits will have broken that we could have helped."

For the time being, we would have to use my money for programs and make sacrifices in our personal and professional lives to get this vision fully operational. I had already lived sparingly at Saddlebrook Resort, working on campus in exchange for room and board. I used public bathrooms often to save on toilet-paper bills. If I did go out to eat at a restaurant, I never ordered the main course. I rarely, if ever, bought things for pleasure. There was always a purpose behind every dollar spent, and I was focused on using the money I had for the benefit of others.

Continuing that way of life was an easy sacrifice for me to make in order to help the children. Now I was asking Heidi to also deplete her savings account, commit to at least forty hours a week at her position—but usually more than that, not get paid for the work for at least five years, and get another job to help pay regular bills. Heidi would need an unparalleled leap of faith toward God on this calling presented to her, along with an incredible amount of trust, faith and belief in me. With no hesitation whatsoever, Heidi made the choice to go forth in faith, completely dedicating her life and resources to the calling God gave her.

Heidi was committed to the vision of helping children with cancer. She didn't only step out in faith, she soared in it. Heidi was heaven-sent with a mission in mind, a calling in her heart and purposes directing her spirit. With God's guiding ways and Heidi's angelic support, we were on our way.

The time had come for us to find jobs that would bring added knowledge and financial means for our living expenses and growing programs. We would need to have time during the week for our regular foundation responsibilities, so the job could not entail nine-to-five hours. Also, it could not be a desk job, since my injuries were far from healed and sitting still bothered my back.

Heidi and I both found jobs that fit the bill perfectly: working as station agents for Continental Express at Aspen's Pitkin County Airport. Our shifts were seasonal, from October 1 to May 1, either 5:30 A.M. to 2:00 P.M. or 2:00 P.M. to 10:30 P.M. One of the benefits was free or heavily discounted airline travel fares. A round-trip cross-country fare was twenty dollars, with overseas flights only a few dollars more. This would help tremendously if we needed to go on program and fundraising missions. Uniforms were provided, so we didn't need to worry about buying a new wardrobe. In addition, one major requirement for the position was that station agents stand the majority of their shifts.

Heidi had lived and worked in executive and management environments her entire adult life. Being ten years older and a lot wiser than me, she also had additional corporate customer service and social skills, which I had yet to acquire. I was excited that my new job would hone my skills as an international public service representative for the foundation.

It was an absolutely enjoyable and challenging experience. Besides checking people in at the airline counter, the night shift had the responsibilities of cleaning airplane ashtrays (these were the days when planes still had them), removing barf bags, vacuuming aisles, stocking the drink cart and closing out the plane cockpit area for its overnight stay.

Aspen was a celebrity mecca, especially during peak season. Recognizable faces could be seen on the ski slopes, in town, or flying in and out of the Pitkin County Airport. I checked in many people, some famous, and often passengers gave me that look that said, "I know her. She used to play professional tennis. No, that can't be her working here." My name tag provided only my first name, so many people didn't know for sure. A few of the bolder customers asked for tips on their forehands, much to the amusement of the counter staff.

I also had my share of angry passengers, as did we all, especially when snowstorms hit or mechanical or other problems disrupted flight schedules. The treatment we received was sometimes downright abusive. I'd never dealt with anything like that in my job at the Time offices back in Tampa. At Continental Express, we stood there and took the abuse like true service industry pioneers. It was part of the job we signed up and were trained for. It was actually incredible frontline training in learning diplomacy and keeping your cool in adverse situations.

Even with those rather sad public displays from people, my shifts, interchanging between morning and night, became very special. I worked with a great group of people. Teamwork and a good sense of humor were required for a number of situations, and we all became very close, even hooking up during the off-season. We were like a big, protective family.

For two years, I chose the Continental route, while Heidi went for four—the last two years sharing shifts with Beene and Kate. Of course, I never again would look at any station agent the same. They were real people who deserved respect and kindness.

While improving my customer service and business skills at the airport, the fund-raising I worked on day and night for the foundation could be described as dismal at best. I was sending out grant and donation requests by the handfuls. In complete and utter frustration, I bounded into the local post office one day asking, "Why isn't all of my mail being delivered?"

The post office employee had a perfect response after I gave him the box number to check. "Miss Jaeger, you are not getting any more mail than what is being delivered." The post office box was empty every time with the exception of junk mail, bills and program responses. The fund-raising area was proving to lack the first three letters it started with: fun. There was no fun in working so hard and receiving no financial donations. Every time I came from the post office, Heidi asked, "Anything?"

I'd reply as optimistically as possible, "No, not this time. But don't worry, one day there will be donations. One day, the mailbox will be filled every day with donations."

Heidi and I persevered during this period of financial drought. We managed to keep our spirits up despite the lack of funds because we stayed focused on helping the children, knowing that we were where God wanted us to be and that soon, when He saw fit, He would release resources and donations to us in abundance.

We both had a deep inner awareness and faith that God did not bring us this far just to back out and leave us stranded with our dwindling personal funds. My prayers became longer and more detailed, meals became smaller, and credit card bills started climbing higher. Still, we kept our faith.

Chapter Fifteen

I will abundantly bless her provision; I will satisfy her poor with bread. I will clothe her priests with salvation, And her saints shall shout aloud for joy.

—Psalms 132:15–17

One stormy day, I was watching television, trying to find the Weather Channel, when I recognized a friendly face on ESPN. It was John McEnroe, chatting along in his typical high-voltage way. I stopped to listen. The reporter asked John why he rarely talked about being a frequent donor to children's charities worldwide. I didn't wait for his answer. As the program continued I shouted, "That's it!" I hopped off my bed and raced upstairs to find my address book. I had to know someone who could put me in touch with John. As fortune would have it, I did.

I made contact with John but, instead of jumping into the conversation with gusto, I was actually quite shy. John was a legend on the circuit and the fact that he took my call in itself was an honor. Fortunately, he took command of the discussion: "What does your foundation do? Where do you need my help the most?" His questions opened up perfect opportunities for me to explain all the incredible programs that the foundation was venturing into. I enthusiastically described in great detail the programs, goals and financial needs.

During our chat, John asked, "Can you hold on for a moment, I need to change my baby's diaper." It was the first time I felt the tenderness in which John lives outside the tennis court. He said those words with such genuine affection, as if nothing comes before the love, needs and care of his children. After the diaper change, we continued the conversation with his baby cooing in the background.

It felt so surreal. I had been sitting, wondering again how I was going to get money for the foundation. Then it snowed. The snowstorm led me to watch TV, which brought me to see John on ESPN at the precise moment he was talking about his work with children's charities. One second I was watching John on television and the next I was asking him to donate.

That is precisely what John did. He donated. For the first time, I didn't leave my mailbox empty handed without a donation. John McEnroe, Grand Slam winner extraordinaire, Nike poster boy, humanitarian, and tennis's so-called bad boy became our first donor! With the large check in hand, I ran onto my balcony, pumping my fists in the air more excited than I had ever been at winning a tennis match. At the top of my lungs, I screamed, "Thank You, God!" followed by a resounding, "Thank you, John!"

That was only the beginning of John's support. He became our number-one ambassador. His donation had a snowball effect. He convinced Nike to donate clothing for the children. Boxes of T-shirts, shorts, sweatshirts, socks, bags and shoes arrived in a variety of sizes so care packages could be filled to the brim with special items.

John encouraged other current and former players to lend us a hand as well. When I came up with the idea to get a job at the Grand Slams to cover program expenses and get access to talk to new sponsors and interested players, John stepped up gallantly.

He made me his assistant for his NBC commentator position at the French Open championships and Wimbledon. It was a dream job opportunity, thrilling me to know I would have to be constantly on my toes. I had a fabulous boss who would be educational and entertaining to work for, but in reality I received far more than expected.

During the two-week Paris event, John took me to art galleries, played soccer and tennis with me, and invited me to meals during our free time. At one point, waiting for the on-air commentary to begin, John pulled out a photo of one of his children. He glowed when he talked about his boy and became teary-eyed because he missed being at home with his kids. John's heart was even bigger than what I imagined, and it didn't stop there.

During our French Open work schedule, John found out, through the tennis grapevine and media announcements, that it was my birthday. He could have easily disregarded the information. His television broadcast coverage wasn't going to be enhanced by knowing this news, and part of my job was to lessen his load, not add to it. Instead, he turned the day into a special celebration. After showing me the sights Paris is famous for, John played guitar for me at the George V hotel and passionately pleaded with the hotel's room service to make a cake fit for a queen.

Never once during our adventures in Paris and London did he drop the protective brotherly affection that he so kindly gave to me. Amid reporters, large corporate heads, his fellow tour pals and commentators, in the broadcast booth, at meals, on every inch of the tournament grounds, even during all his free time, I was part of John's world. He made certain that anyone we came across was well aware that I belonged with him as part of his team, family and heart.

The best of times in the tennis world, during the most interesting of circumstances, was when I worked for John at tournaments. With

John's support, the foundation had a passageway to a future. God placed him as a protective, loving, wise and supportive angel. Over the years, John has stood by me when troubles abounded and the future looked bleak, never giving up his help or his friendship. Plato once said, "Your wealth is where your friends are." My pockets were nearing empty and yet my heart and spirit were divinely and richly full, thanks, in part, to John.

ඏ   ඏ   ඏ

In 1993, after years of successfully running programs from our Aspen headquarters, bringing joy, fun and laughter to children at hospitals throughout the country, we were ready to launch a new Aspen-based program. The first group of children to take part in this creatively minded venture would be from my hometown of Chicago. My vision and mission took another step closer to coming to fruition.

The first group had to come from Chicago. I would have it no other way. God supported the action, because He knew how much I wanted to thank my hometown for their support during my formative years. It was important for me to keep my childhood promise that I made while passing Children's Memorial Hospital for the first time: to remember and help the children there.

I traveled to Chicago to research and talk to representatives from three different facilities: Children's Memorial Hospital of Chicago, a Chicago suburban hospital and a special service program for children that served both the suburbs and the city.

They were all eager to allow their patients to have this valuable opportunity. They shared stories about the individuals who would apply, and as soon as our respective medical teams approved the applications, we could start booking flights.

The number of individuals Heidi and I would host with Beene, Kate and Mary, was fourteen. The Foundation would pay all expenses: airline, hotel, transportation, meals, activities, gifts—everything would be provided for by the main supporters, John McEnroe, Heidi and myself. Beene and Kate had chauffeur licenses so transportation needs were one of their many duties. Mary decided to fly across the country to lend us a hand. I contacted the local hospital and doctors in town and lined them up on a standby, round-the-clock basis. The hotel we selected had a mountain backdrop, pool and open private areas for activities such as arts and crafts and barbecues.

Standing at the airport, waiting for the first participants to arrive, I looked at the foursome I had come to love. There were no cameras, applause or fans heralding their efforts. We didn't think anyone was watching us at all, but someone was. God was taking in the entire scene.

We were all ready to welcome very special guests—children who, for one reason or another, could use a good dose of fun, laughter and joy amidst a serene, protective environment. While other kids were going to school and playing sports, these children spent their time in hospitals, being poked and prodded, getting tested and hooked up to medical devices. These kids knew the sun would always come out tomorrow, but they were not sure how many times they would see it happen.

Heidi, Beene, Kate, Mary and I were full of anticipation as the plane made its landing. We felt comfortable in the airport surroundings, having worked behind the scenes for years. As the plane pulled into the gate, we pressed our faces against the glass door. Our wonderful airline supervisor made sure the plane was greeted with her tender care. Knowing each child from their descriptions, pictures and applications, I started shouting out names as the passengers disembarked: "There's Rhea! Jackie is right behind! Look, there's Caroline!" One after another, I announced names as if I were introducing royalty.

There was no tennis tournament trophy that could compare to the exhilaration I was feeling as those special foundation participants walked across the tarmac and came through the security doors to greet us. This was way bigger than me. It was larger than all the efforts we put forth. This was from God and it was a miracle.

Every detail fell into place; all the arrangements came together. This was life at its best, because we were giving everything of ourselves in order for those less fortunate to have the time of their lives. The week would include lots of fun-filled activities: horseback riding, scenic walks at Maroon Bells, arts and crafts, whitewater rafting, tennis, dinners at popular Aspen hangouts, roasting marshmallows, swimming, fishing, and a last-night celebratory dinner and music extravaganza.

Every participant was unique, gifted in different ways that enhanced the week's events. Jackie took in the majestic beauty around her as if permanently storing it in her heart, to pull up memories to get her through hospital visits. Andrew was sweet, kind and polite in every activity in which he participated. Rhea, the oldest participant at eighteen, was a born leader. She was well aware that her particular cancer, rhabdomyosarcoma, discovered at stage four, was rarely beaten even if discovered at an early stage.

Cancer can take children from their normal, routine environment and place them in a blender with the mix button on high—and that's on a good day. What can come out is a child with not only physical changes but also different ideals and emotions. Their experiences give them a deep wisdom, appreciation and awareness that each day could be their last.

My toughest ordeal at fourteen years of age was figuring out what to order on a hotel room-service menu. These children, at all ages, with Caroline being the youngest at ten, were confronted with the diagnosis and treatment of a disease that would make a grown man, a very strong grown man, fall apart.

The strength and courage that the children and teenagers muster are beyond my comprehension. They enter a medical world full of tests while being examined on a daily basis. In many cases the children endure surgery and lose hair and even limbs. With all that they have been through, their main concern is usually, "Is my family okay with the news?"

Even though the children participating had experienced difficult pasts, and even worse, faced uncertain prognoses for the future, the children had to keep our curfews and follow our rules. Cancer was not allowed to be an excuse for misbehaving. Having been treated differently since their diagnoses, the children enjoyed having boundaries, often pushing them, but knowing we weren't going to pamper them.

Caroline was a playful entertainer as she shared, in a variety of ways, what her world had become since her cancer diagnosis. She had a brain tumor and had been through many surgeries, including the removal of one side of her nose. The doctors chose not to perform cosmetic surgery on her open nasal passage because of the high probability that they would again have to remove a tumor through it. Caroline thought nothing of her facial disfigurement, often joking about it to make others feel at ease. It was the same with her cumbersome oxygen tank that she had at all times, making it her sidekick to bring laughter to the group.

This was certainly a far cry from my childhood antics of blowing bubbles with a straw in my drink. We were all in a different ball game and we knew it. However, our preparatory training and, most importantly, God's grace and love were the reasons that our program worked. The motive behind the staff's involvement was based upon serving God, not obtaining selfish glory. The kids knew that and, unbeknownst to us, so did God.

We couldn't understand how it felt for Rhea to wear a wig and be told she didn't have much time, or for Jackie to have a port device installed in her chest to dispense medicine, or for Caroline to have disfiguring surgery on her face, or for any of the things the other children were going through. But we knew how to give completely, purely and unconditionally from our spirits, hearts and souls.

That is what mattered to the children. They weren't the outsiders, we were, and they loved that. They accepted our noble intentions. They adored us for our efforts to bring fun back in their lives. We became one big family that week. At horseback riding, Rhea exclaimed for the entire group: "You mean to tell me, you all are doing this for us to have fun? You're working your butts off just to help us?"

I had to chuckle at her candor. I was glad she stepped forward to confirm her thoughts. I answered, "Yes. That's right. Is it working? Are you having fun?"

Rhea said, "Are you kidding? This is amazing! This is so cool! I wasn't sure what to expect. This is the best. All of you are awesome."

God had already validated us because He had so generously lined us all up. Now the audience we were serving in His glory, the children, were telling us of their approval and appreciation. God was watching everything, and He had another miraculous surprise to release to increase our efforts.

One of our most celebrated events of the week was a special afternoon at the home of Merv and Thea Adelson. Heidi, Beene, Kate and I spent hours sharpening the tennis skills of these well-known Aspenites. Instead of charging a lesson fee for our personal financial benefit, all lesson proceeds went to the foundation. In the process of sharing tennis tips, Merv and Thea grew fond of our enthusiasm to help children with cancer and they took us under their wings, offering up their home for a festive lunch and an activity-filled afternoon.

In making preparations for all the session's activities I had been in continual contact with the local pediatrician's office. On one specific call, instead of trying to receive vital medical information, I offered an invitation. "Dr. Mitchell, we are having a celebration for the children at the Adelson's ranch, and I wanted to invite you and your staff."

Dr. Mitchell and I went over medical updates and other information. Before we finished the conversation, he said, "Andrea, I know you don't bring outsiders into the program, because you have enough volunteers and you don't want to overwhelm the children with too many adults, but would you consider inviting Fritz and Fabi Benedict? They are an older couple in Aspen, and they love children. They adopted three of their own children, who are now grown up. I am sure Fritz and Fabi would love to be invited."

I was surprised by his request, because he knew of our strict standards in regard to outside people. At the foundation, we conduct criminal background checks and fingerprint all staff and adults who will be assisting in supportive roles with the children's programs. Other protective protocol is also followed. I told him I would think about it and asked if he had the Benedicts' phone number. He didn't. We hung up and I directed my attention to pressing matters at hand. Then I felt a strong pull on my spirit to talk to Heidi about the possible Benedict invitation.

I had never met the Benedicts, but would soon learn from them that they were two of the most prominent long-term residents in Aspen. Fritz was a renowned architect who designed the master plans for the Vail, Snowmass and Breckenridge ski resorts. Dr. Mitchell's request seemed a bit strange, yet Heidi felt the same urging in her spirit that we should invite the couple. We discussed the matter further. Fritz and Fabi had adopted three children. They were siblings and the Benedicts wanted them to be together in a good home and not have their family broken apart and sent to an orphanage. To ensure the children would be brought up together in a safe and loving environment, they adopted them all.

The foundation and the children we care for have created a protective energy in me. I feel blessed by God to have the honor and privilege to spend my life helping children. I expect any individual who is in the children's company to feel the same: that the time is sacred, and it is for the children's benefit, not the adults. An invitation to be part of one of the foundation's programs is a priceless treasure given to us by the children, families and God.

Acknowledging all this information, Heidi and I unanimously decided that Fritz and Fabi Benedict would be invited to take part in the afternoon festivities. With countless items on my to-do list, I bypassed them all to grab the phone book. As I dialed the Benedicts' number, God was in the process of releasing a huge miracle for us.

While I was looking for the phone number in the white pages, Mrs. Benedict was standing in her kitchen, looking out the window across ten acres of prime Aspen real estate that she and her husband owned. This exquisite piece of property had been in the Benedicts' possession for decades. Mrs. Benedict had been carefully keeping the secluded, tranquil and exclusive land for a special purpose, a purpose God had yet to reveal to her. As Fabi surveyed the winding river, tall pine and evergreen trees, the lush fields and majestic mountain atmosphere that made up her property, she felt it was time for the vacant land to take on a higher purpose. At her kitchen window, she prayed to God: "Please give me a sign of what to do with the land. I want it to be for something special; not just a park."

The exact moment Fabi finished declaring those words, her phone rang. Turning from the kitchen window, Mrs. Benedict made the few short steps to answer her phone. "Hello," she announced in a friendly voice.

"Hi. My name is Andrea Jaeger," I said. "Is Mr. or Mrs. Benedict available?"

This initial conversation between Fabi and me lasted only a few minutes. I briefly described the foundation's goals of bringing fun and laughter to children fighting cancer. I extended the luncheon invitation and was happy we could provide some surprise cheer for a dear elderly couple. Mrs. Benedict confirmed all the information, making sure it fit into their schedule. I gave her my home number in case any other questions came up. Fabi Benedict gladly accepted the invitation for herself and her husband.

Before the conversation ended she asked, "Would it be okay to bring the children little gifts?" I explained that it was not necessary but if she wanted to I was sure the children would love presents. The chat was completed and I began focusing on other matters at hand. A few minutes later, the phone rang. Mrs. Benedict did have another question. She decided to call back to get an answer. "Do you have land?"

Did we have land? Not only did we not have land, we constantly worried about where the money was going to come from for the next meal and activity. Most meals Heidi and Beene would prepare in our kitchen and bring to the hotel for everyone to enjoy. The local Hard Rock restaurant learned of our plight and provided a free dinner, and the Caribou Club gave free use of their space for a closing-week dinner and music event, but besides that we didn't even have enough McDonald's coupons for a group meal. When we went fishing with the children at a location that charged for every fish caught, we had to plead with the owner not to charge us the total price as we didn't have the heart to stop the kids from catching fish after their first reel-in. Thankfully, the owner obliged. No, we didn't have land; we existed on dollars stretched as thin as they could be to still keep us afloat. The grace of God kept us going on our shoestring budget. It was like the story of the fish and loaves of bread in the Bible that kept multiplying by some miracle. We were living proof that miracles were happening, because every time we were about to go broke, we looked in the mailbox and a miracle donation was there.

We didn't have land, but oh, how we prayed for it. Heidi and I had walked around countless pieces of property for sale, dreaming and praying that one day we would have land to build a permanent facility for children with cancer.

When Fabi heard the reply that, in fact, "No, we don't have land," she couldn't have been more pleased. "Good! We have land for you."

This incredible miracle, generously bestowed on us from God and Mrs. Benedict, wasn't received with pumping fists and shouted exclamations. Heidi and I were so stunned by the unselfish charitable offer of land that we spent most of our reaction reliving the details to confirm with each other that the miracle really occurred.

"Could it really be?" we kept asking. This land, worth over $10 million, was in the heart of Aspen, only a few short blocks from town. The surroundings were beautiful and would be the absolute crowning jewel for our future children's ranch. Mrs. Benedict was decisive about her wanting to donate the land. In our brief history of fundraising, we had already encountered people who made false commitments. Our hopes would be raised but the donations never came in. Those episodes had been disheartening and damaging. We decided it was a gift in itself to meet the Benedicts. We would hold off all land donation celebrations until after an endorsement came in person. By the time the luncheon arrived, we were immersed in the event at hand.

The sky was a brilliant blue. Crystal clear river water danced over the rocks as it made its way downstream, and the manicured lawn expanded out to welcome our large group. The hosts prepared the picnic tables with brightly colored plates and napkins. Horses and ponies were saddled up for rides. As lunch was about to be served I saw two gentle-looking elderly people making their way down to the picnic area. Light glowed all around them. I motioned to Heidi that Mr. and Mrs. Benedict had arrived. I walked over to greet them and help with the big bag of toys Mrs. Benedict brought. Mr. Benedict had large blueprint plans rolled up under his arm.

Their smiles immediately warmed the hearts of everyone around. In a moment's time they were in the middle of a crowd of children welcoming them to their picnic. Fritz and Fabi adored that their hands were grabbed as if they were the grandparents of us all. We had not made a formal announcement about the land donation, as we wanted the Benedicts to meet us and be sure about their large commitment.

With great delight, Fabi passed out her gifts, which were a big hit with all the kids. The sound of chirping birds, laughing children and festive music echoed throughout the valley. It was a Norman Rockwell scene in full action. As the children finished lunch, Merv and Thea asked who was interested in meeting their horses and ponies for the rides that would happen later that day.

The children eagerly made their way over to pet and learn about their rides. Heidi and I sent Beene, Kate, Mary and the medical team to help watch the children, as we volunteered to clean up the lunch area. With one table cleared, Fritz and Fabi asked if we could sit with them a moment. Fritz spread out the blueprints on the tabletop. With a sparkle in her eyes, Fabi declared, "This is it. This is the land we are giving you." I had to ask. "Are you sure?" That was when Fabi told us of the story of what had occurred between her and God moments before my phone call. Heidi and I had tears in our eyes as she recounted the story. Fabi finished by saying, "We know God wants you to have this land. We are so happy to give it to you."

I stared at the blueprints of the land and looked up at our generous contributors. For months I had been working on transparencies, detailing my hopes for a permanent facility with brightly colored markers. Now the drawings would have a home. I reflected on the past and how everything had progressed to this point: my injury, meeting Heidi, the car accident, moving to Aspen, the approval of the foundation on my birthday, John's donation—these were not random episodes of life. They were all connected. They existed for a purpose bigger than I would ever be able to comprehend.

The purposes glowed with God's love, and their evolution was made possible by His grace. Heidi and I stood in faith and God delivered. Heidi believed in me and in the foundation before anyone even cared to listen. Now we were looking at land on paper, and before long, the kind, generous people before us were going to take us to walk on it. Soon the land would take on a life of its own, too, under the direction of God.

The confirmation from the Benedicts made my heart beat so loud I thought it was going to burst out of my chest. As if on cue, we all jumped to our feet and began hugging and thanking each other, as if we had all grown up together under the same roof. Under God's watchful eyes, the foundation family grew again.

And God still had more blessings to come.

Chapter Sixteen

But he who looks into the perfect law of liberty
[God's Word], and continues in it, and is not a
forgetful hearer but a doer of the work, this one
will be blessed in what he does.

—James 1:25

The further I became encamped in my children's foundation world, the more distance I was creating between my former life and the present. My parents' hope that my shoulder would miraculously repair itself for an immediate return to the tennis courts, in top form, was never going to be realized. While most people who knew me as an athlete applauded my new role, others were decidedly unsupportive. A fellow tour player passed me on the streets in Aspen and voiced her strong opinion about my choice of dedicating my life and tennis earnings to help children. "What's the point? The kids are going to die anyway," she said nonchalantly.

The comment stunned me. For a split second I thought about responding in the same rude tone. But instead of sounding off like a foghorn on a gloomy day, or bellowing out like a volcano, I gave a speech that expressed the responsibility we all have to protect and help children, sick or not. I was so exasperated by her remark that I hardly took a breath. I responded with, "These children are not dying of cancer, they are *living with* cancer."

That clarification summed up our program's mission. As long as there was life, let's do something about helping the children live it. We were going to be the factors in making a difference for children to live fully each moment.

Our philosophy included providing long-term support to enhance the lives of children with cancer. Instead of using negative lines we heard from people such as, "He is terminal," or "She is a goner," we decided to use phrases such as, "We are here to do something to help support you beyond this week of fun and laughter." One girl approached us and said, "Before I met you, I sat at home depressed about my cancer. I was waiting to die on the anticipated schedule the doctors gave me, which is months out. But I am going to go home and live with cancer and throw out that D-day I have been given."

That girl lived three years longer than what the doctors predicted. We helped fulfill one of her biggest dreams by paying for part of her college tuition. She was an inspiration to countless people and made a direct impact on hundreds of cancer patients and other individuals as well. Days before her death, she said, "Thank you. You helped give me extra years that had a purpose."

Often, we didn't understand the full impact the foundation had on benefiting the children and their families. We kept our focus, as if propelled to a destination known only from above. The thank-you's and appreciative letters we received from hospitals, children, families and donors were touching, heartfelt and overwhelmingly positive. We were, indeed, making a difference.

One of the children, Sonia, also loved writing. Had she lived longer, she would have graced the world with volumes of her wisdom and teachings. Despite Sonia's death at a young age, her words have found a home in many people's hearts. She wrote:

> *I went there [the ranch], with a frightened, hopeless and fearful soul and left with a confident, hopeful and cheerful one. Since the first day I was there I could feel a transformation taking place. If there were any doubts, fears or insecurities, there were always words of encouragement, support and inspiration that drove them away.*
>
> *All the staff from the Silver Lining Ranch just opened the doors of their hearts to all of us and made everyone feel welcome. I felt I was surrounded by angels who were shining rays of hope, faith and trust in my heart, which was lacking and yearning to regain all three.*

Every time I thought the children's foundation work should be the sole focus for my spiritual growth, God changed my opinion. He wanted me to have a balanced perspective, along with increasing my knowledge on the importance of prayer. During one of Chris Evert's pregnancies, God nudged me several times, with His audible voice, that Chris should be included in my nightly prayer routine. I was obedient to His request, assuming that the subject was over. Again came His voice on my spirit, "Call Chris. She needs to pray, too."

That part felt a little strange. I grew up around Chris on the tennis circuit. For years, we had played on the same team representing the United States in international competitions. We had traveled to worldwide destinations together, shared the same locker room, learned two-handed backhands from our fathers and played tennis in front of thousands of people. Yet we were not close friends.

The age factor contributed to that. When Chris had already

established herself as a tennis icon, helping create a huge tennis boom in the United States and abroad, I was a kid romping around, having fun, searching for my true calling and purpose in life. We were decidedly different, from our personalities, to the way we conducted ourselves, to the life goals we strived to achieve. Chris had reached the number-one ranking, won numerous Grand Slam events and was focused on her tennis career. I loved training and working hard, playing tournaments and traveling the world exploring my interests in hidden ways.

My 1982 victories over Chris at the Virginia Slims of California tournament, the French Open and the Family Circle Cup Tournament were certainly satisfying wins, but mostly because they paid tribute to special people in my life. My sister, Susy, on a weekend break from Stanford, cheered me on when I won the Oakland, California, event, defeating top-seeded Chris in the finals. It was an important victory because Susy sacrificed a great deal in order to ensure my success. I wanted her to see firsthand what she helped make possible for my tennis career.

The challenge to beat Chris on clay at the Family Circle Cup event had the added notoriety of Chris having an incredible clay-court winning streak in progress. Susy and my mom watched the match on television, so winning that match brought extra joy. Defeating Chris in the French Open semifinal was another victory that my family could be part of, since their support helped groom my successful venture on the pro circuit.

But those results were in the past. My world was different now. I didn't want our history or any old wounds caused by the competition to resurface. Leaving the tennis circuit kept those memories in the distance. With an open heart, I prayed for Chris on my private time. God's request to call Chris and deliver a personal message to her felt altogether different. I was not sure how she would react to my public declaration of faith.

I no longer had Chris's home number, nor did God give me direction on how to rekindle communication with her. I went back in time again, trying to muster up some method that would help. My mom had wanted me to grow up, behave, dress and be like Chris Evert, cringing every time I dove for a ball and bloodied up my knees, or when I questioned a call ruthlessly, and when I went off on my exploits of curiosity. Whenever she said, "Why can't you be more like Chris?" I answered simply, "Because I am Andrea."

None of those recollections were helping my case. Then I remembered the all-important point. It didn't matter what I thought, felt or wanted. The issue was: How did I want to stand before God? I chose to stand in faith and obedience to His request even if it might mean I would feel foolish, could appear crazy to Chris, stumble on my words or reopen old wounds. None of those possibilities mattered as I started my investigative work to find Chris at home.

It was an uncomfortable call that I rehearsed over and over. I fluctuated between going through pleasantries and ending the call with the message or doing the reverse. With each touch of the number pad, I hoped for the answering service to pick up. After a few rings a familiar voice came on the line. I chose the latter course of action, diving right into the message. I stammered out quickly, "Hi Chris, this is Andrea. Well, here's why I am calling. God told me to pray for you and call you. Is everything okay? And you are supposed to pray, too."

I held my breath, waiting for a response, secretly thinking a dial tone about now would help. Surprisingly, one didn't appear. Chris was a little surprised to hear from me, but she held on to the receiver. Perhaps because of the concentrated delivery of my message, she said, "Excuse me, what did you say?" I repeated the information. She sounded slightly taken aback, but she was receptive to talking longer. She told me that her doctor advised her to spend the last trimester of her pregnancy in bed, for her and the baby's health. The conversation became more comfortable with each line. Finally, we said our good-byes and I hung up, letting out a huge sigh of relief.

I knew God had an inside track to the information on her pregnancy. More was needed than bed rest, and He wanted Chris to know that. The prayers were important. Happily, Chris delivered a healthy baby boy a short time later.

Another episode where God told me to pray and call someone happened with a friend and coworker. Rachel's father was a long-time president of one of the largest corporations in America. Rachel could have followed in her father's footsteps, amassing a great amount of wealth, but instead followed her heart and chose to become a social worker. Her studies kept her in New York during the school year, but her summers and winter break periods were devoted to assisting the children in our Foundation's programs. Her enthusiastic involvement was met with joy and excitement from the children and foundation staff alike.

Rachel was back in New York, working at an inner city high school, when God commanded my spirit while I was in Aspen to "Pray for Rachel." This was an immediate assignment. Always attentive when God urged me to help others, I continued to take in the message. "Call Rachel and give her a warning to be especially watchful in the coming days." Responding to the need at hand, I addressed God's heavenly kingdom and asked for an army of His obedient angels to convene and step in to guarantee the safety of Rachel. This particular warning included the defusing of a dangerous situation.

Relationships involving God can be very sensitive and personal subjects to broach with others. A forceful statement, even a well-intentioned one from a place of love, can strain or ruin a friendship and trust between people. Disagreements about religious beliefs have been the root cause of countless conflicts between individuals and nations.

I did not want to intrude on Rachel's religious beliefs, yet I had to be obedient to God to share a message of great value. Rachel and I had talked about God and prayer on various occasions, but the subject never approached a deep level in the way that one holds his or her most sacred truths. We worked together well and held great respect for each other. The message and my need to follow it completely, by calling Rachel, was crossing into new territory of a more personal nature that could also affect our professional relationship. My action involved revealing deeply hidden parts of my relationship with God, both past and present, in order to give Rachel the background of the reason for my phone call.

Calling Rachel out of the blue with this kind of subject material was going to be a new experience for both of us. God urged me on and I proceeded. I dialed each number very deliberately, as if the dialogue of the conversation was being created with each digit of the phone number. Rachel answered with a welcoming tone. It helped relieve some of the apprehension I was feeling about how she would receive the intent of the phone call. The comfortable nature I had with Rachel directed the flow of the conversation to how God sometimes communicates with me. The words didn't flow completely effortlessly, but as time went on, I felt more at ease in describing how God occasionally gives me warnings about things to pray for.

I recounted a few examples of how God had delivered messages to me, including a few times that involved warnings. The topic took a more personal turn toward Rachel as I relayed how God was releasing a warning for her, and she needed to be protected from an upcoming dangerous situation. Rachel was her usual kind self and didn't seem too rattled by what I was saying. She took it all in with her calm demeanor, and said, "Everything is okay." After I felt I had given her proper warning to be careful, we hung up the phone.

A few days went by. God was still giving me urgent messages to pray, which I did. I wanted to call Rachel to see if anything was amiss, but God didn't give me any further instructions to phone her. I kept up my prayer instructions and waited. I felt a sense of heaviness and then all of a sudden a release. The burden from the message was gone and with it, I assumed, the danger.

Shortly after, I received a call from Rachel. I knew things were okay but waited to let her tell me herself. Rachel began the conversation with, "The weirdest thing happened to me. I was sitting at my desk at school after classes were over. I was facing away from the door, when all of a sudden I thought of your call and sensed danger." Rachel continued explaining, "The hair on the back of my neck went up. I thought of our talk, remained calm, so as to not startle anyone. What I felt was danger in the classroom doorway."

Indeed, Rachel was right. Standing in the doorway to the classroom, staring at her, was a student with a gun. Rachel made no quick or jerky movements in her chair. She knew not to alarm the student. After the armed pupil gazed at her for a bit, he left. Rachel was not harmed. The police found the boy, still armed, and arrested him. After Rachel finished her emotional story, I said, "I am so glad things ended up okay. See, God was watching over you."

Partnering up with God is the best way to discover purpose. In all the years, the decades actually, of God communicating to me, He has never been wrong regarding what I should be praying about or who I should be delivering a message to. His messaging service is infallible. Of course, listening and being obedient every time has been a challenge for me. I felt ridiculous calling both Chris and Rachel to say, "Hello, I recently received a warning message from God for you," however, the trust I had in God knowing the bigger picture far outweighed any apprehension I felt at how the message would be received.

It was crucial for me to be a messenger of God's Word and not only a recipient. In doing so, He allowed me to further the extent of my calling and purpose.

Chapter Seventeen

Do not forget to entertain strangers,
for by so doing some have unwittingly
entertained angels.

—Hebrews 13:2

One day in 1994, God provided me with a special message of love that told me to go overseas. I was not overjoyed with the plan God had in mind for me, because I didn't see how I could get away. I was busy as usual, diligently researching new and operating children's programs while keeping up with the foundation's day-to-day affairs.

God was urging me to accept an invitation I had received. But interrupting my routine to travel abroad to the opening of Paul Newman's Barrestown Gang Camp in Ireland seemed out of the question, both financially and time wise. God, however, had other ideas. I had researched and visited Mr. Newman's East Coast camp for children battling diseases in past years, and for some reason I was placed on the invitation list for his Ireland camp opening.

With God's strong message to go to Ireland for the one-afternoon event, I knew I had to make the trip happen, but complications swirled in my mind. Then, as I thought there was no way I could pull it off, I received my Last Eight Club credential from the Wimbledon Tennis Championships. Any player who makes the advanced stage of the tournament is honored by qualifying for an annual renewable pass to attend the two-week championships. Since I had played in the finals, I, and a guest, could take advantage of this privilege every year. This was a blessing that I had the fortune to be reminded of. I would have access to the grounds during the two-week summer championships, and the dates coincided exactly with Paul Newman's event.

I had long desired to manage a program for children from London at Wimbledon, since Wimbledon tournament director Christopher Gorringe, the entire tournament support group and fan base, had been so overwhelmingly kind to me during my playing years. Now I needed funding to make the trip a success. After a lengthy discussion with Heidi, it was decided I would accept a two-week tennis commentary position that was open for an international network—if they could guarantee me one day off to attend the Newman camp festivity.

The graces kept flowing: Airline, hotel, and meals would be covered, and the television pay would cover all the children's program expenses. The added bonus included getting one day off to fly to Ireland and attend the gala. I took advantage of the opportunities and made my voyage to London. Commentary duties secured, I worked diligently until it was time to depart for Dublin. The evening I arrived in Ireland, there was a message at the front desk about a pre-event cocktail party at a pub down the road.

I glanced at my watch and realized the party was to begin in a matter of minutes. Still in my television wardrobe, I hustled to my room, quickly changed, and made my way to the pub. Navigating my way through the crowded drinking establishment, I noticed a private, sectioned-off area outside that was designated for the party. All the tables were full and people seemed to be deep in conversation. I felt tremendously out of place; I didn't fit in with the crowd and, surprisingly, I felt like a foreigner in my own field of work.

I took a sip of my sparkling water, leaned against the wall and silently implored God to, "Please show me if I am in the right place." I had over six days of commentary work left to do. I loved the staff I worked with, but I was weary of talking about forehands and backhands ten hours a day. I had wrapped up the children's programs after the first week of the competition; more tennis analysis was all that remained for me. I started adjusting to the reality of a long week ahead. I began to wonder if I was really supposed to be here. All I wanted to do now was go home.

With that thought, God stepped up mightily. As quick as a crack of lightning the entire horizon changed. I overheard a couple talking about a blonde lady leaning against the other side of the pub wall, removed from the crowd. I listened intently. "I heard she recently returned from a trip to Africa where she studied animals. What a crazy thing to do." That was it—a sign that I was in the right place!

I've always loved animals and even studied zoology in my free time. I briefly reminisced about the incredible visit I had taken to a cheetah breeding facility while playing a tennis event in South Africa. I had a captivating close encounter with a king cheetah. I was photographed with another cheetah, and the picture is still one of my favorites.

I rapidly made my way through the group and approached the elegant, graceful blonde-haired woman, who was quietly positioned away from the core gathering of people.

"Hi. Did you really just get back from an African safari trip?" I asked. Sure enough, the woman, whose name was Daphne, did make such a journey. She then proceeded, with her delightful British accent, to captivate me with countless, detailed stories of every animal species she came across. Discovering I was part of

God's purposeful and special encounters, I bathed in the light of the visit with this stranger who was quickly becoming a friend.

Daphne's eyes held vast wisdom with a sparkling dose of heavenly character. She was fascinating and worldly, yet humble. The more stories Daphne shared, the more apparent it became that this was a blessed trip. After Daphne had spent a lot of time with me, other people approached her for a visit. She looked at me before leaving the party and said, "Find me tomorrow at the camp opening."

Waiting for my taxi outside the pub entryway, I acknowledged God's presence and effect on the evening. I looked into the night sky and said, "Thank You." I was thousands of miles away from my country and home, yet God made sure I was nestled close, right in His pocket.

The next morning, I awoke with a comfortable sense of belonging. After making notes for the following day's Wimbledon television duties, I headed over to the camp opening ceremony. Sure enough, there was Daphne, happily waving me over to her position by the lake. She welcomed me into her family and circle of friends—one being Paul Newman. I eventually learned that Daphne grew up with the Newman family in Connecticut. Her mother, Mrs. Warburg, was a neighbor and good friend of Paul's.

Rarely, if ever, did I operate with preconceived notions of a person. I didn't like it when it was done to me, so I avoided doing it to others. However, I made an exception in Mr. Newman's case, because his good works were found everywhere. They weren't too good to be true; they were good *and* true. Paul has meant a great deal to millions of people around the world. His creative artistry is legendary, having accumulated an Oscar and countless other cinematic achievement awards. Newman's Own products have provided millions of dollars for innumerable charities. Mr. Newman's children's camps have touched thousands of special souls. He is a father, husband, philanthropist, grandfather, race car driver—the accolades could fill volumes of books.

My thoughts were concentrated on keeping up with Daphne, which was no small task, and taking in the extraordinary celebration of children enjoying the jubilee. Television crews, photographers and curious onlookers were all part of the audience at the opening of the Barrestown Gang Camp.

Casually, Daphne announced, "I want to introduce you to Paul. Follow me." Since the event was about children, it didn't dawn on me that he would actually be in attendance. She escorted me to a manor, up stairways and through corridors. As I thanked the fact that I was still in good enough shape to keep up with Daphne's lead, I decided to forgo a lifetime tradition. In all my years of meeting people, I never prepared an introduction ahead of time. Even representing the United States as a teenager, when I was invited to the White House to meet the president, I didn't prepare a statement or remark beforehand, choosing instead to speak off the cuff, from the heart.

Now I was choreographing an introduction. "Mr. Newman, what an honor." I tried ten different variations of the same line. We were nearly at the end of the top floor, taking the last turn, when it happened. We bumped right into Paul. Daphne didn't hesitate for a second. "Paul, this is Andrea Jaeger." I was about to stammer out my practiced, polished lines when Mr. Newman took over the floor.

"Andrea, I have heard great things about you. It is a pleasure meeting you," he said. It was a warm and genuine greeting. His mouth did keep moving; I just couldn't hear anything he said after those first few lines. Eventually I regained my composure and it became a natural, comfortable, friendly conversation and we talked for several minutes. A representative of the press staff for the event came to usher Mr. Newman away for an interview. He refused to end the conversation rudely. Without rushing, he politely excused himself.

Daphne looked at me, pleased with the encounter, and said, "He likes you." I didn't agree or nod or say anything articulate. I just continued following Daphne around as if God had designated a fleet of angels to watch over me in this foreign land that was feeling more comfortable every second.

Eventually, the Barrestown opening ceremony festivities came to an end. I spent the afternoon at Daphne's side, being schooled and directed in exciting and inspiring ways. I assumed it was time to say our farewells, but I was pleasantly surprised when she graciously invited me to a special reception being held in Paul's honor with Irish dignitaries. I could attend the royal affair and still make it back to London in time for my Wimbledon duties the next day. I could hardly believe my good fortune, especially after my initial reluctance to come to the U.K. I had ventured here alone and, thanks to God's support, came away with more members of the foundation family.

Our group—made up of Mr. Newman, Daphne, Daphne's son and mom, and me—walked along the perfectly manicured lawns of the dignitary's estate. The conversation flowed effortlessly, bonds were being established and I felt God's carpentry work in action. He was chiseling away parts of me—which had been hardened by disappointing interactions with people in the past—to make room for these ordained encounters to take root.

Besides the lifetime friendships I made with Daphne and Mr. Newman, windows and doors of opportunity were opening up for the foundation on behalf of their generous efforts. Mr. Newman—who continuously and lightheartedly corrected me by saying, "You can call me Paul"—would be responsible for introducing me to the highly sought after, legendary philanthropist and humanitarian, Michael Bloomberg, who is now mayor of New York City.

Back home in Aspen I received a phone call from Mr. Newman. He said, "Andrea, why don't you come to New York so I can help introduce you to some very special people?" It wasn't in our budget to go to New York, because I had no access to jobs that I could work at to pay my expenses.

I answered, "Mr. Newman—oh, sorry, I did it again—Paul, are you sure I should call you Paul?"

"Yes, I prefer Paul," he said.

"Okay, well, I would love to come to New York to meet people who may be interested in helping with the programs we are running," I answered, trying not to sound stunned.

"Great, then it is settled. Where will you be staying?" he said.

I answered, "I don't know anyone that I could stay with in New York, so I will have to get back to you on that."

"You don't know anyone in New York?" Paul replied incredulously.

"No, not anyone I could stay with," I said.

"Then you will stay with us at the New York City apartment. Call Darice and she will set it all up." Darice was Paul's longtime loyal and gifted assistant. I hung up the phone and called Darice. It was all arranged.

I explained to Heidi, "Mr. Newman invited me to New York to meet possible donors, and he said I could stay at his apartment." What I loved so much about Heidi is she never built up anything beyond what it was—a gift from God. She never thought we were special, never let the famous people we met affect her pride or ego. It helped keep our mission in focus and prevented us from becoming starstruck.

Heidi's response was perfect, "Stay true to yourself by letting God guide your ways."

I boarded the plane for New York, and studied my philanthropy and business management texts for the entire flight. At Paul's apartment, I had my own bathroom and bedroom. Still, I tried to pitter-patter around the place so as not to disturb anyone. In reality, if I thundered through the floor it wouldn't have bothered Paul, Joanne or Darice. Paul was always up before me, using the morning time to work out. Caring in a variety of ways, Joanne Woodward, Paul's enchanting wife and a star and philanthropist in her own right, saw

Paul and me off to a dinner event. As we stood in the hallway, Joanne lovingly came over to help get my attire in order. I still had my dry cleaning tag on the inside of my long winter coat and a small piece was sticking out. "Let me give you a hug before you go," she said. As Joanne hugged me I felt a tiny pull. In her hand, where she tried to hide it for fear of embarrassing me, was my dry cleaning tag. God, in His love, cares about the smallest of details. I smiled at the heartfelt gesture Joanne showed me, as if I was her daughter, getting ready to go out in the world for the very first time.

The intimate, private home dinner Paul brought me to was a veritable who's who of the celebrity, business, entertainment and humanitarian fields. Paul made sure the host of the event placed me at a very specific chair. I took my seat and as the chairs filled, I realized the dinner was a fund-raiser for Paul's camp in Ireland.

Not wanting to take donor dollars meant for Paul's cause, I never volunteered my field of work and how desperately the Silver Lining Foundation needed funding. A gentleman walked up next to me and said, "Hello. I believe they have assigned me this seat."

I looked up to see a charming, handsome man in a well-pressed suit and tie. As the gentleman was trying to get into his seat, several people came over hoping to make a connection. Others took great pleasure in introducing him. "This is the one and only Michael Bloomberg . . . New York billionaire, philanthropist, and head of Bloomberg News. . . ." The list went on and on.

Mr. Bloomberg was confident and, like Paul, did not need his accolades listed as part of his introduction. The more they flowed, the more it looked like he just wanted to sit down, like everyone else had the opportunity to do so. However, people were so totally enamored by his presence that they refused to give him the space to sit. I watched in admiration as Michael handled the situation with poise, charm and extreme patience.

Finally, the host escorted the individuals away and Michael

grabbed his chair. Immediately, he politely introduced himself and we struck up a friendly conversation.

Michael Bloomberg's high profile, business acumen and humanitarian efforts meant he was often covered in the media. During my research on the business and philanthropic worlds, I read *Forbes* magazine features on the people I wanted to learn more from and possibly meet one day. They were all strangers when I cut out their pictures and the descriptive paragraphs about them, and taped them on my bedroom walls. I thought if I went to sleep and woke up with these influential people staring back at me, I would become familiar with them and might even be able to cross their paths. I was hoping each of the people I studied would help me grow to become an ambassador on behalf of children.

What none of the news accounts on Michael Bloomberg captured was his humor, charisma, protective nature, engaging personality, sparkling eyes and special smile. When conversation at the table centered on Michael and how we all had had our first privileged meeting with him, I spoke up in turn. "Does it count as a meeting if Michael's *Forbes* features are on my bedroom wall? I didn't meet Michael before tonight, but in a strange way I always knew this day would come."

Our table companions looked at me stunned. I wasn't a socialite like many people in the group. I certainly wasn't an actress, singer, celebrity type or a woman looking to land a rich, successful husband. Being a millionaire was no longer an issue since I gave away all my tennis earnings, and I was comfortable picking up odd and different jobs on behalf of helping children. I didn't head up a famous corporation and I was most definitely no longer a tennis professional. People were intrigued with my remark and asked why I would do such a thing. I said, "I studied the profiles so I could learn from the best how to run a children's charitable organization." I continued, "If even a small part of me can be as wise, caring and giving as Michael Bloomberg, then God will have done a terrific job with me."

I truly meant it. Giving isn't about the money, even though money is critical to help fund programs. Bigger than the money is the motive, the spirit in which the giving is conducted. And of even greater importance is making sure the love involved in the action is filled with God's love. A person might only be able to afford giving ten dollars a year to charity, or maybe ten prayers, or one dollar or one prayer, or, in Michael's case, upwards of $350 million—which he has done in a three-year span alone. Whatever the amount contributed, the percentage of the donation given from the heart and spirit should be the same—100 percent. I knew Michael based his actions—from a personal, professional and philanthropic standpoint—on the 100 percent scale, and that is what I wanted to achieve.

During the dinner, I would catch glimpses of Paul looking across the room with great approval, well pleased with what he had lined up. Paul Newman and Michael Bloomberg were two incredible men who God gifted to the world, and here I was having the privilege of getting to know them beyond a formal introduction. In the handful of the dearest, significant, influential and lifelong relationships I would ever have in my life, three new heavenly additions were added: Michael Bloomberg, Paul Newman and Daphne Astor.

Chapter Eighteen

I will not leave you orphans;
I will come to you.

—John 14:18

In 1994, I won *Family Circle* magazine's Player Who Makes a Difference award. A fund-raiser dinner was scheduled in my honor during the Family Circle Cup tennis event, and the award came with a much-needed donation. I returned to Hilton Head, South Carolina, for the festivities, where I had played many matches in my tennis career. I was totally unaware that God was arranging yet another partnership to benefit me and children around the world.

Eager to help the event, beyond my appreciation for the prestigious award, I signed up for the tournament charity clinic for physically and emotionally challenged children. The professional tennis players who decided to teach their tennis skills could choose any court and proceed in a fashion that suited their talents. Due to my numerous shoulder problems, I decided to move past the serve court in order to avoid my shoulder coming out of its socket. My seven shoulder surgeries, including one that removed part of my scapula where it was rubbing against my spine, did nothing to help with the continual subluxation issues.

I came upon a volley court and decided to grab a basket of balls and start some fun drills and instruction. During a free moment of ball collection, the tour player on the court approached me. Her name was Maja Muric, a young Croatian player.

In a distinct European accent, the twenty-year-old promising athlete came up to me and said, "I know you help children with cancer. Where I am from, children not only have cancer, they have the war to deal with. Do you think you can help kids from my area who are suffering from war and cancer?"

I was impressed. It was obvious Maja was more interested in helping children from her war-torn country than being number one in the world.

The tennis court we were on was full of children with different challenges, all trying to learn how to play tennis, so we had to concentrate on the task at hand. The next time we had a chance to talk was at the player party. The tournament organizers were pulling out all the stops for my arrival. I had a two-bedroom condo to use for the week for free and great support in running the on-site children's cancer program that I arranged to head up. The kids visiting for the day from a cancer hospital were sponsored by the foundation. They would receive special guest badges, prime seating at the center court matches, a buffet lunch, a tour of the pressroom that included meeting legendary tennis columnist and television commentator Bud Collins, and multiple gift packages—all a far cry from the hospital environment.

The event committee asked if I could attend the player party to meet corporate sponsors and I happily obliged. As I was departing after my duties, I heard a familiar voice. I turned around to find Maja, the same player who approached me at the tennis clinic, frantically trying to get a ride back to her housing. It was apparent that no one was helping her. The seeded players and top pros are always given special treatment; it was a well-known perk of the position.

Maja, not having a high-level ranking, rarely received any special privileges at tennis events. She was highly agitated that no one at the players' transportation desk was interested in her need for a ride back to her accommodations. I pulled up in my rental car and asked if she wanted a lift. I seldom ate at player parties because I wanted to meet as many people as possible, so I asked Maja if she wanted to get a bite to eat. We ended up grabbing dinner and discussing ideas about helping children in her war-torn hometown.

Maja spent the evening passionately describing why the programs were needed in her native country. She told me of bombings, mortar shells and sniper shootings, and how this had an effect on the country's children. The exclusive vacation environment of Hilton Head Island was a far cry from her homeland—war-battered cities with buildings that were reduced to rubble; hospitals lacking basic supplies; shortages in food and clothing—but Maja refused to forget the children so desperately in need. Maja felt assured I was going to be someone who could help make a difference.

It was getting late and I wanted to be refreshed for the next day and night's activities, so we decided it was time to head back to our respective locations. On the drive back to Maja's housing, I was flabbergasted to hear police sirens behind my rental car. Thinking the patrol car was racing to get to an emergency, I pulled over slightly to the side. Then the reality of the situation hit me full throttle. I was being pulled over by a police officer. "Please get out of your car," the policeman's voice on the loudspeaker said authoritatively, completely interrupting my thoughts about helping kids in Eastern Europe.

I had no alcohol to drink that night—in fact I have only had a drink on five occasions in my entire life, and this was not one of those festive or toast situations. Still, I was being pulled over for drunk driving. It was hard to make out the street signs in Hilton Head at night, so I was driving a bit slowly—stopping often for us to locate Maja's street. Maja tried to contain her laughter. She had never experienced seeing someone pulled over for drunk driving when the driver had not even been drinking. Now, instead of being impressed by my past history of assisting those less fortunate, Maja was getting entertained by my not-so-enjoyable circumstances.

Because I was driving so slowly, the police officer assumed that I was heavily intoxicated. He asked me to step outside the car and perform a variety of sobriety tests. Saying the alphabet backwards was not my forte. I failed that one. Walking in a straight line in fancy shoes was not my talent either, and it was made worse by the fact that I had a policeman staring at me. Unbelievably, I stood a very real chance of being booked for something I didn't do. Meanwhile, my new friend Maja tried desperately to hide her laughter. It was becoming quite comical to both of us how dire the situation was becoming. I finally pleaded to take the breathalyzer test.

When all looked hopeless, the officer asked me one simple question again. "Did you have anything to drink tonight?"

"No sir," I replied. "You can call the restaurant if you like. I promise, I swear to God, I have had nothing to drink. We were lost and trying to locate the right street. Please believe me."

The police officer went back to his patrol car. Ten tense minutes went by. When he came back, he handed me my driver's license and said the words I was hoping to hear. "I believe you. I believe you were lost." I wanted to jump out of the car and hug him.

Too rattled to go to sleep, Maja and I stayed up sharing stories. Our introduction on the tennis court certainly wasn't a random encounter. God set it up. Maja told me many personal stories about herself that night. Her mother had tried to abort her when she found out she was pregnant with her. The abortion plan didn't work and Maja's entry into the world was not very welcomed by her natural family. Maja's mom left her when she was eight, and Maja's dad

We care about your opinions. Please take a moment to fill out this Reader Survey card and mail it back to us.
As a special **"thank you"** we'll send you exciting news about interesting books and a valuable **Gift Certificate.**

Please PRINT using ALL CAPS

First
Name [   ] MI. [ ] Last
Name [   ]

Address [   ]

City [   ] ST [ ] Zip [   ] — [   ]

Phone # ([   ]) [   ] — [   ] Fax # ([   ]) [   ] — [   ]

Email [   ]

(1) Gender:
____ Female ____ Male

(2) Age:
____ 12 or under ____ 40-59
____ 13-19 ____ 60+
____ 20-39

(3) Marital Status
____ Married
____ Single
____ Divorced/Widowed

(4) Did you receive this book as a gift?
____ Yes ____ No

(5) How many Health Communications books have you bought or read?
____ 1 ____ 2-4 ____ 5+

(6) How did you find out about this book?
Please fill in ONE.
1) ____ Recommendation
2) ____ Store Display
3) ____ Bestseller List
4) ____ Online
5) ____ Advertisement
6) ____ Catalog/Mailing
7) ____ Interview/Review (TV, Radio, Print)

(7) Where do you usually buy books?
Please fill in your top TWO choices.
1) ____ Bookstore
2) ____ Religious Bookstore
3) ____ Online
4) ____ Book Club/Mail Order
5) ____ Price Club (Costco, Sam's Club, etc.)
6) ____ Retail Store (Target, Wal-Mart, etc.)

(9) What subjects do you enjoy reading about most? Rank only *FIVE*. Use 1 for your favorite, 2 for second favorite, etc.

	1	2	3	4	5
1) Parenting/Family	O	O	O	O	O
2) Relationships	O	O	O	O	O
3) Recovery/Addictions	O	O	O	O	O
4) Health/Nutrition	O	O	O	O	O
5) Christianity	O	O	O	O	O
6) Spirituality/Inspiration	O	O	O	O	O
7) Business Self-Help	O	O	O	O	O
8) Teen Issues	O	O	O	O	O
9) Sports	O	O	O	O	O

(14) What attracts you most to a book?
(Please rank 1-4 in order of preference.)

	1	2	3	4
1) Title	O	O	O	O
2) Cover Design	O	O	O	O
3) Author	O	O	O	O
4) Content	O	O	O	O

BB1

TAPE IN MIDDLE; DO NOT STAPLE

FOLD HERE

Comments:

soon after that, even though he stayed in her life in some ways. Maja's grandparents raised her, but it was still not a good situation. Maja was severely abused by her father—whenever he was around—throughout her childhood and adolescence. The experiences were so traumatic that she blocked many of them out in order to survive. Despite all the pain and suffering she endured, her spirit was never broken. That is what God does. He makes His children whole regardless of physical or emotional pain and suffering, by urging their spirits to move toward God and their divine callings.

Maja took up tennis as a means of fun and escape. She was a gifted athlete who practiced hard but didn't care about being number one in the world. She hadn't received worldwide fame and fortune in tennis yet, because her true rewards were to be found in serving God to help children. Like me, Maja was given the honor of having tennis be the catalyst to meet others with a like-minded mission of helping children. Also similar to me, Maja still needed knowledge, direction and salvation—all things God was ready and willing to deliver.

When I met Maja, she had already lived through twenty years of difficult circumstances. Her grandmother had died. Maja had no money to get back to Croatia for the funeral. She was in such bad shape financially that the clothes and shoes she wore no longer fit her properly. But she had a heart as big as a mountain. Out of all the players that God could have picked to be on my court during my award ceremony week, He chose one who would become a lifetime partner in helping bring fun and laughter to children around the globe.

At the Family Circle Cup awards gala, Heidi arrived for the dinner and ceremony with a great group of Aspen community and foundation well-wishers. I accepted the award and looked forward to the foundation's new horizons. The ceremony took place in April; by autumn I was on my way to Croatia. The foundation, and through Heidi and my personal support, was able to secure medical supplies, clothing and toys in excess of $50,000 to give to children in Croatia and Bosnia. The cargo vessel—paid for by the kind-hearted, Croatian-born, superstar professional tennis player Goran Ivanisevic—loaded with the supplies, arrived in Zagreb where Maja and I met it to go through customs. This was not an easy assignment, because there was no cease-fire in the war. But we held firm that the children, especially the children left orphaned by the war and also undergoing medical treatments, would receive a welcome surprise.

Safety was not an issue we took lightly. I landed at the airport under very different circumstances than what I was used to. No commercial planes were in sight out of my window. In fact, the only plane I could see during my descent and taxiing into the gate was a United Nations plane. United Nations uniformed military guards were everywhere.

People back at home were understandably worried about my visit to a war zone, but it only made the visit more important to complete. Many people balked at this opportunity to help the children, but God kept providing for us. The children needed us and we had to be there for them.

No news report or television documentary could fully reveal the hardship and devastation the children had to endure. Visiting the local hospital, we saw it together, and it was horrifying. Medical supplies were so low that needles were being reused and medicines were a rarity. Countless children were left orphaned and had sustained major wounds. They were innocent victims caught in the crossfire. I was glad that we could do our part to help, and I kept the children in my prayers.

The trip was such a success that we set even higher goals. We would continue to expend our efforts in hospital facilities in as many foreign countries as we had access to. We would not forget the orphans and other suffering children of the world. Heidi and I parlayed our resources, adding to the support by asking friends to help and getting the foundation to step in whenever possible. I contracted myself out for a variety of tennis commentating duties to help cover expenses as Maja and I traveled together to obtain additional assistance. Nike stepped up in a big way by providing great bags of shirts, socks, hats and other clothing items.

Throughout the initial phase of the foundation's international programs, Maja and I visited children in more than nine countries, bringing supplies and gifts, and spreading laughter and smiles. Hundreds of heartwarming stories of how our programs were making a difference poured into our offices.

I read a story in *People* magazine that moved me to act in another way. On March 13, 1996, a madman armed with four guns walked into Dunblane Primary School in Scotland. Within three minutes he shot twenty-eight students and three teachers. Sixteen of the children and one teacher died from their wounds. It was a horrific, tragic story that struck me deep in my spirit.

I needed to visit the children and see if I could help with the healing process. I wanted them to realize that not every stranger has such evil intentions. Not having this overseas trip in the budget, again I looked to secure a way to work in order for the trip to become a reality. A perfect opportunity opened up. In May there was a mixed-doubles tennis event in which I could participate—in, of all locations, Edinburgh, Scotland. God was using me and I was excited to participate in His plan. I had to practice to play at a competitive level, which was not easy on my shoulder, but I was bound and determined to get to Scotland. Heidi told me as she watched me wince during our practice sessions: "It is great how God is using us to help children in ways we could never pull off on our own. Make sure you pack extra ice bags—I have a feeling you will need them."

Maja met me in Scotland, fresh from a European tour event, to help me practice for the doubles competition and to distribute the presents and goodwill. We had school supplies, tennis and sporting equipment, all sorts of gifts packaged with God's love.

Maja and I were taken in by the stories we heard. The horrors these innocent children had to endure were beyond comprehension. During the Dunblane visit, there was one boy in particular who wanted to share his experiences of the shooting with us. The boy seemed relieved to give us the details of this terrifying episode. Maja and I listened closely as he told us his story:

> *I hid under my friend. I knew my friend was dead. His body was not moving and blood was coming out of it. I thought if I hid under my friend and pretended to be dead, I wouldn't get shot. It was scary and hard. When my friend's blood dripped on my face I thought I would scream. But I didn't. I stayed really still even though I wanted to run and get help. My friend, who was dead, helped save me from being shot to death, because his body covered mine.*

We hugged this cherubic little boy with the soft, tender eyes. We taught tennis to him and other students, hoping and praying that they, in turn, would not resort to violent acts of their own to deal with the trauma. The boy was excited about all the volleys he hit over the net. His smiles were genuine and his laughter real.

The children carefully guided Maja and me to the exact place where the shootings took place on their school grounds. We moved through the classrooms to the hallways and then to the outside area where we touched the precious greenery planted in memory of friends lost in the shooting. We said prayers, fervently asking God to help heal the children, teachers, school, families and community from the violence it had endured.

Unfortunately, there are people in the world who perform

unspeakably evil acts on innocent children. Can a wound so deep, pain and suffering so severe, or an act so viciously inflicted ever heal? God says in the Bible He can heal all, and we stood on that promise, believing its truth. God had to watch His only Son be persecuted, tormented and eventually killed. He knows about pain and suffering. God knows how to heal anyone's pain and suffering, no matter the cause and result.

Children can always use another prayer. Every morning and night I pray for the protection of children. It is critical to be more aware of a child's needs, whether the child is your own or not. Oftentimes, it takes a tragedy for people to incorporate prayer into their routines, but prayer is for both good and hard times, not only for help but for thanks. Prayers make a difference. In Dunblane, parents, surviving teachers and children said, "We felt the prayers of people all around the world." The lost, ailing, sick, orphaned, hurt and abused children of the world need prayers.

The loss or the harm of a child is a burden too heavy to bear alone. The best way to survive such devastation is to pray and bring the heavy burden to God. Living in torment forever is no way to live. Placing any and all grief, pain, and suffering in God's hands will help heal the intensity of heartache.

Maja and I had an interesting experience during a children's program in France. A young girl had had her leg amputated to stop the spread of cancer to other parts of her body. She was distraught, spending the majority of her time blankly staring at the wall. We entered her hospital room and started our fun act of selecting a present for the girl. It is a routine we do with much fanfare to build up the anticipation. Before long, the child was smiling and happily enjoying our entertainment and company. Venturing out of the room, the girl's mother approached us, and in broken English said, "That is the first time in months that my daughter has smiled. Thank you."

We also met with other children who had been severely injured from various outbreaks of violence, war and fighting throughout the world. They were sent to the Paris hospital to receive specialized treatments. Maja knew several languages and that certainly helped in explaining to the children and families that the gifts we brought were free. Most of the children we visited had never received presents during their extended hospital stays. The language that translated with no trouble at all was the language of unconditional love.

One little boy's doctor explained how his injuries were sustained when a bomb exploded near him. He had shrapnel wounds all over his body. He was all alone in a room, looking lost in thought about what surely was a very traumatic episode. When we came bounding in with presents, his entire demeanor changed. He was excited to receive gifts, managing a big smile and a wave as we left the room.

Another time, we were in London, making our way through a hospital corridor with our bag of fun surprises. Down the hallway, we heard several machines making noise. A young boy was attached to more medical devices than I thought humanly possible. He was conscious and well aware of his surrounding but his eyes were fixated on the ceiling. The nurses were very careful with him and obviously taken with the boy's situation. It was hard to keep our composure with the life-support machines clanking away, but the last thing this child needed was a visit from a squeamish adult who could not handle for a short time what he was living every second of every day.

It was not a scene for the faint of heart or spirit. I reached the end of his bed and said a prayer. The boy couldn't move to hold his present, but we were able to show him what it was. He beamed with joy. This incredibly brave and composed youngster had to lay flat to stay connected to the tubes. The intrusions on his body looked painful, yet the boy smiled when he saw his gift. A grin brighter than the voltage in the light high above took over the entire room.

Maja and I have shared countless laughs, experiences and enjoyment together as we have helped children all around the world. The privilege and honor of being in a child's company and watching as they choose faith, joy, light and love rather than darkness and decay is a blessing that grows and grows.

Still, God was not finished in building our team and releasing blessings.

Chapter Nineteen

I will instruct you and teach you in the way
you should go; I will guide you with My eye.

—Psalm 32:8

Heidi and I felt the constant existence of God making miracles out of what could be perceived as dismal circumstances. Every cloud had a silver lining. Thus we decided to name the permanent facility capital campaign project the Silver Lining Ranch. The Silver Lining Foundation would be the umbrella organization for all the programs.

Every night before I went to bed, I followed two rituals. First, I recited the Lord's Prayer, something I had done for many years. Second, I prayed for God's will to be done for our Silver Lining programs.

A disciplined prayer routine was great, but in order to gain more knowledge in the Word, ways and will of God, I needed to step things up quite a few levels. Heidi and I prayed for a teacher for me and God sent me one of His best. I found an excellent tutor, mentor and instructor in Pat Theissen. We met at a Bible study weekend event in Orlando, Florida, where we were paired up as roommates. I certainly received the better end of the bargain. I was in my twenties and had very little sound scriptural knowledge. Pat was the self-assured, confident, knowledgeable participant, and I was the high-energy, desperate-to-learn, curious student.

Pat was willing to go to the depths with me, so I could find truths that had eluded me. She was brilliantly educated in the Bible; scripture effortlessly rolled off her tongue. She was a wife, mother and career woman, but her devotion to God, to serving Him with obedience, was foremost in her life.

Pat was comfortable in the charismatic provisions God amply provides to His believers. The gifts and fruits of the Holy Spirit were all familiar and in working order in Pat's life. Calm and patient, with a great sense of humor, Pat was always available to give scripture-based advice.

The difference between Pat and other religious authority figures I sought out was that Pat defined real-life problems, supernatural occurrences and areas of life within the context of how they related to scripture in the Bible. Religion can isolate an individual as easily as it can embrace a believer. Embracing and enhancing a relationship with God was my priority, and I didn't want to ruin that by becoming too entrenched in religious dogma.

Pat's Christian knowledge and Heidi's strict Catholic upbringing provided me ample opportunities to digest information and proceed to receive further direction on my quest to know God and the Bible more intimately. It became a balancing act, a recipe of sorts, to get me headed in the right direction in all areas of life, not only a few.

Anytime I was tripped up, I would seek out God and my mentors and say, "What is this about? Please explain this and help me understand." Every day I was learning how to progress in my walk and calling with God. It was like my tour days: Some days were good and others were major character-building moments. I looked at all the challenges before me as exciting.

The biggest misconception I had, and had lived with comfortably my entire life, was that knowing God exists is enough to be protected and saved. I stumbled upon prayer as a child, not because my parents made me, but because I truly loved having a relationship with God. However, Bible reading never took hold. The words were not always easy to comprehend right away, as I had expected. I didn't operate under the false assumption that Bible reading is simply an extended version of a Hallmark card, but I did expect to feel the heavenly moment of truth in my spirit the minute I opened the book and committed to learn more about God. In truth, there is a special process involved in learning and being instructed in God's Word. A baby cannot be given solid foods when it is only ready to digest milk. A ten-year-old isn't given keys to the family car, and certainly I was in no place to understand the depth of what the Bible entails without an anointed and guided instructor to help me along.

The purest joy I knew about God that was validated by my Bible studies was that God loves all His children—and I was included as one of His children. God didn't love and provide salvation for me because I was working hard, doing good deeds and actively seeking His approval. He loved me because of the constitution of His heart. The unconditional love God gives to His children is without flaw. I wanted to have that.

During my tutelage program, God kept stirring my spirit to call people for a variety of reasons. This particular time, the phone call—which would end up in hundreds of attempts made—had to do with contacting someone to help the foundation. God urged me to contact supermodel Cindy Crawford, and again I went forward in obedience.

The same week I had this message, I had the fortune to receive, out of the blue, Cindy's New York phone number from a dear friend. I proceeded to make twice-weekly notes on my "to do" lists to contact Cindy and leave a message if there was no answer. Then I'd call every day at a variety of times without leaving a message if no one answered. I had no idea what God had in mind. With as much curiosity as obedience, I kept my call cycle going. Several months had gone by when I said to Heidi, "Either Cindy is going to change her home number after all my calls and messages, or she is going to help us in a big way. But something is going to happen very soon."

Sure enough, it did. I was on perhaps my three-hundredth call, waiting to hear Cindy's now familiar voice on the answering machine. Suddenly, the automated message changed to a live person. "Hello," she said warmly. I was so stunned that I surprisingly replied, "Hello?" as if inquiring, "I know I am here, but are you sure you are?" Finally my intentions kicked in. "Hi, my name is Andrea Jaeger and I . . ." then I was kindly interrupted.

Cindy said, "Andrea, I am so sorry I missed your previous calls. I was overseas and arrived home yesterday. For the past few months I was traveling in Moscow and Africa." I could hardly believe Cindy Crawford was apologizing to me. Cindy took hold of the conversation and brought it to places I never expected to go on our initial call. She said "Andrea, do you know my younger brother died of cancer?" and "I would love to help and visit the children," and "I will gladly attend your fund-raiser." I didn't have to push, prod or plead to have her support.

Exactly to her word, Cindy arrived a few months later in Aspen for our year-end fund-raiser and December children's session. The commercial flight she was on was delayed several times due to inclement weather and mechanical problems. The scheduled afternoon landing became a late-night arrival. The unfortunate delays did not dampen Cindy's enthusiasm. She walked off the plane glowing.

On our short walk to the baggage claim area, several people grabbed her arm to demand a picture. I was astonished. I was inclined to turn the people away, but I wasn't sure what my role should be. As it turned out, my intervention was utterly unnecessary. Cindy had the situation addressed in moments. Without flinching, she turned with polite amusement and asked, "May I help you?" Flabbergasted, I watched the gawking onlookers happily saunter away having their questions answered. As they fumbled for their cameras and autograph pens, Cindy patiently took on every attack on her personal space with respect and kindness.

The children's visit was more aptly suited for Cindy's genuine and caring nature. Within moments of the exciting introductions, where one teenage boy actually fell on his knees in the snow in complete disbelief, a planned snowball fight started. I tried to position Cindy on the children's side of the snowball fight rather than the staff side. She would not have it.

"Cindy," I said, "the children's side is the safer side. The staff never throws high. We make sure no one gets hurt. The children get to throw with youthful abandon. Even if we tell them to avoid throwing high, we can't guarantee that you won't get pelted."

Cindy looked at me surprised, saying, "I will be fine." She took her position on the staff side and firmly planted her feet, with a pile of snowballs at the ready. The kids targeted her with glee and laughter. Everyone wanted to be the one to exclaim, "I had a snowball fight with Cindy Crawford."

Afterward, Fabi Benedict hosted us in her lovely home, serving hot chocolate with whipped cream, warm apple cider, hot dishes and a variety of desserts. Toasty warm and with full bellies, the children gathered by the Christmas tree to receive presents, autographs and souvenir pictures. The setting was perfect.

Heidi and I surveyed the blessed scene. The kids laughed and romped joyfully with eyes as wide as saucers. Cindy's charm, beauty and generosity of spirit sparkled and filled everyone in the home with happiness. Mrs. Benedict loved being involved in our programs. She knew that one day we would be having festivities like this in a permanent place of our own on land that she gifted us. Her spirit would infuse the facility with the love she always held in her heart. This wasn't a Kodak moment, it was a Kodak life.

⚯   ⚯   ⚯

Cindy answered the girls' questions about makeup and offered them beauty tips. She presented herself as if this was the most important photo shoot of her life. Models get paid well for how their bodies, hair and faces look. The children's battle wounds and scars from cancer were apparent. Many had lost all their hair, including eyelashes and eyebrows. Cindy made sure that every child felt like a cover girl or boy. She respected them for who they were on the inside and that generated love and acceptance on the outside as well. That afternoon, it wasn't so much what was said, but rather who said it and how it was said, that made an impact on the children. Cindy made sure everyone understood that "Beauty comes from the heart. How you feel and how you act always comes from your heart. Your hearts are truly beautiful and so is each and every one of you."

The festivities did not end there. The Foundation's first-ever major fund-raiser was on the agenda for the adults. It was an important step in establishing much-needed support in the Aspen community. If it went well, we would make it an annual event to help fund our programs. The night of the event, Heidi, Beene, Kate and I donned our pantyhose and evening wear and gathered in Cindy's hotel room where I attempted to safety-pin my top together. Cindy marveled at how we had gotten so far with the Foundation on our own. Of course, we didn't do anything on our own. God was our partner from the beginning, and He was always in charge. He was responsible for all the blessings we received.

Cindy was the highlight of the evening gala and the foot traffic flowed continuously past our table. As the celebration wound down, I leaned over and whispered in Cindy's ear, "It's time to get going. Before I take you back to the hotel, can I introduce you to someone?" She agreed, though she was probably wondering how she could have missed someone at the event. The place was filled to capacity, and Cindy had made the rounds of the entire ballroom, greeting people, asking them to donate to our cause, as well as thanking individuals for supporting the Silver Lining Foundation.

With permission from Heidi and me, the children, along with the counselors and medical staff who were chaperoning them for the night, crashed the party. They were amused to see us in our fancy get-ups. The children were the reason we were all there in the first place, and their entrance made everyone beam. Cindy and the youngsters enjoyed a few more group hugs, tips and laughter before it was time for the children to leave and get to bed. I took on the host duty of returning Cindy to her hotel.

The stars outside twinkled brilliantly in the cold, clear mountain air. Cindy and I made our way on the icy walkways to the small foundation office. Navigating the ice in high heels was no problem for a supermodel; I, however, slipped and slid the entire way.

Flicking the office lights on, I prepared the introduction. Cindy made her way to what Heidi and I fondly call the "Wall of Life." A picture of every child who ever visited our Aspen programs, and our outreach, on-the-road programs, smiled back at us from the wall. It was easy to see how quickly life can go by. I stood before the pictures and every story, each moment I had spent with the children, played back in my mind. As I walked into the room reminiscing about all the special times, I came across Rhea's photos with the first participating group from Chicago; the strong-willed girl had been one of our first participants. Rhea's remissions and relapses during her late teenage years and early twenties had a profound effect on her emotionally, spiritually and physically. Never once did she complain about unfairness, or show anger, hatred or bitterness in her long battle with cancer. As the world closed in on her, and the cancer fought to steal her last breath, Rhea still found compassion for others.

During what appeared to be a solid remission phase for Rhea, I received a very different message. I was on a plane, traveling home from Australia after a month of international children's cancer programs and tennis commentary work. The captain announced the flight time to the States and I winced at the length of the journey. Grabbing my study book from the overhead compartment, I settled in for the ride. We hit some turbulence, so I decided to combat it by trying to go to sleep and get some much-needed rest. I rarely slept on planes, but I closed my eyes anyway. A few minutes passed with no success. Suddenly, with no warning, I started choking. I immediately opened my eyes expecting to see someone holding my neck, constricting my airway. No one was there. The person seated next to me was gone. I was alone. I kept gasping for air. Everything was happening in slow motion, yet my mind was racing. I kept asking myself, *What is going on?* Then I received an answer. In my spirit, I knew what had occurred. *Something has happened to Rhea,* I thought. *I have to call home to see what has happened to Rhea.* With that realization, I was able to breathe normally again.

I'd had Rhea's phone number memorized since her participant application came in years before, and with our long-term support programs, her number came to mind easily. There was no reason to call in the middle of the night and startle her and her family. I would wait until my arrival in Los Angeles, wake up Heidi, and see if she had heard anything. The hours crept by so slowly. I knew something was wrong. The seconds ticked by, tearing at my heart each time the clock moved.

When we finally landed in Los Angeles I phoned Heidi. Immediately after saying hello, the worry came spurting out, "What has happened to Rhea?" I asked desperately.

Heidi replied, "What? Who told you? Rhea phoned yesterday on the home 800 number saying that the doctors told her she had relapsed. Fluid and tumors are in her lungs. They are saying she has very little time, and she may end up suffocating to death, because of the buildup of tumors and fluid."

I wanted to drop the receiver and run as fast and far as I could. I didn't even know where to run; I only knew the motion would do me good. Instead, I listened to the painful explanation of the doctor's theories and information. It was still too early to call Rhea in Chicago. I would have to wait until landing in Denver for that conversation.

The flight from L.A. to Denver was emotionally painful, as I thought of the days ahead for Rhea. She would not make her next birthday. She would not reach her goals of getting married, working with us at Silver Lining through her adulthood or having children of her own. Now her decisions and schedule would revolve around how much morphine she could take to reduce her pain, planning her funeral arrangements and giving away her belongings. I landed in Denver, sick to my stomach from the horrible news, and walked to a pay-phone stall. I methodically dialed Rhea's home number.

I spent my life refusing to let my emotions dictate my life when my heart hurt, my soul was tortured, my space invaded or my progress stunted. This was more than a survival instinct; it was a way to stay in the spirit and joy of life as God intended. I was a veteran at staying in the light, because I didn't want to succumb to the destructive ways of the darkness. Despair and dread were not going to rule my days—that was for sure. My method of dealing with pain didn't mean I never felt it; it meant that I rarely reacted to it, because I didn't want it to control me.

I was thankful for the youthful talent I had acquired of being able to suppress tears at will reflecting instead on blessed and joyful times. It wasn't the best gift I had mastered as a child, but it did serve its purpose. If gaping wounds appeared and I had to tend to other pressing matters, I was assured that God would help with the cleansing and healing as I went about my business. As I grew older and closer to God, those scars did heal, leaving me more whole than when I started. God picked me up and I ended up cleaner than when I went down in the first place. However, this medical news threw me for a loop. Now I needed that on-and-off pain switch, because I had to be strong for Rhea.

When Rhea came to the phone, I said, "Hi, Rhea. It's Andrea. I heard the news. How are you taking all of this?"

She answered, "I knew it came back. The doctor didn't even have to tell me; I felt it. You know that cancer emotional roller-coaster you promised to ride with me, and that we have been on together for a few years now? Well, it took a big dive."

"Look, whatever, whenever—I am here, you know that, day or night," I said.

"Yeah, good thing you have that 800 number," she replied, chuckling slightly.

"Rhea, what else did the doctor say?" I asked.

"Well, it wasn't pneumonia like we hoped. The cancer came back. I don't have much time. It is growing really fast. I am planning my funeral service now," she said.

Because Rhea worked for the foundation, we talked on a more in-depth level than merely keeping in touch or checking in. We knew each other well enough to often finish each other's sentences. She told me her worst fears and darkest moments and naturally we became accustomed to registering the things that brought the greatest joys.

Over the years she was part of our Aspen foundation programs for winter and summer sessions, as well as our Washington, D.C., and Chicago programs. It was as if we were siblings who never had a fight.

Rhea proceeded to tell me more. "The tumors are growing, fluid is filling my lungs. I was told that when I die it might be like suffocating to death. I am scared to go to sleep, because I may not wake up. I am starting in a hospice program so I can stay at home." Before I could respond, Rhea continued, "Andrea, are you okay with this news? I know this is hurting you. I am sorry I have to leave."

I sat in this special phone booth area sickened by the news and admiring that Rhea, despite the odds against her, was being so calm.

"Rhea, please don't worry about me. I mean, sure, like you, I would have loved to have heard better news. That didn't happen, and we will deal with it. So, what would you like to be the first order of things? How can I help?" I asked.

With that, Rhea said, "I am going to miss you so much."

The intercom went off in the airport announcing arrivals and departures. Passengers kept moving along, and I thought of what the world was going to lose with Rhea's death. I would have plenty of time to think of the impact later. Now there was still time to comfort my good friend, so I responded, "Rhea, I am going to miss you, too, but you are going to a place where we can still keep watching out for each other. This is obviously not ideal, but it's not over. It will be different, but it's not over. Remember, God has this under control, and I am sure you will always be watching over a lot of kids and somehow, some way, He will make sure we can still be close."

One could describe Rhea as "an old soul." Wise beyond her years, she came into people's lives with purpose and a passion. She didn't welcome everyone into her life; she carefully chose those she was to teach along the way. I had the good fortune of being one of this youngster's students. Rhea was the Foundation's first paid employee—many years before Heidi and I received a salary. Rhea took on her position with great pride and success.

The first letter, and countless letters thereafter, I ever received from Rhea came with lengthy descriptions of all the ways she wanted to say thank you. Her signature reflected her soul: "Love, Your Kindred Spirit, Rhea."

It was from that point on that I knew these children, teenagers and young adults were our teachers in many ways. But we also had the responsibility to protect, provide for and support them. The programs had their purposes, but it was the people who acted on them that made the difference. The foundation staff was jumping out in faith, in ways that we did not quite comprehend. The value and positive impact on a heart, soul or spirit can't be measured or quantified on a piece of paper as well as medical treatment to the body can. We couldn't necessarily see every positive result, but the children's hearts and spirits were most definitely registering them.

I took on the parental role with the foundation and children we were helping. My driving principle was to protect the children at all costs, regardless of the hardships of fundraising. I would never, ever, surrender my calling of helping children.

During the last days of Rhea's life, which were coming rapidly after our airport discussion, I took a trip to Chicago to see her. As the taxi drove me to the trailer in which she lived, I stared out into the darkness, trying not to think too much about the difficult days ahead for Rhea. I had learned that Rhea could experience a "bleed out," losing blood from all parts of her body, during my visit. The thought of her life transcending out of her drop by drop as we watched, not able to do a thing about her demise, certainly affected me in ways words couldn't even describe. However, years before, when Rhea asked me to help by going on what she called "the cancer emotional roller-coaster," I made a promise to be there for her. As time would have it, we already had been through many ups and downs on the treatment, remission and relapse journey, yet none as severe as the one she was about to encounter. Now, it was more important than ever to be there, and knowing the reality of the dire situation was certainly not going to stop me.

When I arrived at Rhea's home, I was amazed at the resilience of the human heart and spirit. Although her physical state was declining rapidly, it did not affect her love, humor or generosity. We laughed about the talent show acts and my lack of ability to ever get one dance move down. She reminisced about the best times of her life, joyfully telling each story. Visitors popped in and out of Rhea's room, saying their last good-byes, as she gave them her personal belongings. Death doesn't always have to be dark and depressing. Rhea let her light shine brightly in the trailer home and refused to let her friends and family go into premature mourning.

Sleeping on the living room couch, with Rhea's grandmother on a sofa a few feet away, I stared at the ceiling. Hearing Rhea's screams of fear in the middle of the night were more frightening than the scariest horror show, for these shrills were real—and again, there was nothing anyone could do to stop the end result. After a hospice nurse rushed over to administer more morphine, I sat at Rhea's bedside, both of us unable to sleep. It didn't help soften the blow when the nurse matter-of-factly explained, as she looked at her watch, "Well, it won't be much longer before you die."

There is something about death that humbles us all. My inability to keep her alive devastated me. I couldn't pray or will Rhea's death away no matter how hard I tried. None of us had the power to control what was happening. There were times when I stared at the trailer ceiling asking why the blueprint of Rhea's life entailed this trauma. I knew it was in God's hands so I handed my confusion over to Him.

The last conversation Rhea and I had was one of great depth and love. She said, "Pretty soon I will be going to sleep forever."

I was taken aback and replied instantly. "Rhea, no way. You will be in heaven with God, helping all those kids who had to go before you and certainly continuing your efforts for us here. You have always believed and followed God," I continued, my eyes welling with tears and my voice cracking, "so He has a plan for you—even after you are done in this body."

I continued, "When I have crummy fund-raising days, you are

going to help me out. You will shout, 'Keep going, Andrea. Don't give up.' It will be like you are there. When I am driving in a snowstorm and can't see a thing, you will guide me to safety. You will be around, just in a different form. In a presence that God will give you with no cancer, no sickness or disease. And you will have your hair that you missed so much and that beautiful smile that you have brought to everyone's life."

Rhea responded with the most distraught look I had ever seen. She stared deep into my eyes, down into my soul and spirit. Slowly, carefully and decisively she said, "Everyone is going to forget me." Tears formed in her eyes, gently falling down her hollow cheeks.

I never thought my final words to a friend days from death would be ones of defiance. Pleasing, comforting and loving should have been the order of the day; however, I had to be true to myself, and in this case, pleasing did not have a role. Rhea's remark, made in despair, was not going to exist, especially not in my world.

The cancer pressed on in Rhea's cells and tissues, breaking blood vessels. I took a stand. "Rhea that will not happen. I am going to make sure you are remembered. I promise you, you will not be forgotten." Her tears rolled stronger, this time with a hint of joy and happiness. I held her hand softly as the gentlest touch caused her more pain. Her mouth, full of blisters and sores, spread into a smile. A sparkle returned to her eyes.

Rhea proceeded to give me a list of things she expected of me. The remark I had made was set in stone, and she knew I would keep the promise. "Andrea, you have to work on your dancing skills." An immediate chuckle came to both of us. Rhea grabbed her sides in pain, but kept advising. "Remember when I got us tickets to sit in the audience at the *Oprah Winfrey Show*? And how you refused to leave before finding a way to introduce me to Oprah?"

"Yes," I said.

"I was so embarrassed. But you went up and took me along, and before I knew it, Oprah was saying, 'Hi.'"

I answered, "Yes, Rhea, I remember. I told her about your cancer and she came over and affectionately touched your hair, which was growing back in little soft patches."

"Well, you shouldn't be sitting in the audience next time; you should be a guest on the show," she said.

We went on for hours: laughing and sharing, Rhea crying at times and, of course, being human, which entailed wanting more time. Each moment was sacred, but light and joyful, as if we had a lifetime left in each other's company. When almost all her wardrobe and personal effects went out the door with her visitors, Rhea said, "I want to give you something."

Barely able to hold back the tears, I stammered out, "Rhea, your friendship has been the greatest gift. I will always hold on to it. You don't have to give me anything."

"Well, I am. I am giving you a piece of my heart."

Rhea got up to take part in our traditional "See you later" hug. During my entire tennis tour life, I was made fun of because I didn't want to hug people. I would step back, trying to remove myself from as much physical contact as I could. I was ridiculed for it. Now, when I wanted to give a hug that would last forever, I had to be careful because Rhea was so fragile and in so much pain. We managed the biggest hug her body could handle and in unison, as though it were scripted, we both looked in each other's eyes and said, "Thank you."

Ending the visit, Rhea said something that totally caught me off guard. "You know, I have to thank cancer in a weird way. I met you and you changed my life. Cancer may have taken some things, but it gave me a lot that I am thankful for. I appreciated things better after my cancer. I spent so much time with wigs I forgot what real hair was like there for a while, but it taught me an awful lot.

I didn't wish for cancer, but I did receive a lot from it."

In a role I was getting used to playing—the student—I walked over to the teacher and declared, "Rhea, remember you will be watching over us. Will you give a hug for me to Caroline, Keith and all the kids who are in heaven and in our prayers and hearts forever?"

The teacher responded, "I will take good care of them. I will watch over the children in heaven, and I will make sure you are getting help down here." We didn't say "good-bye" as we had faith our relationship would carry on. Rhea died a short time thereafter. Her memory and spirit will live on forever, as has our friendship.

Taking Cindy to see our Wall of Life was not only a declaration of faith in what God wanted Heidi and me to be doing; it was a declaration of a promise kept to Rhea and to all the children—that they would always be remembered. "Cindy, I wanted you to be able to meet all the kids." I proceeded to name the children and teenagers who were pictured. "And this is Rhea. She would have liked you," I said.

I pointed to an architectural colored rendering of the ranch. "See that tower, that is what we are calling Rhea's Tower. It is the highest point of the ranch, the closest part to the stars. It is to assure Rhea and all the children that they are being remembered."

Cindy listened to every word with interest. It was well after 1:00 A.M. when I finished telling Cindy the stories of Rhea and the other children on the wall. I handed her a video and pictures, so Rhea and the other children could be fondly remembered. Cindy handled the videos and pictures with the special care they deserved. As we walked outside, the stars illuminated the pathway. I explained how Rhea loved looking into the Aspen sky hoping to find a shooting star to make a wish upon.

I dropped off Cindy at her hotel. Before leaving my car, she said,

"Thank you. I will make sure I do my part. Rhea and all the children will continue being remembered. See you later." The Silver Lining Foundation motto made up the last words of the night. I was full of excitement and adrenaline from the festivities, so I decided to harness my energy into some administrative and fundraising work. At 4:00 A.M. I drove to the office. The moment I put the car in park, the largest, brightest, closest shooting star I had ever seen in my life flew across the sky right in front of me. I stepped out of the car, looked up in the sky and announced, "Rhea, I knew you and the other kids would like Cindy. Thanks for letting me know that you are well aware you are all being remembered."

Chapter Twenty

Now God worked unusual miracles. . . .

—Acts 19:11

O ne of the children's activities included special nature tours by Fritz and Fabi Benedict on the appointed land that would one day host the Foundation's Aspen program. Bird and flower species were pointed out, as Fritz shared compelling stories of Aspen before it was a world-class ski resort. Tales of Fabi riding her horse to the grocery store, Fritz's hopes of buying land in the mountain town after he returned from World War II, and the use of vehicle headlights to illuminate the airport runway captured the children's attention. Each step that the children took on the property, following Fritz and Fabi, anointed it for the release of God's miracles and blessings. Sadly, Fritz would not see our dream realized. After reaching his eighty-first birthday, he succumbed to a heart attack.

Heidi and I were frantically fund-raising to meet the needs of both our program and building funds. We stood on the claim that children's sessions would continue even though at least $4.7 million would be needed to construct the 18,000-square-foot facility that had already been designed. It became apparent that we needed another permanent member of our administrative, fund-raising and program team.

Weeks later, after several calls, conversations and prayers, the Foundation was blessed with a major victory. The immensely talented and personable Chris Wyman would fill the position. Chris was essential if we were going to progress at the pace that God placed before us.

During the construction research phase, I traveled the country checking out large medical, ranch and camp programs and centers to make sure our design plans were as solid as they could be. The days on the calendar were clicking by, and we still had not located an individual who would step up with funding to begin construction, as well as attract more donors to contribute to the construction project and children's programs.

For three years, I had been trying to get an introduction to Ted Forstmann. Mr. Forstmann was a leading philanthropist whose large donations to children's causes were legendary. Head of the Forstmann, Little & Co. investment firm in New York City, Ted set standards in humanitarian giving. I had sent word out to everyone I knew, friend and foe, who might help secure a conversation with Ted. Finally, that day arrived. Ted called my cell phone on a balmy late summer day to arrange a meeting. However, there was a problem. He was available to meet with me on the same day I was to attend a friend's fund-raiser in Las Vegas, where I was hoping to gather up ideas and secure new financial support.

I explained the situation to Mr. Forstmann. He said, "Andrea it is your decision. This is the time I can meet in Aspen. Will it work for you?" I had been fighting for one opportunity to open up and now two were facing me on the same day. In a matter of seconds I had to make a choice. I quickly consulted God, asking, "What do I do? Help me make the right decision." God answered me, as swiftly as I had asked Him, "Meet with Ted Forstmann." That was enough guidance for me. I confidently said, "Mr. Forstmann, where would you like to meet?" We agreed to a time and place. My heart was racing. I meticulously planned for the occasion. Fabi was ready at a moment's notice, so I could introduce the two of them. It became an absolute must to introduce the person who provided the land with the individual who might get the building off the blueprint and under construction.

Mr. Forstmann didn't arrive with an entourage. He stood outside a hotel, casually dressed yet elegant and handsome, possessing a serenity and purpose of the highest sort. Our first stop was the Benedict home. I shared the story of how God touched Mrs. Benedict to bless us with the land donation. I pointed out the boundaries of the land as we proceeded to walk the property. We wound through trees, hiked up embankments and stepped over delicate wildflowers. Ted carefully asked questions and listened intently to my responses. All of his inquiries were insightful and knowledgeable. He had obviously heard thousands of pitches for money in his time, and he wanted to be sure of what his participation might entail.

The visit was capped off by a "Thank you" from Ted. He left my car without a decision about his support. I was demoralized. Fabi was excitedly waiting in her home for good news about when we would break ground. I promised Fabi, who had cancer and other problems, that if she could hold on a little longer we would show her that the children would get their special place built.

Fall was settling in and the urgency for funding became more apparent. A grant came from a Paul Newman contact. The Kellogg contribution required one of the executives to attend fund-raising school. Heidi and I looked at each other, knowing we were the only full-time fund-raisers. Still unpaid, but with the passion for helping the children stronger than ever, we divided up the responsibilities and arranged for the trip. Heidi would cover the Aspen administration and program organization duties, and I would venture to San Francisco and attend the weeklong fund-raising workshop.

My private research in the basic fundamentals of fund-raising proved to be highly accurate. The class became a refresher course for the first few days, until we entered into charitable remainder trusts on the last day. During the lunch break, I headed up to my room to check messages. As I was about to leave the room, the phone rang. I picked it up and heard, "Hello. I have Mr. Forstmann calling for Andrea Jaeger." I immediately gulped in a large breath before answering. "This is Andrea."

"Hold on please." This was most unusual. How did he even know where I was?

I knew I left him my entire schedule for the next year, hoping he would want to contact me—but here and now, on my last day of fund-raising school during the limited class break? It was more than a coincidence that he called at this exact time.

Finally, Ted came on the phone, "Andrea, I really love what you are doing. The children should have the ranch you want to build for them. I am going to help you. I am donating $1.7 million to you so you can start building."

Every tip from fund-raising class flew out of my head. The calm, professional persona the class talked about achieving was not me, and it became obvious. "Mr. Forstmann, could you hold on for a second." I didn't even wait for a reply. I covered the phone with my hand and screamed at the top of my lungs.

Attempting to regain my composure, I returned to the phone. "Mr. Forstmann?" I heard a slight chuckle and a "Yes?" "Please hold on for one more second." I could hardly believe my ears. The impact of this donation was astounding. The children were going to have a permanent facility! Groundbreaking was imminent! Fabi would see the efforts of her land donation come together! The miracle happened!

With every thought, another huge scream of pure joy bellowed out of me. I returned again to the phone, this time sure I could keep calm. "Mr. Forstmann?" He was still on the line, this time his chuckling more apparent. I proceeded to say thank you in every way my heart knew how. All the doubters, all the naysayers, perhaps they would now turn and join the bandwagon of getting the facility built and helping our programs. It was going to happen with or without them because one man stepped out in faith in a miraculous way.

Ted saw beyond the blueprints, beyond our grassroots staff. He believed in the vision and he wanted to be part of it. We were on our way. Before hanging up the phone, I went one step further. "Mr. Forstmann, would you consider instructing me in business? Your friendship and support in taking me under your wing business-wise would be greatly appreciated." Again, I held my breath, hoping I didn't push our relationship out the door.

"Yes, I will help you," he said. I felt God arranging a partnership with Ted that would be essential in ensuring the Foundation's long-term success. After the discussion ended, I ran around the room screaming with excitement. Glancing at the clock, I realized my lunch break was over. I grabbed my cell phone and briefcase and raced out of my room.

Waiting for the elevator, I called Heidi. Between the "Oh, my God!" and "Can you believe it?" Heidi couldn't make out a thing. She said, "Andrea, are you okay? What happened? Just breathe." I couldn't slow down. I said the same words, this time even louder. Then Heidi started screaming.

I returned to my class nearly ten minutes late. All eyes were on me as I walked in the door. I scribbled a note to the instructor saying, "I am sorry I am late. I received a call from a donor. The foundation I work for will be getting our largest cash donation ever. That is why I was late. Sorry." She beamed with pride when she read the note. During the next break, she came over to talk to me.

"I have to say, it is most unusual for such a small grassroots organization that is not taking the pyramid approach to fund-raising to
receive such a large contribution. Congratulations! I am so happy
for you. I know the children will reap the rewards." She was right
on every account. It was a miracle! One that would definitely make
a difference for children all around the world.

God's miracles of unusual proportions continued to appear. Ted
Forstmann didn't stop with his initial contribution. He stayed true
to his promise of leading us and taking our growing Foundation
family of support under his wing. Ted became a voice, a beacon of
the grandest kind for the foundation's mission. Before the groundbreaking ceremony, Heidi and I felt compelled to give the ranch a
name: The Benedict-Forstmann Silver Lining Ranch.

God blessed it from the beginning. Still, there was a lot to do and
God continued providing miracles, in the nick of time, before our
bank accounts zeroed out. I read an article in *USA Today* that Garth
Brooks was going to Peoria, Arizona, for spring training with the
San Diego Padres baseball team. I had the impression that Garth
was a man of God. Seeking a higher authority on the subject, I
asked God if I should try to seek Garth out to help the foundation.
The familiar stirring in my spirit said, "Yes, go to Peoria." I presented the idea to Heidi.

In explaining the opportunity, outsiders questioned the logic.
They asked, "Do you know Garth Brooks?"

"No," I said honestly.

Another question came. "Do you know anyone who knows
Garth Brooks?"

Again my reply was, "No."

The conversation continued. "Do you have an idea of how to
contact Garth Brooks?"

Finally I could answer positively, "Yes." I continued, "Garth has
to drive into the parking lot at the San Diego Padres spring training

site. I will sit on the curb and wait for him to come in." I felt several pairs of eyes looking at me incredulously, as if to say, "That is it? That is the only plan you have?" Eventually, people did say those words, trying to protect me from venturing into a disappointing situation.

I needed to get to Peoria. I knew it sounded like an unusual plan to receive a donation, but it would be more troubling to my spirit if I stayed home, rejecting the urging from God to go. My decision was final. If the Foundation would not cover my expenses, I would cover them myself. Heidi lived by faith and knew to trust me when God was directing the situation. With others casting doubt, Heidi stepped up to approve the expenses.

Upon arrival, I took my place outside the security gate, sat on the curb and confidently waited. While I was sitting on the curb, one of the players recognized me from an HBO Sports feature that Ross Greenburg produced on the foundation. Before I knew it, I was inside chatting with Garth Brooks, meeting members of his family, sharing stories with John and Rebecca Moores, the co-owners of the San Diego Padres, and enjoying the friendly atmosphere. I knew in my heart that the conversation I had with Garth and the Moores was divinely appointed. Donations from Garth and the Moores were promised and secured.

Before I left the ballpark, I had commitments for a donation that would be the third largest donation we had ever received. In respect and appreciation for the Moores' contribution, we designed a San Diego Padres baseball room with a Peoria, Arizona, backdrop at the ranch that the children love. Heidi and I insisted that all the bedrooms, and certain other play areas, have wall-to-wall murals, each one unique, and all with fun and innovative themes. This haven was going to be colorful, warm and fun—as different from the sterile, blank white walls of a hospital as it could be.

According to past national studies on philanthropic organizations, the average return on soliciting financial support ranged from between 4 and 8 percent. That means for every one hundred people researched and approached for donations, only four to eight people will respond positively. The amount of no's I have received over the years has certainly added up. For every miracle moment and divine donation received, I have experienced at least seventy-five rejections. Fortunately, giving up is not in my vocabulary. I focus on the knowledge that there are people who will respond positively; it is a matter of God lining us up together. There is always someone just around the corner who will help. I made this delightful discovery through a couple of journalists from Los Angeles who made me realize why L.A. is called the city of angels.

Bill Dwyre, sports editor of the *Los Angeles Times,* had been trying to contact me through regular tennis channels. When those avenues failed, Bill found me on his own. We struck up a pleasant and engaging conversation, parting company as if a new friendship was formed. That informal chat resulted in a series of stories on the foundation that ran in the *Los Angeles Times* from 1994 to 1999. Bill and his popular sports feature writer, Bill Plaschke, wrote emotional articles telling readers how they could support our noble endeavors in helping children. Stories titled "Prodigy to Protector," "Guardian Angel" and "Care Package" brought us closer to the L.A. community.

Because of their tenacious efforts, we developed a team of loyal followers. One eighty-two-year-old reader living on his Social Security checks sent twenty-five dollars. Children in the greater Los Angeles area sold baked goods and lemonade and participated in walk-a-thons to help us. Moms, dads, children, business executives, professionals, men and women, and a few celebrities stepped in to lend a hand. Valerie Bertinelli read Plaschke's column and both before and after raising funds for us from her appearance on

Who Wants to Be a Millionaire, she wrote personal checks to support our cause. As a direct result of the *Los Angeles Times* articles, readers sent in enough funds to complete an entire room. These caring readers, who sent their hard-earned money, heartfelt cards and prayers, indeed made a difference. In tribute, the ranch has a specially named area called the Gathering Room, complete with vaulted ceilings, picture windows and cozy furnishings. The plaque announces its sponsor: The City of Angels, a tribute to the support of thousands of people from Los Angeles who made miracles possible for the Silver Lining Foundation and children we assist.

Bill asked, "So, after the ranch is built, are you done fund-raising? Can you sit back and relax?"

I answered, "Far from it. I still have an annual budget in excess of $2 million, along with a $40 million endowment to raise. When we get our endowment, then I will feel funding falling into place. I will continue running programs and projects, but it will be a great relief to get the endowment raised, so I don't have to worry where the next meal or activity is getting paid from. The endowment will take care of those needs."

Hearing how far I had to go, Bill took his own steps to help offset program costs by setting up a fund-raiser event for us in Los Angeles. He enlisted Irv Grossman, and suddenly the women's tennis tour stop in Los Angeles had a charity event assigned to it for a short time. Sponsors came on board and the dynamics of our programs increased.

During the L.A. fund-raising and program event, Heidi, Beene, Maja and I played host to children with cancer from a Los Angeles area hospital. I heard that Arnon Milchan, producer of megahits *Pretty Woman, City of Angels, L.A. Confidential* and numerous other successful films, was taking a keen interest in finding the Women's Tennis Tour additional recognition. Maja provided useful party information details and after the children returned to their hospital, Heidi, Beene and I went off on a midnight quest to get Arnon on our team.

The party was in full swing when we arrived. Arnon was the host and the center of attention. The clock was ticking. The timing didn't feel right as throngs of people always surrounded Arnon. Finally, after 1:00 A.M., I saw an opening. Arnon was returning from hailing a cab for one of his guests. I would have seven to ten uninterrupted seconds of his time. I went for it. Arnon, sharp, charming, witty and intelligent, made his way back to the private room at the restaurant. I pounced. Before settling back into the party, Arnon decided to give me proper attention to hear my Silver Lining Foundation pitch. Within minutes, I walked back to Heidi and Beene. "I have a meeting at his house in Malibu tomorrow."

The foundation's programs and staff's devotion moved Arnon. At his beachfront home, I politely said, "Arnon, the ranch construction project needs your help. If you could come see it, perhaps you would be inclined to help with its completion."

Arnon looked at me with complete sincerity, "Andrea, I know what the ranch looks like. I can see it in your eyes." With that, he took out his address book and agreed to write people financial support solicitation letters. Before my departure, Arnon guaranteed long-term financial support of his own. The Hollywood Safari children's bedroom at the Silver Lining Ranch reflects Arnon's style and zest for entertaining people with love, laughter and generosity. It was another unusual miracle from God to help get the ranch completed.

Chapter Twenty-One

*God also bearing witness both with signs
and wonders, with various miracles
and gifts of the Holy Spirit . . .*

—Hebrews 2:4

In 1997, I was dining in a restaurant during a fund-raising and program trip to Los Angeles. Madonna was at the same restaurant, apparently having a business meeting. Trying to be a polite children's activist, I didn't want to interrupt her meal. The second she completed her meeting and headed out the door, I flew out of my seat to follow her.

In a confident but soft voice, so as not to alarm anyone who might have been in earshot, I said, "Excuse me, Madonna, excuse me." No answer. The walkway was dark, I looked around quickly, and with the realization that we were alone, I raised my voice, "Excuse me, Madonna, may I speak with you for a moment?" Her small frame turned around. "Hi! My name is Andrea Jaeger and I run the Silver Lining Foundation for children with cancer." In my normal desperate fund-raising role, I kept speaking without pausing or taking a breath for fear that it would disconnect our encounter. "Perhaps you have read about us in the *L.A. Times* or seen the feature HBO Sports ran on us."

Watching her facial expressions and body language, I didn't seem to have hit a mark. Out of my pocket I pulled out the business card that I had worked on at the restaurant, which now contained my home and cell phone numbers and additional foundation information. I handed her my card announcing, "I used to play professional tennis. Have you ever followed tennis?"

She curiously asked, "What is your name?"

Thrilled that I received a response, I continued, "Andrea Jaeger. I played a long time ago. I turned pro at fourteen, pigtails, braces. I look a lot different now."

"Okay, I remember," she said. At that point she was being so accommodating, I didn't know if she really recognized my name or was being polite. Either way, she kept her stance in my direction and relaxed even further.

There was a big black SUV—it looked like a Range Rover—only a few feet away. I had the feeling it was going to whisk Madonna away any minute. I kept waiting for a team of bodyguards to jump out and pin me down, but it never happened. As I talked to her, I kept thinking, *Doesn't she have somewhere to go? Why isn't she cutting me off?* She never did.

I kept talking. "I have been helping children with cancer since my tour days. After my shoulder injury, I devoted my full attention to helping the children. I could really use your help."

"What kind of help are you looking for?" she asked.

I was amazed that in this bustling area of the city we did not have one interruption. It was a sign for me to keep going. "We have received a $10 million land donation and Ted Forstmann donated $1.7 million so we could start building a ranch for children with cancer. People are donating dollars they have saved up for years. I know you help a lot of causes, but what we could really use is a financial contribution."

Throughout the conversation, I had been holding out the card. As

Madonna took it she asked, "This is the information?"

In a louder voice than I used for the conversation I exclaimed, "Yes! And all donations are tax deductible."

With that she looked over the card, and then back up at me to make eye contact and said, "Thank you. Nice meeting you."

I had seen Madonna's bold, outspoken ways in interviews, her music videos and in the movie *Truth or Dare.* There were no cameras around, no reporters or crowds for her to perform for. Madonna appeared in full form before me. She was incredibly kind, sincere, unassuming, compassionate, purposeful, patient and enlightened. It wasn't an act; it was real. Madonna was gifted and special in a way that far surpassed her music, film and book sales.

From Madonna's Ray of Light Foundation, we received not only one, but several donations. The Ray of Light Children's Bedroom at the ranch has colorful murals reflecting the obvious nurturing and caring qualities that exist in Madonna's heart. What a miracle encounter God lined up that night in Los Angeles.

Support also came in from closer to home. Aspenites Stuart and Lynda Resnick, Merv and Thea Adelson, Esther Pearlstone, RJ Wagner and Jill St. John, Ana and Michael Goldberg, Tom and Bonnie McCloskey, Gerry Wendel, Jonathon Lewis, and Marcia and Greg Abbott headed up their own fund-raising efforts by donating and soliciting their friends to help complete the ranch.

The foundation's annual fund-raiser in Aspen had an array of angels and divine appointments from God coming from out of town, as well as from down the block, to help our children's cancer programs. David Foster, his wife Linda; music superstars Faith Hill, Tim McGraw, Luther Vandross and Kenny G; supermodel Cindy Crawford and her husband Rande Gerber; pro wrestler titan Billy Goldberg; musical talent newcomer Josh Groban; and entertainer David Brenner were a few of the special guests taking the stage.

The majority of entertainment support arrived because I was given a last-minute seat on Michael Milken's plane from Las Vegas to Los Angeles in 1998. Days before, in Los Angeles, I was a guest with Michael, Cindy Crawford and other speakers on the Larry King show in support of the upcoming Cancer March in Washington, D.C. That in itself was an honor, and I followed up the experience by heading to Las Vegas to lend a hand in Michael's prostate cancer celebrity fund-raiser event by teaching tennis. To close out the trip, I was placed on a plane with the musically talented couple, David Foster and Linda Thompson. David is one of the most successful music producers of all time. He has worked with Barbra Streisand, Whitney Houston, Celine Dion and countless other artists, winning Grammy awards for decades. To have David's ear was a blessing in itself.

I said, "David, I saw your performance at Michael's event. You were great. Is there any way you could come to an event I am putting together in Aspen to help children with cancer?"

David looked surprised at my bold request. "Andrea, I am really booked out. Some of my charity and professional commitments are made years out. Sorry, I wish you well."

"David, please. The only entertainment I have is me tap dancing, and I don't even know how to do it. Could you please reconsider?"

David looked at his wife and they seemed to understand that this was my life's work and their help was to be part of the calling.

David said, "When is your event?" The date I provided was only a few months away. "Andrea, I definitely can't make that date, but I promise you next year I will be there."

David's positive response, even though secured for a year away, was certainly a miracle. After the hugs upon departure, both Linda and David warmly said, "See you next year." They kept their promises. David and Linda came two years in a row to make our Aspen fund-raiser into a star-studded affair.

David, Linda and the other God-appointed ambassadors, viewed by the public as superstar celebrities, visited with the children, took tours of the ranch with great interest and performed passionately for the gala crowd, with no performance fees. And then one of those chosen angels, Faith Hill, took the stage. I was all ready to hear her incredible voice singing one of her popular tunes, when Faith decided to start her stage performance by saying a line that took me totally by surprise: "Andrea, thank you for being an angel."

When I heard Faith make that comment, I looked around to see whom she was talking about. I thought, *Isn't that sweet. She is thanking someone who has helped her.* It was then that the person sitting next to me bumped my arm and smiled at me. I was surprised to see tears of joy in the person's eyes, and it was only when I looked back up at Faith and felt the crowd applauding that I realized what had happened. Faith's anointed presence, as well as the other supportive people on stage and in the crowd, helped shine the Holy Spirit's light brighter on everyone.

The ranch was getting closer to completion. Every stage became an activity in which the children could participate. Groundbreaking had children and staff digging into the earth with a ribbon-wrapped shovel, declaring that the purpose for the land and facility was set in motion. Children painted walls with their names and creative artwork for everyone to look at and enjoy. Murals showed their smiling faces. Dates and words of wisdom adorned the arts and crafts room, showing that, in spite of the children's cancer diagnoses, their spirits lived on forever.

Construction workers cleared the site at the ranch in order to prepare cement blocks where the children and staff could place their hands and initials. These blocks were then placed in the viewing area near the handicapped walkways. The individuals who came before would then watch over the ones who came later.

A blessing ceremony over the children and ranch was given by

David Robinson, an "admiral" in many ways. We had heard that the heralded San Antonio Spurs world-champion basketball star and his family had bought a home and would be spending the off-season in Aspen. Heidi came to me and said, "I really believe God is trying to line us up with David. Why don't you leave him some information and a number where he can contact us?" I went in faith that Heidi's direction came from above. David, a Christian and a military man, a father, husband and longtime pro basketball star (now retired), was dedicated to serving God in every aspect of his life.

The direction and connection was a success, and our Silver Lining family spent a great deal of time with the Robinson family at Bible study, tennis outings, children's visits and meals. David has such enormous enthusiasm for Jesus. The Bible stories David shared came alive in his eyes. He said, "God sent His Son for our sins. Isn't that awesome? God gave us a way to receive salvation! What an awesome God we serve!" David most definitely walked the talk.

Hearing David say grace before meals, watching his endless joy and love for God and those around him, and being enriched in the knowledge he shared were blessings that kept on giving. When David and his wife, Valerie, heard that Heidi and I were adamant about having a prayer room at the ranch, they stepped up to donate the needed funds. The Spiritual Retreat Room received a sponsor in the Robinson family.

Before, during and after the ranch's opening, David led prayers at the ranch, including this one:

> *God, we come together before You at this special place You have placed in Your heart. Bless, protect and provide in Your mighty ways for the children, Andrea, Heidi and the entire Silver Lining Foundation staff. Thank you for sending Your Son, Jesus. You have brought us here together, Lord, and we thank You for*

all the blessings You have given us. Amen.

The sun always shined brilliantly during the prayers, glistening off the ranch's roof while the children enjoyed their special guest. Another one of the countless poignant moments of special guests visiting came during a holiday children's session. The children were all up on stage for the finale of the talent show performance. Their own version of the "Twelve Days of Christmas," created as a thank you for the staff and the week of fun, was going to have a surprise visitor. The children took the stage, donning their Santa hats.

In place, ready to sing, the children waited for our, "Begin whenever you are ready" line. Right on cue, as I started making the announcement, "We have a special guest who has graciously taken time from her busy schedule to hear you perform," Mariah Carey entered the room, walking toward the children as she went to take her front row seat.

There were gasps of astonishment, mouths agape in glee, eyes widening as if they couldn't believe what was before them. A touching moment none of us expected came as well. One of the children from the United Kingdom dreamed of becoming a recording star before being diagnosed with cancer. Voice lessons had taken a back seat to treatments, and unbeknownst to us, Mariah was her hero. When Mariah walked in the room, the youngster burst into tears.

The reactions were genuine and appreciative. I continued with the message, "I would like everyone to welcome Mariah Carey."

Mariah said, "I am excited I have the opportunity to visit the ranch and hear your performance. I know you will all be great." After a few nervous moments the children began, their voices singing with such beauty and love. Upon their completion, Mariah rose to her feet, applauding and showering glorious praise on the children.

The children beamed with pride. The entire room of special guests and staff approached the performers for congratulatory hugs.

Mariah received a ranch tour from one of the children, and we all ended the evening by decorating the Christmas tree with handmade ornaments from the arts and crafts activities. Once again, God blessed us.

As Heidi often states in prayerful moments and conversations, "This has never been about us; it is about God. We are vessels for God to do His work."

When the doors first opened, welcoming children with cancer to the 18,000-square-foot Benedict-Forstmann Silver Lining Ranch, Heidi announced, "There is no safer place than the center of God's will." We both stood and continue to stand in awe of what God created.

Prayers and declarations of faith make a difference. The completed ranch and joyful supportive programs were proof of that. Whether or not a person is a superstar athlete, entertainer, business tycoon or in any other celebrated category, financial support and prayers make an impact. The humblest, weakest, smallest of prayers and support from people in any walk of life matter in big ways. Because of the grace and love God bestowed on our calling, because of our prayers and other people's prayers, and because of our walking in faith, we have been provided such tremendous miracles, signs, wonders, blessings and gifts.

Chapter Twenty-Two

Pursue love, and desire spiritual gifts,
but especially that you may prophesy.

—1 Corinthians 14:1

In late August 2001, I was in New York City for fund-raising meetings, as well as to run some new and innovative children's cancer programs. The first stop on my nearly three-week trip was Ted Forstmann's Huggy Bears charity gala in the Hamptons. Ted and his close group of family and friends put on the annual Huggy Bears tennis event with much anticipation from the East Coast audience. At the end of the weeklong tennis event is a social fund-raising extravaganza attended by celebrities, athletes, influential business people and other individuals from around the world. Ted was excited and grateful, and his presence on the stage set the tone for the evening.

The Silver Lining Foundation had recently celebrated its eleven-year anniversary of helping children with cancer. The multimillion-dollar Benedict-Forstmann Silver Lining Ranch was completed. As promised, Ted had brought an entire new area of the business sector to acknowledge and support our efforts. Our $40 million endowment fund-raising effort was underway. Every dollar mattered, and

I greatly needed to generate funding to continue our worthwhile programs.

Ted, as the master of ceremonies, asked me to say a few words to the audience. I walked to the center of the stage and looked out at the massive audience—many of whom were long-time contributors from the incredible donor base we were building on the East Coast—in a few short weeks many of those in the crowd would be fleeing for their lives from the World Trade Center. Not everyone made it out alive.

Philanthropic fund-raising was always an uphill journey for us, subject to fluctuations in the economy and unforeseen events. It is always challenging to keep up with program expansion costs and inflation. The Little Star programs, introduced in the late 1990s, and the Silver Lining Foundation programs took a tremendous hit from the September 11, 2001, attacks. Millions of dollars in commitments were lost. By October 2002, the economy had not yet swayed in our favor and donations were down.

The Little Star programs were developed by Heidi and me to provide additional follow-up and outreach for Silver Lining, while also supporting the family, caregiver support system and other children afflicted with hardships. The programs provide educational, spiritual, medical and financial support around the world.

Our new program construction projects—including the family retreat center, lodge, sanctuary, chapel and indoor arena/convention center—were especially hard hit by the depleted funding. Still in its infancy, the $40 million endowment was at a standstill. It was a dreadful fund-raising phase. The children's programs were continuing with great success, but it was only a matter of time before something had to give.

On October 19, 2002, my old high school was going to present me with their prestigious Heritage Award—the first time it had been given to a former student of Stevenson High School. Stevenson High had grown from nine hundred students, when I attended, to four thousand students and five hundred faculty members. It had been twenty years since I had been on campus or in my old Lincolnshire neighborhood. The years had passed so quickly and so much had changed since then.

I loved being back in my old hometown. Despite the town's growth, I felt like I was in completely familiar surroundings. From my downtown Chicago hotel, I drove the rental car down the same expressway that my parents used for years. At the turnoff, instead of going left toward Lincolnshire and the high school, I went right. To the right stood the tennis club complex where I trained as a youngster. Next to it was the field where I had run countless laps on the orders of instructors. I didn't need to see the sign for Trinity University. I knew where I was.

I didn't have much time to spare before the ceremony at Stevenson was to begin. However, I felt God calling and pulling me toward Trinity Chapel just as I was drawn to it as a child. Without hesitation, I realized there was an important reason for me to get to the chapel.

The college campus had grown by leaps and bounds, yet I found the chapel without one wrong turn. I was excited because God was leading me. I stepped out of the car and veritably skipped toward the chapel. With every footstep, I felt God's presence guiding me. My shoes were bigger than when I was a child walking this same path. The burning sensation in my heart and spirit to do God's work had also grown.

Walking through the chapel door, I understood the importance of my tennis career being a training ground for my long-term purpose, my life of service to God. The calling led me to the chapel as a child and drew me to it again as an adult.

More than twenty years had passed since I had entered the

chapel, but the moment I stepped inside I knew I was home. I knelt before the Lord and said, "Thank you, Jesus. Please take over every aspect of my life. Thank you for your constant love and companionship. I could use Your handholding to carry me to the path, calling and purposes You have destined for me."

I continued, "Increase Your teachers for me and let me encounter more miracles, signs, wonders, blessings and prophetic anointing. I also need You to decide what is good for me and what isn't and to place those things accordingly."

I profusely thanked God for allowing such interesting people in my life—ones who taught me brilliant lessons. Even the interactions I had that were difficult to digest were essential, because they helped build character and knowledge to run to God for help.

His love was transforming me, and I used that love to help me in my work and other situations, in my relationships with people, and in dealing with problems. Looking at every occurrence with God's love, words, wisdom, prophesy and spiritual gifts became a better formula for me to follow than laboring through encounters searching for answers of my own.

Before I ended my prayer, I took in a long breath and said, "Thank you Heavenly Father, Lord Jesus Christ, and the Holy Spirit, for being there for me always. Thank you for saving me, for Jesus dying on the cross for me and for loving me despite all my sins. Thank you for forgiving my sins, for allowing me to serve you and for being so patient with me. Help me be obedient to Your command, as I know I can't do anything in serving You without Your help. Take all of my life, everything, and do with it as You want. Thank you! In Jesus' name, thank you! Amen."

Refreshed, invigorated and soaring with the love of God, I sprang to my feet in the empty chapel. I was no longer anxious about things. The prayers of requests and thanks in place, I knew God was going to guard my heart, spirit, soul and mind

Talent Show participants and staff with Ted Forstmann, August 2003.

Holiday time at the ranch with Anna and Andrea.

Maja Muric, Katie and Andrea in Las Vegas in 2003.

Pete Sampras and fans from the Foundation during the U.S. Open 1998 program.

Las Vegas resident Katie, age 10, Andrea and Iraniza (1980–2000) at Talent Show.

Carolyn (1985–2003), Andrea and Andrew (1987–2003) at San Diego Ranch on the Road Program.

Andrea, Matisse and Lauren (1986–2000) at the ranch.

Kevin Costner and fiancée Christine's fishing lesson in Aspen.

Heidi Bookout, Andrea and Nelson Mandela at the ranch.

Sonia (1983–2001) and Andrea at Talent Show.

Pete Prado in front of the ranch; Pete passed away in 2003.

Talent Show fun.

Andre Agassi and Sarah during Wimbledon 1998 Program.

Photo courtesy of Art Seitz

Counselor Annie Costner and ranch pool party participant Emily.

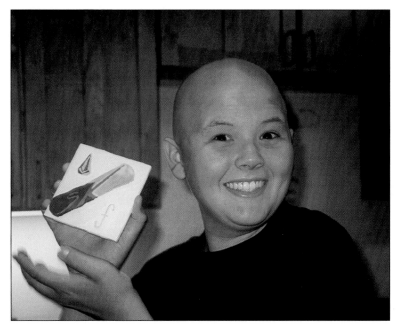

Kaleb "Special K" (1987–2003) at the ranch.

Nick's big catch.

Andrea, Paul Newman and Heidi at the ranch in front of the Jacuzzi Room mural.

Eddie, Pam (1981–1998) and Andrea having fun in Aspen.

At Fabi's house in Aspen. Front row: Mark, Keith (1980–1994), Clown, Leigh, David (1987–1996) Back row: Heidi, Jackie, Rhea (1974–1995) and Andrea.

John McEnroe and Andrea at Wimbledon.

Anna Kournikova and Andrea at New York City fund-raiser.

Cindy Crawford and Rande Gerber surprise children at the ranch.

Tim McGraw and Faith Hill, shining God's light, love and joy on Camile, others and the town of Aspen during their special ranch and fund-raiser performance.

David Robinson and the Epstein brothers in Aspen.

Andrea, Ted Forstmann and Secretary of State Colin Powell at Forstmann Little Conference.

Photo credit: Alice Koelle Photography

Rhea, (1974–1995) Fabi Benedict and Jackie in Aspen 1993.

Cindy Crawford, Tripp and Andrea at Washington D.C. Cancer March.

RJ Wagner, Andrea and Paul Newman at the ranch.

New York City Ranch on the Road Program. Staff (Heidi, Beene, Andrea, Kate, Chris) and the children.

while guiding me through every step of my life.

I made it on time to the ceremony for me at Stevenson High School. I began my walk to center stage on the football field to the background cheers of students, faculty and adults. Before I reached the platform, God asked me a question. I stutter-stepped and caught my breath. He had never asked me a question in my life. God asked me, "Do you want me standing next to you? When you are doing My work for the children, who do you want standing next to you?" He continued asking me the same question in different ways: "These teenagers are cheering for you. Who do you want standing beside you when you do My work in helping children?"

Before taking the final steps to the platform, I answered, with no hesitation at all, "You, God—I want You to be next to me. Please choose the people who serve You to stand next to me. We can all stand together, helping the children, in Your name." That crisp fall afternoon, I felt God's love in a way that surpassed anything I had experienced before. He was bringing me to an entirely new level.

A five-mile fund-raising walk followed the award ceremony. The Stevenson students raised $20,000 through the walk for the Silver Lining Foundation. I walked with the girls' high school tennis team the entire way. They were a great group of kids with wonderful spirits—ambitious as well as community minded. Each one of the girls that I spent the afternoon talking and walking with made me beam with great pride at the ambassadorship we have in the youth of America.

Chris Franken, my former photography teacher, gave me a tour of the school, which now resembled a college campus. I saw the old and the new. I gazed at the lockers I used to be pushed into. I asked to go to Mrs. Schallerer's room. Long since retired, she had been one of my dearest teachers, helping guide me through the pitfalls I encountered during my high school years.

Mrs. Schallerer was living proof of the power of prayer; indeed, without her lending hand I might never have made it through high school unscathed. When I was at school, the lunch period was an especially unbearable time for me. I was often the target of adolescent behavior at its worst when students threw food at me in the lunchroom, and I longed for a way to escape this torment. Mrs. Schallerer saved the day by granting my request to help her grade papers during the lunchtime period. As I looked around her classroom, where I had spent so many lunch periods, I remembered her good deed with thanks in my heart.

These grateful memories flowed in as I continued on the Stevenson High School tour, combining the new experiences with the reminiscing of fond old stories. The current energy of students in the school was incredible. Here it was a Sunday afternoon, and the teenagers were enthusiastic and full of service to their school and community. It truly was a privilege to be in their company. God had certainly blessed me once again.

After an absolutely amazing day, I drove back to my hotel and sang praises to God the entire way in the car. As I approached Chicago, God sent a message to me.

Chapter Twenty-Three

Give thanks to the Father who has
qualified us to be partakers of the inheritance
of the saints in the light. He has delivered us
from the power of darkness and conveyed us
into the kingdom of the Son of His love,
in whom we have redemption through
His blood, the forgiveness of sins.

—Colossians 1:12–14

God's message to me while I was driving in the car from my hometown of Lincolnshire back to Chicago made me stop in my tracks. He said, "You need to be delivered from demons of your past." This certainly was a quick change of atmosphere. Still, even though I knew God was right, I kept singing away, because joy was in my spirit and heart, and nothing was going to silence it. I accepted that it was now time to forever change my life through God's deliverance.

Traveling through the rest of my day, the next remark I heard from God was, "You are going to be with Me on Thursday." I was ecstatic. I wondered if an angel would come to me and deliver a message from God. I pondered the idea of being able to see God in a vision or dream. It was Sunday, late afternoon, and my mind was churning with ideas about what opportunities could arise.

Then I stopped, as if my mind hit a brick wall. I slowed down the car. What if God was taking me to heaven on Thursday, because my life on Earth was over? What if that is what He meant? I realized as sad as it would be to not be around the life I currently knew, I would be obedient and go where God wanted me to go.

Fortunately, I knew wherever God was taking me on Thursday, I would be okay. I would be with Him and He would make sure the things I held so dear to my heart—people, children, animals, the foundation's programs—would be well taken care of.

I tried to assign words to what was happening. God would have nothing of it. He didn't want my mind to rationalize and take over. I actually tried to bring up problems that needed solving, and God patiently and lovingly replied, "The only thing that matters is that you will be with Me on Thursday." God blocked all the old patterns. It felt very liberating knowing that He was taking over everything.

I mulled around in my mind any invitations I had received in the last few days that required travel. I could have virtually picked up the phone and arranged a meeting or children's program in practically any city in the United States—or in the world, for that matter. I did nothing of the sort. I scheduled nothing for Thursday onward. I had more work to accomplish in Chicago on Monday and Tuesday. A special and unique trip to Grand Rapids, Michigan—which God had set up earlier—would take place on Wednesday. But I kept Thursday and the days after wide open.

What I was so thrilled about is I knew I was getting lined up correctly under God's tutelage. I knew I could never go wrong by following God. I was aware that some people might not applaud my actions in following God and being obedient to His Word, messages and will, but the only audience I was concerned with was God.

Come Thursday, I knew I would be exactly where I was supposed to be. How to explain that to people was another story. I wondered to myself, *Do I tell anyone this or will it spook them out?* Trying to live as God instructs can be difficult and in some instances a little strange for people to understand, especially if they have never been aware that God communicates in a variety of forms to His children.

The bigger picture of my Thursday events was yet to be revealed. With each message God has shared with me over time, I have known there was a larger picture behind it. This situation was no different.

From Chicago, on a brilliant October Monday morning, I phoned Pat Theissen to update her on my weekend events. During the conversation, Pat told me about a Christian Charismatic Deliverance conference in Detroit, Michigan, from Thursday to Saturday. I screamed, "That is it! That is where God wants me to be."

I wanted to leap to Detroit immediately, even though the conference was days away. Completely thrilled that my destination to be with God was revealed, I already started the planning process of getting to Detroit. Pat realized the significance of what happened. Before we ended the conversation, she said she would pray and see if God had intended her to be there as well.

I booked my hotel in Detroit. The Marriott Conference Center near Cobo Arena was a place I had previously stayed during my tennis tour days. I loved playing in Cobo Arena. I won a tournament there and had fond memories of the audience support, victories and hospitality. The instant the conference registration office was open I was on the phone. Fifteen hundred people were scheduled to attend the conference, and I did not want to miss out on securing my hotel or conference booking.

That is how fast God worked with me in dramatically changing my life by taking me to an entirely new level with Him. God had been blessing me my entire life, but He waited until I made the ultimate decision of giving Him and coming to Him 100 percent before revealing what other things were destined for me.

Interestingly enough, my Wednesday scheduled trip to Grand Rapids, Michigan, fit in perfectly with the Thursday Detroit conference. Both appeared ordained by God. My first Michigan stop involved spending the entire day with Betsy and Dick DeVos, a well-known Christian couple who helped build the DeVos Children's Hospital.

I had met the DeVoses in Aspen during Ted Forstmann's Forstmann Little Conference. Hundreds of people from around the globe, from all walks of life, gathered for the three-day event that included roundtable discussions with high-ranking officials on a multitude of business topics: politics, education, scientific discoveries, technological innovations and a whole lot more. For the luncheon, we were free to sit at any table we chose. All other meals had assigned seating. I found an empty chair and waited as the table filled up and introductions were made. Queen Noor from Jordan, the owner of the Washington Redskins football team, and doctors, professionals and specialists from a variety of fields took the empty seats at my table.

Dick and Betsy DeVos sat down next to me. After hearing my name, they shared, "We have a daughter named Andrea. She is fourteen years old."

I continued the conversation, "At fourteen, she must be in high school, right? How is she enjoying it?"

As soon as the reply came, "She has joined the tennis team," I thought, *This is more than a coincidence that I am sitting next to a family who has a daughter named Andrea who is fourteen and plays tennis for her high school.*

"If you and your daughter Andrea would like, the next time I am in Michigan I can stop by her high school and join in on their practice session. I used to play professional tennis, starting the tour at the same age your Andrea is now." I felt God trying to stir up a relationship between us, and the only thing I thought I could bring was my tennis coaching skills, so I offered them up for free. I assumed incorrectly that our relationship was to be based solely on my willingness to coach a girl's tennis team several states away. That was part of it, but not all of what God was trying to establish.

The gentleman sitting across the table asked me, "Andrea, please tell Queen Noor about your amazing work with children." I shared enthusiastically. Moments before Charlie Rose was to begin the political presentation at lunch, the DeVoses revealed supportive information. "The DeVos Children's Hospital in Grand Rapids is a facility we work very closely with. In hearing about how you devote your life to supporting children with cancer, perhaps our resources can help with your foundation."

I also learned that Dick and Betsy were instrumental in providing health care, education and information about the importance of having a relationship with Jesus to people well beyond their children's hospital and Michigan borders. The DeVos family was also involved with ownership of the Orlando Magic basketball team, and Dick was the son of Richard DeVos who founded Amway. I was on the verge of seeing, firsthand, the DeVoses' generous philanthropic efforts in building the children's hospital in Grand Rapids, Michigan.

The luncheon provided an informal venue to merge our respective contributions to society, and within a week God lined up the dates to fit in perfectly with our busy schedules. After my Chicago trip, I would fly to the warmth and hospitality of the DeVoses.

The wind was howling outside my Chicago hotel room window with such tremendous power that the windows rattled. Looking outside at picturesque Lake Michigan, I gazed at boats trying desperately to settle themselves. It was still dark when I left the hotel

Wednesday morning. Barely able to keep my coat on, because of the wind's power, I headed to Meig's field to meet the DeVoses' plane. Menacing dark clouds couldn't stop God from opening the skies for our departure. The big storm cleared right before take off. I knew it would; God had plans for me. I surveyed the scene as we left Chicago, my hometown, the place of my natural birth and the location where I first started encountering God's presence and power. I was heading to an even bigger spiritual birth than I had ever experienced before.

Putting on the control tower and pilot information headphones, I took in a deep breath and silently murmured, "Here we go God. I am ready." The Chicago skyline and its tall office buildings majestically towered over the waterfront. God was taking me to a new level in an already enormously blessed way of life. I was traveling toward a destination about which I knew nothing—other than God's presence.

The first stop in Michigan was the DeVos Children's Hospital. The visit began with the distribution of gifts that I had previously shipped. The children, all of them, exhibited such courage and strength, and an appreciation for life beyond measure. A boy in a wheelchair showed the physical effects of his cancer treatments. His head was bald from chemotherapy treatments. Even though the youngster had one leg amputated in an attempt to save his life, he cheerfully managed to maneuver his way down the hall in his wheelchair. He held three roses ever so delicately. Glowing with joy, the boy held the blooming flowers proudly. He pushed along with the wheelchair gracefully, using one arm and one leg.

The youngster appeared before me as if practicing for a role as a dashing prince in a school play. He handed me the roses while presenting me with a welcoming speech so touching that it far surpassed any words I'd read in a greeting card. It made my heart swell and my spirit smile. Secretly, I knew God was behind it. God loves working through His little children.

Betsy DeVos hosted a lunch with members of the dedicated

hospital staff. Grace was said before the meal, and most of the conversation centered on stories of God's glorious ways of forming Silver Lining and Little Star's program work. It was an honor to discuss God's loving hands on our children's programs. People shared Christian testimonies and God's love touched everyone.

I had been visiting children's hospitals bearing gifts since I was a young teenager. Each visit, every child, parent and hospital staff member I have ever met has been unique and special. The wonders, miracles, smiles and laughter experienced throughout the decades have become sacred moments etched forever in my memory. However, this was a hospital visit like none other I had experienced. The luncheon centered around the workings and glory of Lord Jesus Christ. God was working His ways.

It was the first time at a hospital that I shared my testimony of how thankful I was for God's grace, love and guidance. I had no hesitancy or concern about how my remarks would be taken. I felt God urging me along with every word I spoke. In past situations, I was scared to fully share my faith, for fear that a contributor would be affected adversely and wouldn't donate.

God knew where the roots of my hesitancy existed. It was a huge relief to receive a confirmation from God that sharing the depth of my faith would not take away from contributions but rather enhance them. With a $47 million goal for the capital campaign and endowment project, I didn't need to be placed behind the starting blocks with nowhere to go. The fact that I could share my faith to heighten the children's programs, without any repercussions on fund-raising efforts, was a cause for celebration.

The timing of the special visit at the DeVos Children's Hospital during such a pivotal period in my life was the work of God. Dick and Betsy DeVos were chosen for a grand calling. They had lined up with God in great appreciation and thereby touched the lives of everyone they crossed paths with, exuding the light and love of God.

Visiting with the children battling cancer, being part of the luncheon hosted by Betsy and joining in for tennis fun with Andrea DeVos's high school tennis team made for a most memorable visit, and God shined His glory with every step.

The DeVoses arranged for my transportation that evening to Detroit. I was greeted on the plane by at least seven men elegantly dressed in tuxedos. Dashing from the tennis clinic, I boarded the corporate plane in my sweaty tennis clothes. The group didn't care. In fact, they saved me a seat in the front of the plane. While we were on the flight, I felt compelled to ask the group what they thought was the biggest life lesson they had learned. The men's answers, given individually, didn't center on the career positions they had in the world, goals achieved, things conquered, big homes, cool cars or toys acquired. Every answer started and finished with the relationships God brought to their lives. Wives, children, coworkers, friends—the list went on and on about how special and blessed they felt for the people they had in their lives: All made possible by God interacting in their lives.

From my plane window, I watched the sun start to set. The scenery slowly faded out of sight. Another day was coming to a close. Certainly a day like no other. God was building additions to my life with His mighty hands. I reflected on the way the DeVoses chose to live their lives—in serving God fully. I thought of the remarks from my fellow passengers. I walked on the plane a stranger to everyone. The DeVos family members and hospital staff I met in Grand Rapids were not randomly selected people who luckily fell into my life; neither were the people on the plane simply ordinary passengers. They were all people on a mission from God, serving their purposes and callings to the fullest, and God planned for our lives to intersect.

I landed safely in Detroit. Courtesy of the DeVoses, a car was waiting for me and whisked me away to my hotel—where God had a big appointment waiting for me.

Chapter Twenty-Four

"And I will give you the keys of the kingdom of heaven, and whatever you bind on earth will be bound in heaven, and whatever you loose on earth will be loosed in heaven."

—Jesus says in Matthew 16:19

Standing in the hotel's check-in line, I received a call from Pat saying that she was boarding a plane to Detroit. I was thrilled. I phoned Heidi with the good news. Heidi was pleased Pat would be with me during the conference, because Pat has always been a positive force for getting me lined up with the purposes God intended for me.

Pat and I were going to catch up over a late dinner, so I used the time before she arrived to send off a few e-mails. God decided He was going to make sure I was paying full attention to the conference. The last e-mails I was able to send or check my entire time in Detroit occurred on Wednesday evening, moments after checking into the hotel. By the time Pat landed an hour later, and throughout Thursday, Friday, Saturday and Sunday, my power button was mysteriously broken on my laptop computer. I tried numerous times to boot-up the machine but to no avail. Pat and I were rooming together and she asked, "Has that happened before?"

I said, "No. God really doesn't want anything but Him coming through while I am here at the conference. He has made that obvious."

Every day while I was in Detroit, I checked to see if the power button was working. It never did. God took care that the only messages coming into my heart, soul, spirit and mind would be of His choosing.

Taking the step of turning my life over to God seemed so easy. I couldn't imagine living any other way now.

On Thursday morning, I woke before dawn waiting for the events to unfold before me. At 7:00 A.M., Pat and I headed down to the convention hall to check in and claim our seats. I gladly pulled out my credit card to pay the conference fee. Pat would have nothing of it, making sure the historic occasion would be presented as a gift in every sense of the word. Despite the capacity crowd, we had perfect seating—up front and center.

Worship started at 8:00 A.M. I had no idea what to expect. My schedule card said worship 8:00 to 9:00 A.M., followed by numerous speakers intertwined with breaks, lunch and dinner. I could expect to be back to my room around 10:00 P.M. Everyone had a Bible in tow. The place was packed and worship started right on time. I assumed wrongly that worship was private or group prayer time. Worship was also singing, praying and dancing in praise and celebration of God.

From 9:00 A.M. until the lunch break, I was engaged in every word of the speakers' messages. Becoming involved with anointed and appointed believers, prophets, apostles, teachers, ministers and pastors serving God was truly making a difference. God loves helping ordinary people do extraordinary things. He had worked that way in my life, and now the control knob was being turned up a few notches.

All the long years and devotion I put toward my own private study time in the Word of God were enormously successful in helping me get to this next level in God's training process. I had also done course work for my Institute of Theology and Ministry Training associate's degree, which helped make it possible to start relating to subject areas covered as the conference progressed.

After taking the designated thirty-minute break, Pat and I entered the conference sanctuary area. God spoke to me then, very clearly and concisely: "Go to the jewelry table now." Right outside the conference sanctuary was a makeshift bookstore with videos, tapes, books and CDs.

All the speakers had special areas for their materials, and it was a great setup to purchase educational tools. In the middle of the book tables section was a tiny jewelry table. The moment God spoke to me, I said to Pat, without hesitation, "I will be right back." The next session was going to begin any second. Our seats were held from the previous morning's teachings, but everyone was crowding in, returning from the break, eager to become more absorbed in God's Word.

Turning toward the gift shop area, I told Pat, "I am going to the bathroom." I didn't want to make us both late by taking the time to explain what was going on. Pat, in her always helpful ways, asked for my backpack to help speed up my return. I handed it to her hoping I had money in my pocket. I sprinted to the jewelry table faster than I had ever run after a tennis ball.

Months ago, per God's instruction and with enormous love, I had given away my holy dove ring to a very trusted, gifted and special soul. The piece of jewelry was anointed with God's miraculous protection. Now, I was thrilled with the potential opportunity that God was going to replace the ring with a new one.

I arrived at the table to find a minimal amount of jewelry. No rings at all. I thought, *Oh well, maybe God will give me a new ring another time.* I thanked God for making my spirit spring with delight, knowing my old ring was in a deserved place on a purpose to bring love, protection, healing, peace and joy. As I was about to head back to the conference, God spoke to me again, loudly and clearly: "I am giving you a key to my kingdom. Take the key." I looked on the table and sure enough there was one key on the table—it was huge. I thought it looked gaudy. It was a huge key with fake diamonds in it on a thick gold rope chain. As I looked at it, I asked God, *That key?*

God responded immediately. "Yes, I am giving you a key to my kingdom. Take that key." I was obedient. Despite the key being a style that was quite different and not my taste in jewelry, I followed God's instruction. I headed for the cashier, thanking God along the way for showing me the necklace and giving me a key to His kingdom. I paid the forty dollars and slid the box with the contents secure inside my pocket. Racing to my seat, I made it in time before the next speaker was to begin.

The speaker said, "Promise comes when you have God's heart and vision. There is a key. The Lord wants to give us a key. Do not be distracted from what God is saying. The Lord goes out of His way to reveal this stuff. The God of heaven will give us success."

I was well aware of how powerful and incredible God's messages could be, having lived with them since I was a child. However, this was perhaps the most significant situation God had orchestrated for me. I had an immediate reaction to what had occurred. On Thursday, God gave me a key to His kingdom. He gave me a key, which I could wear around my neck so I could always remember who I was, where I was going and who I was with at all times. I was a child of God. My Heavenly Father gave me a key to His house. On the previous Sunday, God made me a promise. On Thursday, He kept and granted His promise. The day God guaranteed I would be with Him, I was.

All my life I was searching for God's house and kingdom, never coming close enough, because I stretched myself out on the wide path. The footing to get into God's house eluded me. I had been looking for the key since I was eight years old, and I never quite found it. God knew how much I wanted it. I prayed for it daily. I was scattered in my knowledge of the Bible and many times I grieved God, the Holy Spirit and Jesus because of my lack of knowledge and obviously much-to-learn-from actions. But they stuck with me.

I was not going to miss this escort. As soon as the speaker finished, I told Pat, "I didn't go to the bathroom. God told me to go to the jewelry table. He told me to take this key, saying it was a key to His Kingdom. He wanted me to have it. It was forty dollars."

Pat replied, "Jesus was in the wilderness for forty days. God has brought you out of your last forty days of trouble. God definitely has some plans for you."

I was ecstatic over the recent developments. During the next break, I went back to the bookstore cashier. "Do you have any more keys? I only saw one on the jewelry table."

The cashier said, "No. We only had one."

I went back to my seat and stared at the key. It had an inscription on it: Matthew 16:19, a passage from the book of Matthew. Before the next speaker approached the podium, I looked up the scripture in my Bible to see what it said.

In Matthew 16:19, Jesus says, "And I will give you the keys of the kingdom of heaven, and whatever you bind on earth will be bound in heaven, and whatever you loose on earth will be loosed in heaven."

God was granting me authority, in Jesus' name, to rid myself and my life of things from the darkness and the enemy's domain, and replace them with things from God and the heavenly kingdom. I had received some amazing gifts from God before, but this one touched me with incredible love and depth. I knew my joy and passion in helping people and children were gifts from God, and the gifts kept coming.

Another declaration God was making to me was just as obvious. Currently, the extreme lack of knowledge I had could no longer be excused. I had graduated from my old way of life and thinking, and now I had the added responsibility of living in a new way, from God's perspective instead of my own or humanity's. I wasn't expected to be perfect, but I was schooled enough to be progressing on a daily basis toward more Christ-based thinking and behavior rather than my old secular ways of thought and actions. I wasn't forced to go this route, but rather I felt called to it, and excited about choosing to learn more about God and His ways, will and Word. I was ready to immerse myself.

God giving me the key to His house and kingdom was a message of acceptance. I was accepted as a joint heir with Jesus—a co-laborer with Christ. I had authority to bind the enemy's strongholds. I was given the authority to loose God's glorious blessings. It was a hugely significant occurrence in my relationship with God. The grace and love of God, the prayers God heard from people on my behalf and all the prayers I prayed, led God to present me a key to His house and kingdom on Thursday, October 24, 2002.

The previous Sunday, in my hometown, God told me I needed to be delivered from demons of my past. God was also going to take care of that at the conference. The next speaker's expertise and gifting from God was to cast out demons and curses from people. God states in the Bible that everyone is born in sin. God provided a way for people to be reborn in the Spirit. At one point during the speaker's message, people who wanted and needed to be delivered from abuse of any kind could come up to the stage. This included generational curses of abuse, and also adultery, wrongful sexual partners, rape and other things. A great deal of the audience rose up and went forward. I stepped forward having no idea what to expect. I was a little skeptical of the shows I saw on television where people were prayed over and they fell down. I wondered if people were planted in the audience to perform in such a way.

Everyone who stepped forward was told to keep his or her eyes and heads forward while they were being prayed over, ministered to and delivered. I was in the very closest row to the stage, right in the middle. Even with my eyes closed I could hear people thumping to the ground. One man to the left of me started vomiting. There were screams and sounds of people falling to the floor under the power of the Holy Spirit. I had never experienced such a situation. It was difficult to keep my eyes, head and focus forward. What was happening was not choreographed. There was no stage trick. It was real. God had the Holy Spirit working through the room and delivering abuse, curses, sins and demons out of people, including me. It was wild.

Then I sensed the speaker right over me, inches above my head, praying. I did feel a shift from God occur. It was like a big whoosh that went right through me. I didn't fall down, but I most certainly felt a power that was well beyond my own, taking over to change things inside of me.

At this point people could open their eyes and select an intercessory prayer warrior, specially trained to minister. I chose an African-American woman with friendly features and a gentle voice. I was so taken that this woman would make an effort to help heal others that I immediately asked God to one day gift me with that responsibility of giving back and helping advance His kingdom.

My trained minister's name was Linda and she was from Detroit. All of our first names and places of residence were printed on our nametags. No pleasantries were exchanged; it was down to business immediately. The first thing Linda asked me was, "Have you forgiven everyone?" I answered, "Yes," with great clarity, as I knew

God always gave me the ability to forgive people regardless of circumstances.

God made it a point in the Bible that His followers had to forgive others in order to receive God's total forgiveness. Jesus forgave everyone, even those who killed him. It was encouraging to know that since I had forgiven fully every wrong done to me, allowing God to be in charge of everything, that I would be healed and cleansed fully.

I asked Linda to pray for someone I knew who also needed to be delivered from past pain and abuse but could not make it to the conference. She did. Then I joined her in doing a prayer for the person, fully remembering that when two or more come together in God's name, God is with them. After we finished praying, Linda went on to minister to other people, and the speaker was still walking back and forth on stage, declaring prayers of deliverance. I walked back to my seat, stepping over people lying across the floor. The man to the left of me was still vomiting, but fortunately they had found a bucket to put under him.

Back in my seat, I began to say prayers of thanks. Stopping abruptly, I realized I had never forgiven *myself* for things I had done. My entire life I was consumed with forgiving other people while being extremely hard on myself. I very rarely excused any of my actions, so in a strange way I was battling myself seeking the unobtainable—perfection.

There is no such thing. The only place I could go was closer to God, but as for being mistake-free, sin-free, it would never happen. The quest was in trying to be more like Christ every day, fully knowing that this lifetime effort would require close daily support from the Holy Spirit. The purpose instilled in everyone's spirit is to reach his or her own pinnacle relationship with God.

I wanted a stronger and deeper bond with God. I craved that connection. If God said it was okay to forgive myself, well then, I was up to the task. Leaving my seat, I walked up to a speaker and murmured, "Could you pray a deliverance prayer over me. I don't think I ever forgave myself for things, sins that I have committed." The speaker took some oil, placed his hand on my head and said a prayer over me. I returned to my seat with a skip in my step, a smile on my face and God embedded securely and permanently in my heart and spirit.

God's work was in progress and miracles were happening all around. I had a quick education and a very up close and personal look at the act of deliverance. I could see the truth of it before my eyes.

It was after 10:00 P.M. when Pat and I returned to our room. What an incredible full day God had presented to me! I went to sleep clutching the key, God's gift to me, knowing that He lived within me and that He, and His kingdom of heavenly and celestial support, were all around me.

Chapter Twenty-Five

Every good gift and every perfect gift
is from above, and comes down
from the Father of lights.

—James 1:17

I awoke at 5:00 A.M., still gripping my key. Indentations were on my hand from holding it tightly all night. I went in the bathroom and stared at myself in the mirror. I wanted to see if I looked different now that God had given me a key to His kingdom. I stared at my reflection, looking for the changes since my deliverance experience from the night before.

Even if I still looked the same, I felt different. No longer would I veer off my path in an attempt to please people, constantly trying not to disappoint others at the cost of my spirit. Saying no would be easier and guilt-free because God, not me, was going to be in charge of all parts of my life.

I had a new strength and peace in being a servant of God. It wasn't the old me staring back in the mirror. The new me had a greater partnership with God. I now had a calling and purpose behind *all* of my actions and steps. I wanted to wake up Pat and call Heidi with the great news and say, "Look what you helped create—a child of God, a joint heir with Jesus, whose purpose is to help advance the kingdom of God."

I couldn't contain my energy any more. I knew if I stayed in the room any longer I would have to wake up Pat and rattle on about how the Andrea sharing her room today was not the same Andrea who checked in on Wednesday. I decided to go reserve our seats in the sanctuary and get in a workout.

I jumped on the Stairmaster, tuning in to Fox News, which was playing on four of the television sets in front of me. Reports of a possible war filled the screens. It was a strange sensation to be so completely full of God's love, and be in a world that had such tremendous turmoil going on.

Continuing with my workout, I wondered how God felt about the state of the world. He gave up His only Son for people all around the world. Jesus paid the price for my sins, cleansing me with His blood and death. God watched it all. God and Jesus lived it all because of their love for all humanity. The truth of the sacrifice God and Jesus made for me resounded in my heart. That basic truth had never dawned on me in its full reality. It was exactly as written in John 3:16: "For God so loved the world that He gave His only begotten Son. . . ." I had to know, believe, confess and follow—and that is what God was working on with me. My successes didn't save me. It was Jesus who jumped in and saved me.

After completing the first day of the conference, God graduated me from an old program of teaching and placed me on a more dynamic path. As I dressed for the second day of the conference, I felt the Holy Spirit moving in me, asking, "If God appeared before you right now, what would you want Him to say?"

Without hesitation I responded, "You have done well, my faithful and loyal servant. I have accepted you as you are, but I am not going to keep you as you are. You will grow more in the nine spiritual gifts given by the Holy Spirit: wisdom, knowledge, faith, healings, miracles, prophecy, discerning of spirits, tongues and interpretation of tongues. You will perform these gifts with My love, in My name and for My glory to benefit children and people around the world."

When it was time for the dinner break, Pat and I went to the hotel restaurant. We were discussing the ways God blesses His followers when my cell phone rang. I excused myself and took the call. To my delight and great surprise, I received a call from the office of a terrific, generous humanitarian. I had been trying for three years just to get a contact number for this person. I returned to the table and told Pat what had happened. She acknowledged the divine gift by responding, "God has something in mind for the two of you." The short intermission came to a close, and we eagerly headed to the evening session of the conference. It was a special way to end our last night, exploring and learning more about the ways of God.

That night, before drifting off to sleep, I heard Pat praying. I reflected on what an incredible week it had been. My life was heading in the right direction, on the exact path God had appointed for me. I went to sleep holding my key necklace, pressing it against my heart.

Now it was time to incorporate the new knowledge I had acquired at the conference into reality—for the benefit of the children I served as well as the people I interacted with. I had been wanting to incorporate specialized spiritual programs—something I had researched before, but not on as grand a scale as I was planning now. I boarded the plane in Detroit and settled in my seat, prepared to spend the flight catching up on my journal from the last day's activities. Instead, I was given a new course of action. God spoke to my spirit and declared, "It is time for you to write a book: *Soli Deo Gloria.*"

My first reaction was that this role was for someone else. I wasn't an author. I loved writing about and to God in my journal and sending off letters to the children I worked with, and to anyone who cared to learn about the children and God. A book, however, seemed way out of my league. I knew gifted and talented authors who had dedicated their lives to writing books, and it took some of them years to get their work published. Besides, I didn't know anyone named Gloria, and I didn't really want to venture into the publishing world. However, I knew I needed to be obedient to God. He captured my spirit again and said, "It is time for you to write and tell people about your faith. My glory can be revealed through your stories. It will release blessings and purposes for people all around the world."

Writing the book sounded like an enormous undertaking, which made me think about my other responsibilities. Funding demands pulled on me constantly. God had always pressed on me the fact that the endowment of $40 million needed to be raised by the time I was forty. That deadline was approaching rapidly, and we were only starting the process.

I had taken out loans to cover some of the various delinquent pledges of financial support, hoping to pay off the loans when the money came in. Various contributors who made million-dollar verbal commitments, pre-September 11, 2001, were now affected financially, and were refusing to return my phone calls. These broken commitments totaled ten million dollars. Our financial position would be nearing the "dire" point very soon.

My quest to complete Little Star's entire Rancho Milagro building project was also still stuck in the vision area. Annual budget needs of over $2 million for program operation were a perennial concern.

I had been working in the fund-raising field for seventeen years, and every year it was a challenge to receive much-needed funds. It was faith in God and my love for helping children that kept me forging ahead. I could not let the disappointments from commitments that fell through affect me. I had to focus always on the achievement of the goals rather than the continuing financial hardships.

Ever mindful of these responsibilities, I asked God, "Would it be okay if I started the book next year? I need to concentrate all my energy on fund-raising to help the children."

The defining moment came through God's distinctive voice. "No. Begin it now. I will make sure funding comes in as long as you are obedient to My Word." I certainly was not going to argue with that reply. I obeyed God implicitly by beginning to concentrate on the book task. I always traveled with a pocket Bible and now began to flip through the pages in search of the name Gloria. The task was overwhelming me, so I left that research assignment for home, where I had an entire library of Christian books.

Right then, with God's confirmation, I began to tackle the book project and eagerly started composing my first page—disclosing the glory of God in my life to help benefit other people. By the time I landed safely back in Aspen, the first chapter was well under way.

Back home, I found the English translation of *Soli Deo Gloria:* "To God Alone the Glory." My entire life could be summed up by those words. God released all my triumphs, victories and blessings. He deserved the thanks, glory and acknowledgment.

During my writing journey, God released major miracles as long as I was obedient to His Word. Indeed, every year of my life God has taken me to a deeper place with Him, challenging me all along the way. I remembered hundreds of times when it would have been easier to go with the flow of the crowd rather than stand up for the truth of God. Then there were the times where I didn't know better, but God kept working on me to awaken me to His ways.

I remembered Romans 10:9-11: "That if you confess with your

mouth the Lord Jesus and believe in your heart that God has raised Him from the dead, you will be saved. For with the heart one believes unto righteousness, and with the mouth confession is made unto salvation. For whoever believes in Him will not be put to shame."

Of course there were days of extreme struggling and suffering, but I never went through them alone. There were countless times when the choices I made hurt my relationship with God, rather than enhanced it; other times I even pushed Him away. But I would realign myself with God and thankfully get back on track. I had always sacrificed fun trips, vacations and holiday outings because I was saving money to give to other individuals. But in all my years of giving, there has never been a time when I went without having some type of roof over my head, clothes to wear and food to eat. God has always provided for me. Regardless of what God asked of me, I would do it. With my accord alone, things were not possible, but with God's guidance all things were possible.

God taught me to give, even when I didn't think I had anything to give. Even if I am going through a period when I have not been given to abundantly, I still try and give to others abundantly.

The sowing of the seed concept, also often called tithing, stated in the Bible, declares that the first 10 percent received goes back to God for others to be helped. I didn't need to find that knowledge in a book to know it in my spirit. I give because I am called to give, and always far beyond the required 10 percent—because giving, serving and helping is what God has placed upon me.

Heidi and I stood on the principle that God would provide no matter what—even if it looked like we had no money in our accounts. We never had to cancel a program or project because of funding; a miracle would always appear at the last possible moment. One incredible miracle occurred when Heidi and I were walking on Little Star's newly purchased Rancho Milagro (Ranch of Miracles) property. We were praying and declaring God's Word to bless the land and project He asked us to take part in. God brought a miracle that very day. I received a call from a special couple in California who felt compelled to donate a large sum to the project. It was a heaven-sent phone call.

By November 2002, autumn was settling in. God decided it was time to challenge me even beyond my regular giving nature.

Our financial horizon looked bleak. We cancelled the foundation's scheduled 2002 fund-raiser dinners in New York City out of respect for other events that were focusing on fund-raising for the post-September 11 rebuilding efforts.

I reflected back to our January 23, 2001, gala. Ted Forstmann was honored for his unwavering commitment to the Silver Lining Foundation. A host of well-wishers and longtime supporters came for the celebration.

Jon Stewart had agreed to emcee the event and Glen Frey of the Eagles took on entertainment services, both coming to lend a hand for free. All speakers, celebrity attendees and supporters not only appeared for free, they also brought in financial support. Thankfully, for the second year in a row and at the suggestion of Ted Forstmann, Gulfstream, headed by Bill Boisture, took on the title sponsorship responsibility at our fund-raiser. Tom Freston, CEO of MTV Networks, and Time Warner head Gerald Levin (since retired) took on the role as co-chairs with great enthusiasm.

John McEnroe spoke from deep within his enormous heart. "I am proud to say I was the first person to donate to the Silver Lining Ranch. Andrea had this idea to try and help kids. And this is some-one who didn't have much of a childhood herself." John continued, "We made a pact back then. One thing we said was, 'We are going to stand up and fight for what we believe in.' And if necessary, Andrea said, 'We have to shout for what we believe in.'

"Now, you have accomplished actually what you set out to do. . . . You wanted to be remembered in the future as a voice for all these young children. And I congratulate you for doing that."

Cindy Crawford was another shining presence in the audience. She said, "I have seen Andrea in action, and I think probably one of her strongest characteristics is her passion for this cause and for these kids. She doesn't take no for an answer as a lot of people here tonight know. And that is how it was with me. I don't know how—somehow Andrea got my number—and she kept leaving these messages and finally I picked up the phone and even in a phone call she convinced me that I had to come and meet some of these kids. . . . The whole way that Andrea and Heidi and their team treat these kids is about belonging."

Cindy went on eloquently and compassionately before closing up her speech by introducing Oprah Winfrey. Oprah brought the guest of honor, Ted Forstmann, up on stage and used her vast abilities to take command of the fund-raising and celebratory gala. Her grace, power and passion set the tone for the evening, demonstrating that this was not your average dinner event.

Oprah shared, "I am honored because this man, who has done so much to help so many, is someone that I am proud and privileged to call my friend. . . . What makes Ted stand apart is that he brings more than resources to the table. . . . He brings passion for what he does, and a compassion for the people that he helps. . . . Anybody that knows him, knows that he never does anything halfway. He either does it right, or he doesn't do it at all."

Oprah continued, captivating the full ballroom at the Waldorf Astoria. "And let me tell you, from firsthand experience since I have been there with Andrea last September, Andrea and Ted did the Silver Lining Ranch right. They have created a place there where . . . children who have life-threatening illnesses can go and just be themselves. Children who play and swim and go horseback riding and white-water rafting, and fishing; and for that time that they are allowed to be themselves, they are allowed to experience and feel a little happiness, and a little hope, and a little laughter. And those of us who have observed that, know that it is as powerful as any of the medicines and treatments known to modern man now.

"Well, as usual, Ted took a risk. . . . He didn't know Andrea from Adam. He really didn't. But he believed in her, and he believed in her dream."

Michael Bloomberg, Paul Newman, Edyth and Eli Broad, Donald Newhouse, Neil Amdur, Gordon Beck, Arnon Milchan, RJ Wagner and Jill St. John, Jerry Murdoch, Viacom, Stephen Goldberg and Starlight International, John Eyler and Toys R Us, Samuel Goldwyn Jr., Diane Sawyer, Gayle King and countless other caring generous people and corporations joined in to buy tables and support the foundation in their own special way. Oprah introduced Ted to a standing ovation.

With the crowd still standing and applauding, Ted began to tell us what the evening and the long partnership he had with us in helping children meant.

"I think what this evening is really all about is vision, compassion, commitment, and heroism. Andrea had a dream, and it is true that I invested in Andrea's dream. But it's been her dream from the start to the finish. She was doing this, she imagined this, she envisioned this long before I came along. And quite frankly, as Cindy mentioned, I'm not 100 percent quite sure that once I got in Andrea's sights whether I had a real choice or not to invest. Her vision was and is compelling."

People could have heard a pin drop when Ted was speaking. I was sitting at Ted and Oprah's table with the talented Gayle King and Diane Sawyer, whose gift of light, joy, exuberance and appreciation for life shines in every action and choice she makes. Other wonderful well-wishers of the foundation were also there that evening, glowing with enjoyment. It was one of those occasions when time went extra slowly to guarantee every word, every tear shed from sheer joy, every moment of what can happen when people come together would stay imbedded in our hearts forever.

Ted continued, "Andrea's compassion can't be described. . . . And if you step back and think about what she really has accomplished, it is absolutely mind-boggling. . . . Heroism comes in many, many different guises. It obviously comes in the form of great historical figures, but it also comes in many others as well.

"I'd like to suggest to you tonight, that one of the forms heroism comes in is as a little ex-tennis player with long blonde hair. A little girl with very, very big and very bold ideas, and it also comes in the form of all those fabulous little kids . . . all of whom were dealt such a really lousy hand in this life. But who take it. When I have visited the ranch, I have never met one child who didn't have a smile on their face. I've never heard a complaint from one of them, and that's heroism. And they have all been benefited, benefited greatly, by this period of time they spend, and the fun they have, thanks to Andrea and her organization."

Ted concluded, "What you are seeing is life at its absolute worst, in the form of this evil, evil disease. And you're seeing at the same time, life at its absolute best, in the heroism of these kids and in the person of this absolutely unique young woman, and I would like to suggest to you, with deference, that we cannot give her enough support."

There was another standing ovation, even louder and longer than before, as Ted departed the stage. I hugged Ted before he sat down and then immediately said, "Ted, you were responsible for us being able to start building the ranch. I believe God has put it in my heart to build a follow-up program and facility called 'Rancho Milagro.' God wants it to be a 'Ranch of Miracles,' and it would be headed by our specialized separate program called Little Star. It is time for us to step up and teach the children about God in bigger ways.

Spiritual growth and healing is so important. I am asking for your endorsement on this exciting venture. I want to call one of the buildings St. Nick." (Ted's brother Nick Forstmann was battling cancer, so in talking about Ted's love of helping children, the topic naturally went to Nick's situation, and how he graced the world with his constant loving and giving ways.) Really, I couldn't have stopped myself from asking Ted if I tried. It was exactly like what Cindy and he had talked about moments before. God brought everyone together in ways none of us could quite comprehend, but we all loved the results. This was a tribute to Ted for what he had already done, and now I was asking him to jump into an even bigger project.

He replied, "I think it is a great idea. I fully support it." On January 21, 2001, Heidi and I had discussed Rancho Milagro, fully knowing God was going to have to bless us again with someone who would take the project off the page and believe in its potential as God and we did.

Now, two days later, on January 23, 2001, we had our first pioneer.

This was not a dinner of strangers thrown together in a ballroom who were counting the minutes until they could get into their comfortable clothes. This wasn't even about how big we had grown. This was about the foundation family that God brought together. God joined us to help children. He formed a group in the most unusual and miraculous ways and for that we were all being blessed. The company that we were gifted with that evening would stay in our hearts and spirits forever, proving what a difference one genuinely caring person can make in a child's life. That is what we celebrated that night, because one person attracts another, and before you know it, there is a family of caring people connected by God in making a difference for a whole lot of kids and their families.

Oh, how that evening stayed with me. Even though our New York gala for 2002 was canceled, I knew God had a plan for the survival of the programs and projects.

Within three weeks, I received a call in regard to a well-known individual who asked to remain anonymous. The caller's announcement was beyond good—it was a miracle. The caller said, "Your $2 million loan has been forgiven." I actually thought the person on the other line had the wrong number. This was bigger than Ed McMahon coming to my door with a big check. I couldn't scream with joy. I was beyond screaming. I was so overwhelmed with God's grace that I experienced my first ever tears of joy.

When a loan is given, it is with the understanding that it will be paid back. It was a miracle in itself that one of the greatest humanitarians of all time agreed to provide the loan. The agreement was done on honor, on word, on faith. I promised to pay the loan back one day. It had only been a short time, well before my deadline to repay the large amount. The children were being supported through the efforts of an enormous angel's loan in the midst of terrorism, economic woes, distressed situations and all types of world uncertainties.

Immediately after thanking God and the divinely appointed donor, I ran to find Heidi to share the joy. With tears flowing down my face, I explained what happened. She started crying. We both said praises to God for the special angelic donor who graced our life. We still had more than $47 million to raise, but we were well aware that God was watching over us.

God had more blessings in store. On December 18, God touched my heart by declaring that in mid-January I would receive a donation with the number five hundred in it. Then, on January 10, the Holy Spirit came in my room in the form of an angel. It was an incredible display of God's majesty and protection. The large angel took over the entire space of my bedroom ceiling. I had completed my nightly prayers, turned off my bedside lamp and was preparing for a restful sleep. Lying back on my pillow, I couldn't help but see the glory of God manifesting on my bedroom ceiling. The form had wings that softly fluttered as I talked to it. A glow illuminated my room. I knew that God was going to release supernatural blessings to me. I felt comforted by the angel. Despite its delicate appearance, I could tell the body, head and wings were powerful and mighty. This angel would be able to destroy any enemy it encountered. It would be victorious, and because I was lining up with God, I would be victorious, too.

A few days after my angelic encounter, God pressed me to again sow a seed beyond what I was giving. I was still struggling financially. Donations were lagging way behind, and individuals continued to pull out of their commitments, because they feared economic troubles and further terrorist attacks. My personal efforts in covering foundation bills continued. Still, I knew I had to be obedient to God, for it would be a sin not to.

I had refused to take a salary from the Silver Lining Foundation for the first ten years of its development and program phase. I was the last remaining full-time permanent staff member still not receiving a salary. At the adamant request of one of the greatest business minds in the world, who happened to be one of our largest donors, a salary was eventually assigned to me. Board members supported the act, and other donors also jumped in stating that they wouldn't donate if I didn't take a salary. After that, the decision became easy to make. Now I had additional income to give away every year, but I had long surpassed that limit.

Within days I received a call. It was a first-time invitation to attend dinner with a well-known Christian couple, who had a vacation home in Aspen, and their friends who were related to the Von Trapp family from *The Sound of Music* story. I happily accepted the invitation.

I was thrilled about being part of a Christian gathering. The evening was delightful and full of intriguing conversation. When it was time for me to leave, the host couple took me aside. They explained that they really believed in how important my children's programs were and they had decided to donate. The amount given on that mid-January night, with the Holy Spirit present in the background, was exactly $500,000. Again, God showed through His miraculous ways the power of prayer and how critical it is to sow seed and follow his direction.

The blessed miracles I have seen through people who have donated to the Silver Lining Foundation and Little Star programs have exemplified the generosity of caring, obedience, and faith-filled love that God equips all of His followers with. Every dollar given and received has a purpose behind it. Contributions bless and change the lives of children worldwide as well as the very people who have opened themselves to give.

God told me where to build the Silver Lining Ranch. It didn't matter that we didn't have the eventual grand total of $5.7 million for the entire ranch, pool, frontierland, furnishing and infrastructure. Heidi and I didn't have $10 million to buy the land and complex, either, yet God provided both through His followers. Heidi and I went in obedience, following God's instruction, and the land and building funding came in. We worked hard day and night, prayed diligently, asked to be lined up in obedience with God's instructions, sowed seeds—and God rewarded our efforts across the globe.

God was showing me what happens when people donate according to His will. I was certainly devastated when ten million dollars in total commitments were lost in the fall of 2001. Yet Heidi and I held onto our faith, knowing full well that the funding would come on God's timetable.

Do we have faith that all of our funding needs will be met, including the recent grand announcement from God to me that I would have to raise $100 million one day to help equip children with more tools to survive? Absolutely! God has said it will arrive, and we stand on His Word that it will.

Sowing the seed into God's work is important because it is a necessary step in a special relationship and connection with God. Donating to programs that perform God's work releases blessings in life for everyone involved—donor and recipient. The greatest power in the world is being connected, in covenant with God. Convenant means being in an agreeing relationship with another. When God asks me to donate financially and to be obedient to His command—wherever, whenever—I step out in obedience to His request, as is stated in James 4:17: "Therefore, to him who knows to do good and does not do it, to him it is sin."

Chapter Twenty-Six

Train up a child in the way he should go. . . .

—Proverbs 22:6

"Speak to the children. . . ."

—The Watchman Anointing, in Ezekiel Chapters 3 and 33

While I was sitting in a Denver church where I was attending a conference in 2003, surprisingly, several children, who were all past guests and participants in Little Star's programs, came bounding up to me enthusiastically. The children laughed as they playfully tugged on my arm to take me to meet their parents. On this day, January 26, I was to be the recipient of—quite simply—pure joy from children I had recently provided for. The kids played host to me in the church they attended, which happened to arrange the conference. Several "Mom, this is Andrea" introductions were made. Shrieks, applause and thank-you's surrounded our little group. It was a marvelous addition to an already exciting event. The results of the children's programs came around full circle.

Any uncertainties about taking time to attend the Denver conference and the following conference in Colorado Springs were quickly dispelled. God was declaring His glory and I wanted to catch it. Upon the healing conference's completion, Pat, Maja and I drove to Colorado Springs for the two-and-a-half day prayer conference. Before returning home, God equipped us mightily while including direct instructions for us to follow.

During a snack break during the January 31, Colorado Springs session, I became involved in a strange encounter. While I was patiently waiting in the middle of a long bathroom line, a woman came out of nowhere and whacked me on my right shoulder, stating loudly and with great purpose, "Move up!" The entire line, myself included, looked at her in astonishment. The line had been progressing at a normal pace, and I was planted smack dab in the center of it. There wasn't anywhere for me to "move up" unless I wanted to topple the woman in front of me. The lady disappeared as quickly as she surfaced with her demand on me. Several of the people in line asked if I was okay, and after reassuring everyone I was, we all went back to our business of standing in line.

The episode still bewildered me, so I felt compelled to discuss it with Pat. As I told Pat the story, she had that look on her face—the one where she knows what God was doing and she is excited He did it for me. She said, "God's instructions can take on a variety of forms. The Holy Spirit wanted you to receive direction. Now it is up to you to decide what to do with the command."

Pat was right. It was time for me to move up in helping advance the kingdom of God. My faith and God's glory were not reaching their potential all bottled up inside me. Another leap of faith would be necessary. Searching my spirit, it dawned on me that every enemy, any assignment against me, could be turned into a weapon and blessing for me to go to the next level of glory in my life from God. All my past trials and tribulations could serve as elevators for me to move up. It was similar to how I learned tennis. By working on my weaknesses—which I had plenty of when I started learning to play, and even later on—they eventually became strengths, tools for victory. This concept presented a new awareness of the workings of God. Angels may have been dancing around my presence while I was in the bathroom line, but the message was a direct statement that came with fierceness, resolution and a determination to confront the issue at hand. The Holy Spirit has always had a busy time keeping me on my path. However, this time, God's efforts were focused on equipping me to join His army. I needed to provide sound tools from a biblical and scriptural basis for the children to determine their own walks. I also felt I was being instructed how to step out in my faith with more confidence, therefore dispelling all hesitations on sharing what God wanted me to present to people.

It was also time for me to receive another dose of His ways in February 2003. A dream occurred where I encountered a great angelic presence. These teachers were assigned to present me a special task force for God. I woke up exactly at 3:33 A.M., with God placing a command to read Ezekiel, chapters 3 and 33, which are about the watchman anointing. I eagerly woke up at 3:33 A.M. to grab my Bible and soak in the Ezekiel chapters.

I was used to working on multiple levels in helping children with cancer. Those practices helped me comfortably adapt to God's new directions without disrupting the purposes I was focused on reaching with God, while helping children in enhanced ways. A watchman anointing had the duty to protect and patrol, and to provide warnings and information to children and people.

Ezekiel 3:11 directly states, "And go, get to the captives, to the children of your people and speak to them and tell them, 'Thus says the Lord God,' whether they hear, or whether they refuse."

That Scripture declares the responsibility people have to share the good news of God. It doesn't demand that children or people behave exactly like one another or follow someone else's purpose, but it does tell the watchman to be obedient to God.

Children with cancer can be at many different stages of the disease. A few can be newly diagnosed; others may have recently relapsed; and others yet may be on cancer treatment protocols for the second, third, fourth and, in some situations that we have seen, even the fifth and sixth time. We have encountered children just entering the remission stage, or in the worse-case scenario, children whose doctors have told them nothing else can be done treatment wise. Everyone is in a different stage and moment with their cancer.

In all walks of life, every man, woman and child has a unique place in the universe. God knows exactly the birth times and places of everyone, and how life will progress for His children. Each individual can be guided with special attention from God, if they so choose.

God pressed on my heart to keep in mind that He always has the full picture and I need to follow in faith in whatever piece of the whole I am given. I inquired of God, "How am I supposed to make sure I am in the right place, thinking the right thing and doing what you want?"

"By getting your direction from the Holy Spirit," He replied. "Pray, live, obey, respond, surrender, receive, believe, love according to My Word, and be with the Holy Spirit always and life will take on an entirely new significance. Then you will always be at the right place, at the correct time and know how to deal with every situation the absolute way—My way."

I couldn't resist continuing the conversation. "I know you have purposes behind everything in life, but are there also purposes behind those not-so-great things, such as diseases and death?"

God supplied no detailed explanation, just a simple, "Yes." I decided not to push the subject further for fear God would reveal answers that I was not so sure I was ready to hear. I thought of how quickly life does go by and how I wanted to use every moment in the way God desired me to. The time Heidi, Pat and other heaven-sent people have spent instructing and equipping me with God's Word and support of the children's cancer programs has been extraordinary, because everyone has his or her own busy lives to attend to, yet they chose to continue on God's path of providing rather than getting caught up in life's hectic ways.

I have seen thousands of children with cancer—very young ones, too—who refuse to let the disease dull their special light and the love that they choose to share with the world. I have watched adults do the same.

One such adult is a progressive advocate for women. Mary Dixon, forty-three years old, is a seven-year breast cancer survivor herself. Mary works diligently as Vice President of Advocacy and Public Affairs for Lifetime Television for Women. The network supports and informs women on issues that matter to them and their families. Mary has made huge strides in raising awareness about breast cancer and has prompted legislative changes to positively support women with breast cancer and women who have had to endure rape and violence.

In her spare time, she has completed four marathons to prove to herself that she could recapture her strength and life as she deals with cancer. By example, she has reassured and, in many cases, rev-olutionized people's way of thinking: that a cancer diagnosis does not have to be a death sentence, or a life lived without the accom-plishment of personal or professional goals.

Every person in the world has a story of getting through pain and suffering. Making choices for healing, peace and wholeness that arise from traumatic and heart-wrenching experiences may not be the easiest path to take, but it certainly is the one God will help any-one get on.

I have a very dear and special friend, Tamara, who does just that. Tamara and her husband, Gary, have endured two miscarriages and a stillbirth. Yet, despite inconceivable pain and suffering, both Tamara and Gary are a tribute to God. It has been incredibly inspiring to get to know Tamara over the years. She and Gary shine with love and joy, and they shower it on people everywhere. Their words and actions demonstrate what the spirit and heart can accomplish regardless of pain and suffering. As they continue praying and standing on God's Word, they show individuals that they are true ambassadors to the kingdom of God.

∽ ∽ ∽

Geri Cranford was born in 1930. Her lifetime of caring for others, loving God and persevering over difficult struggles brought her to Washington, D.C., in 1996—the year I won the Jefferson Award, which was presented in the Supreme Court chambers by Justice Sandra Day O'Connor. Before the national award recipients were given their honors, local caring people from all walks of life were paid tribute, and that is how I met Geri.

Geri works out of her garage, collecting blankets and other necessary supplies to send to people domestically and overseas. Sweet and gentle, Geri and I hit it off when she approached me asking if she could sing the Lord's Scriptures for me right there in the hotel lobby. I was slightly taken aback by the request, but decided that if she wanted to deliver a message, it might as well be on God's timetable and location.

As Geri often says, "I didn't need anything else other than prayer. God provides all my needs and the supplies to help other people. I am no one special, just one servant in many."

Another heroine who changed the world for the better appeared at my award ceremony as a surprise guest. Joanna and Noelle were sisters who participated in the foundation's programs. They enjoyed the nature walks with Fritz and Fabi, laughed as we took canoe rides and enchanted everyone they met. Noelle lost her battle to her disease just prior to my D.C. trip. Joanna, fighting the same disease, attended her younger sister's funeral service days before I was to be awarded for my work with children.

Joanna, in mourning, chose to make the trip to Washington, D.C., so she could be part of the recognition ceremony. Providing her Social Security number to gain entry to the events at the Supreme Court chambers, Joanna came with full congratulatory hugs. Looking across the crowd and seeing her so happy for me during my acceptance speech, the most important words that I could share were, "The real tribute, the real heroes, are the children. This is not about me; it is about them. I would like to ask Joanna to stand, because she is one of those children, one of those special heroes, who so often go unrecognized. Battling her own disease, coming here days after a funeral service for her younger sister and attending the local children's hospital recently to give an inspiring talk, Joanna deserves the recognition for making a difference. She is the hero we should be applauding here."

Anointed angels sent by God come in a variety of packages, amidst splendor, beauty, joy, light and love. One such messenger— the embodiment of how the Holy Spirit loves to work in every-one—is Kellie. Faith-filled, desperate for Jesus, Kellie glows with the gifts God has so wonderfully presented to her. Successful, graceful, intelligent, striking, elegant, fun and ever so humble in the calling and purposes God has chosen for her, Kellie's world dra-matically changed with her father's prostate cancer diagnosis.

Rather than stay comfortable in her New York City way of life, while ambitiously advancing her private jet charter company to fur-ther success, Kellie followed the calling that she knew God had placed on her heart. She went without hesitation to care for her dad, who was declining rapidly with the late-stage cancer diagnosis. Bowing before God, Kellie asked for strength and wisdom to help shoulder the burdens of what was to come. God bestowed on her the ability to be a blessing in her dad's life, caring for him during the days he had remaining, while still allowing her to forge ahead in professional and personal areas as He saw fit.

Relocating to Colorado Springs, where her father was residing, divorced and alone, in an assisted-care living facility, Kellie juggled many responsibilities and issues—which tore into her soul—and managed throughout to bring to fruition a relationship which God had ordained. Sleeping on a pull-out futon in her father's side storage room, living out of a bag for nearly a year, Kellie rose, and in many ways soared, in spirit to provide the answer to what perplexed the doctors as they surprisingly kept explaining, "Your dad is living on borrowed time." No he wasn't. What was happening, in fact, was that he and his devoted-to-God daughter, Kellie, were living on purposeful time.

They hadn't always been the proud papa and adoring daughter. However, father and child were now fully realizing God's grace, and how true love of the spirit could connect them with God's complete glory. Decades before, Kellie's Grandpa read Billy Graham and Oswald Chambers devotions daily. Now, due to Kellie's choice to follow God's guiding hand, a father and daughter's love was coming full circle. It didn't matter if the beginning or middle parts of their relationship had floundered, become broken, even lost, along the way. Kellie's faith in God to reclaim, restore and rejuvenate their connection prevailed. She moved out with compassion to be with her father.

She baked chocolate chip cookies for her dad in the only heating device allowed in the nursing facility—a toaster oven. On Sundays they cheered for the Denver Broncos together. Daughter sat with dad while the chemo was pushed into his body, knowing full well that, in the end, there was no medical treatment that would cure her dad's cancer. But that didn't stop him from smiling. His daughter held his hand, prayed, laughed and shared with him. This was no borrowed time; this was blessed time gifted from above, joining father and child, heart to heart, spirit to spirit.

It is never easy to watch disease take hold of a body, a mind, a soul. But Kellie stood firm in faith, making sure that cancer wouldn't take her dad's spirit. Through their prayers, God assured them that her dad's spirit would make the journey home. Born of God, belonging to God, Kellie's dad would return to God in the same splendor he had arrived on Earth, as a gift.

Kellie's presence, spirit, joy, faith, gifts from God, and choices to follow God and the Holy spirit's urging brighten and change the world, one person at a time. Her dad wasn't the first person, nor the last, that she has touched with God's love and grace. She shines light on all who God brings before her, and I am forever blessed and thankful God gave me the gift of divinely placing Kellie in my life.

God provides the choice of including Him in all of life's adventures and occurrences—good and not so good—not only for the healing that occurs, but for the enjoyment and fulfillment of life.

When I was doing research at hospitals, I talked with people who gave up their fight with cancer, because they were mad at God and had no faith in Him. They were fixated on anger, bitterness, lost relationships, resentment and worldly possessions. Then, despondent over bad medical news, they had no place to turn. They saw nothing in front of them worth working toward.

It is heartbreaking for God and His kingdom to see the pain, torture and suffering of His children, especially when they don't turn to Him to be freed from all the anguish. And then there is the pain and suffering of those who have no voice, who are powerless—children most often, many children—who would ask for help if they could, except they never learned how. However, solutions, freedom and a voice can be found in and with God. I didn't become a servant of God because I had episodes in my life of trauma and abuse. I became a servant of God despite them.

The world is full of medications and so-called cures to help all kinds of ailments and problems. God was the only way for me to be healed and made whole in spirit, and it is a daily process to stay on course. That doesn't guarantee me a life free from pain and suffering. But it does ensure me a life with tools, blessings and gifts from God because the Holy Spirit lives in me. A passage from a book that caught my attention sums this premise up beautifully.

Looking for a few cards in a Colorado bookstore, I was eventually drawn to the Christian and inspirational book section. I pulled out a book and it fell open to page forty. It read: "I was in the central highlands in Vietnam when someone remarked about Christians suffering there. One Vietnamese Christian remarked, 'Suffering is not the worst thing that can happen to us. Disobedience to God is the worst thing.'" —Tom White, director of Voice of the Martyrs; imprisoned in Cuba for seventeen months for distributing Christian literature, 1979–80.

That page was another confirmation of what was already sealed in my spirit. In God's kind ways of repeating a lesson for me, the exact same incident happened to me again. I walked in the same bookstore several months later, was pulled to the same section and pulled out a copy of the identical book—and it immediately fell open to the same passage on page forty.

Chapter Twenty-Seven

Have I not commanded you?
Be strong and of good courage; do not be afraid,
nor be dismayed, for the Lord your God
is with you wherever you go.

—Joshua 1:9

For years, I had vigilantly sought to secure a specific donor who had the financial ability to completely fund the program, endowment and building campaigns I had been working on for decades. In May, I was in the door. A meeting was scheduled and I prepared for it vigorously. Then, instantly, it was cancelled. Devastated, I turned to God to receive an explanation that could soothe my extreme disappointment, as well as gain the leverage to keep plodding along on the fund-raising trail.

The response actually propelled me further into a hole. God answered, "Your $47 million will come, as well as $100 million that you will receive for purposes I have yet to reveal to you."

I wanted to curl into a ball and not move an inch. Hesitant to uncover the even more challenging funding needs to do God's work, I sought refuge in Heidi's sanctuary space where she centers in peace and balance.

The moment I entered Heidi's room, she knew something was amiss. Protecting her from the somber fund-raising update appeared to be a ridiculous plan of action. I announced the dismal news about the potential donor, as well as the recent message I had received from God.

Heidi turned, and with her typical faith-filled, calm demeanor challenged me. "Why are you acting so troubled? Has God ever let you down before?"

She knew the answer. So did I. Yet Heidi made me answer the question out loud. "No, God has never let me down before," I answered.

Heidi patiently waited with her humorous "And?" look. I answered, without even needing to hear the question verbally. "And, I stand on His Word." Heidi proceeded to get down on her knees in prayer position. I followed her actions. We both held the torch for the children's programs—as well as the responsibilities for them. By the time the prayer was finished, the massive disappointment of the loss of a potentially large, multimillion-dollar contribution was cast aside. I was renewed with enthusiasm that maybe another day the gentleman I almost met—who was worth, according to *Forbes* magazine, $1.8 billion—would reschedule the meeting. Meanwhile, I had work to do.

Opting to collect my thoughts and direction on a long run through the country, I laced up my jogging shoes and headed out the door. The serenity of nature cleared my mind. God had an easier time entering my spirit without my whirlwind of frustrations settling in. After eight miles, I bounded back in the door with a new message. "Someone does want to donate today." God told me it was my job to find out how. He gave me the lead and I was eager to follow.

Without changing out of my sweaty clothes I grabbed my large black address book and feverishly flipped through the pages. Nothing jumped out at me, but I felt the message growing stronger that the timing was perfect for a special person to donate. To guarantee the opportunity, I resorted to praying over pages for God to help me locate the person I was supposed to contact.

Thirty-six pages into my address book, God nudged me. I let out a gasp. The person I was being directed to contact happened to be from the exact caller ID number that came in on my cell phone while I was having dinner with Pat during the Detroit, October 2002 conference. I punched in the number. For countless years, I had tried to schedule a call or meeting with this particular person. Nothing had opened. Now, I was assured by God the timing lined up.

Despite God's assurance, I was still surprised that the assistant put me directly through. For forty minutes, I had the most delightful and engaging conversation. The individual and I grew up in completely different environments and had more than a forty-year age difference between us, but our similarities bonded us. She was a huge tennis fan who had enjoyed many of my Wimbledon matches. Our love of tennis came out in stories and favorite Grand Slam moments. We both had dogs that had recently succumbed to cancer. We were both philanthropic, driven and preferred a no-nonsense approach. God was revealing a mentor to me. Only recently had things fallen in place with my parents, but in the process we lost years of great family fellowship. My new friend and I had hit it off instantly on the phone in ways that went even beyond a maternal, nurturing family bond. We laughed, reminisced and established a genuine fondness for each other's company.

At the close of the forty minutes, my newfound friend said, "I really enjoyed this conversation. I had such fun talking to you and I want to help your children's programs."

She proceeded to announce a large donation she was going to send upon hanging up. I was flabbergasted. Engaged in the conversation, I felt less like a fund-raiser and more like a daughter. God was bringing support in for the children and the child within me. He was filling a void I didn't even know I possessed.

As soon as I hung up, I dashed off to find Heidi. I was so excited, my mouth was in hyperdrive. The only words of a ten-minute explanation that she could understand were, "I had such fun talking about tennis and life."

Heidi asked, "What happened?"

I shouted, "It was a gift from God." Then I scampered off to prepare a package for my new friend, complete with pictures of Lily, my dog that had died of cancer. As promised, the contribution came in within the week. My care package included the only gift I thought worthy of a person with such tremendous stature and wealth. Knowing her love for tennis—she had attended Wimbledon and watched the tournament from the All England box seats for thirty-plus years—I offered my services as a tournament host. "I will cover all my own expenses and I will be available to you during the time you are attending Wimbledon as your own personal tennis host."

"Oh, no, you don't have to do that for me," was her reply. "Thank you for the offer. Though it would be nice to have a visit together. If it fits into your schedule, you can visit me when I am in Hawaii."

We scheduled the visit for the first week in June. I would spend my birthday in the company of a person I loved dearly, yet had never met. The contribution was a bonus, but it wasn't the core of our relationship. God brought the complete package because of His ability to provide for a wide variety of needs.

I was scheduled to be in Hawaii the first five days in June. Looking at my planner, I asked God to step in with assistance about whether I should fly directly to Hawaii with no stopovers or not. For some odd reason, I felt God compelling me to go to Los Angeles on May 29, even if critical donor meetings could not be arranged. I booked my air travel and proceeded to make Los Angeles my destination for the Thursday, Friday and Saturday before my Hawaii trip.

My regular Los Angeles hotel accommodations were totally booked. I called the massive hotel directly to confirm that there was really not one room available. There wasn't. Curious, I asked what was happening in Los Angeles. I was told, "Some convention where forty thousand people are coming to town."

I tried the next hotel choice. Fortunately, two rooms were still left unoccupied, but only at the higher rate. Again, I asked why there was such a run on rooms. I had been in Los Angeles on previous trips during the Golden Globes, Oscars, MTV Video Awards and various sporting extravaganzas and never had such a hard time making room arrangements.

The concierge replied nonchalantly, "There is a book publishing convention coming to town. It is not open to the general public, but forty thousand people are expected to attend."

Now it was crystal clear why I was supposed to be in Los Angeles. I told Heidi the surprise news. Enthusiastically, Heidi replied, "Congratulations. That is certainly a confirmation that you are writing the book according to God's will." Pat was equally excited and responded with the same reply. When I phoned Maja about the update in the itinerary, she nearly dropped the phone in shock.

The Los Angeles trip happened so fast. The entire miracle of a book publishing convention occurring during my exact travel dates in Los Angeles didn't even have a chance to fully settle in. In only a few days' time, I would have to pull together a better presentation than the raw and unfinished manuscript I had saved on my computer. I had to secure convention passes, pack for the Hawaii trip and follow up on arrangements for the scheduled children's summer sessions that were geared to begin on June 6, all while organizing the chapters, inputting new material and getting page numbers, spelling, grammar, index and cover pages in shape. Heidi and I handled foundation phone, fax and e-mail communications that needed responses and we prayed daily for God to watch closely over my journeys. He did just that. Maja stepped in to help with printing out the entire book, seeking the assistance of technology whiz and prayer warrior Yanaris Nieves. It was a bigger procedure than we thought. They worked through the night, putting together page after page.

I prayed for God to lead me to a publisher divinely selected and anointed by God. Maja, who was to accompany me, asked, "There will be thousands of publishers attending the event. How are you going to know which one to go to?"

I answered with complete faith: "God is going to lead me to the right one."

Maja's anxiety filled the car as we took the early evening drive to the Los Angeles Convention Center. She knew how important the project was, and she was hoping for everything to fall into place. The convention halls were massive. We stood in a long line to check in. As we moved closer, we heard the check-in lady ask someone, "What category are you with?" Maja and I looked at each other quizzically. She ran to grab a brochure from the counter. I asked, "What categories are there?"

"Vendor, buyer, author, speaker, publisher . . ." the list droned on and on. Maja and I again looked at each other and proceeded to check things off that didn't pertain to us. The list was dwindling rapidly and we were almost the next to be called up in line. As if on cue we both announced victoriously, "The Hope Chest. Silver Lining writes, edits, prints and publishes the Hope Chest."

"I can help the next person in line," the woman said. Maja and I confidently walked forward. "We are here to pick up our credentials." And with that we paid for every workshop, program, breakfast, lunch and opportunity that we could fit in the schedule.

As we carefully placed our name and credential badges in a secure place, we pulled out a map to establish our bearings in the massive complex to prepare for the next day. Before exiting the enormous arena, I gazed at the largest banner I had ever seen in my life. It hovered above Maja and me. I stared at it, mouth agape. Trying to see what had absorbed my attention, Maja repeatedly asked, "What?" At first I could not speak. I only pointed. While Maja marveled at the banner's announcement of, "Make your plans to attend the 2004 Book Expo, June 4-6 in Chicago," I said confidently, "My book will be at that convention. I was born June 4 in Chicago. God is giving me a birthday present in my hometown. Of course God will help me find a publisher here, because that is a purpose already destined to happen. God has guaranteed it."

I was supremely confident God was going to reveal a publisher to me the next day, May 30, 2003. The next morning was a welcome sight because it inched me that much closer to securing a publisher.

Praying extra long for guidance, Maja and I made our trek back to the convention center. The trunk of the car was full of foundation videos and materials, as well as copies of the manuscript, still raw and unfinished but with a pretty plastic cover and black binder. Upon arrival, we filled our backpacks to capacity and headed in prepared for a big day.

Thousands of booths, countless vendors and scores of participants filled the convention center. We had to push our way through the crowded halls. Numerous times, Maja would ask, "How about them? Try talking to that person. That looks like a good booth." I bypassed every suggestion.

Maja's exasperation was showing as she carried both loaded-down bags to ease my shoulder pain while trying to keep pace as I walked through each vendor booth without stopping. Giving her a reprieve, I stated, "God hasn't nudged me yet, but I think I know where He wants me to go." There was a tall, elegant man freely talking to interested passersby. He had command of the large vendor area. I approached slowly to join the listeners. As soon as I heard one individual address the gentleman as Peter, I knew I was in the right place. Peter Vegso, cofounder of Health Communications, Inc., the publisher of the *Chicken Soup for the Soul* book series—which have sold tens of millions of copies—was also a name I recognized from donations that had come into the Silver Lining Foundation.

The rainbow journey had a beginning and an end. I boldly stood on God's Word that He would direct me to the publisher for the book. This was it. I politely introduced myself as soon as there was an opening in the conversation. "Mr. Vegso, my name is Andrea Jaeger. I want to thank you for your financial support to the Silver Lining Foundation." The surprised look on his face was priceless. This wasn't a tennis event or a children's pediatric cancer program. He certainly didn't expect me to appear here.

Peter and I talked for several minutes. I refused to leave until I planted a seed about the book project God had me working on. Pushing further, God gave the green light. "Peter, I have been working on a book about how God helps people pursue their purposes."

The moment the words came out of my mouth, I could feel my heartbeat speed up in excitement. The response was more than I anticipated. "If you get me a copy of your manuscript, I promise to read it."

While roaming the complex in search of the exit area, Maja interjected, "Do you want to check out any other publishers?" Without breaking stride, I responded, "No."

Maja stammered out, "You have worked so hard to get this far. This is such a huge opportunity. Are you sure you don't want to research any other publishers?"

I knew it seemed incredible, even outrageous, to pursue only one publisher at the conference, and that one publisher would guarantee a book contract, but I decided to take my chances on what God was proposing. The only agent I had was God, and I was sticking by Him. The decision was set in stone. In agreement, Maja and I walked quickly to the car.

The trip was turning into one extraordinary experience after another. I returned to my hotel room well past midnight—after a celebratory HCI dinner that Peter had invited me to—ablaze with a desire to work on the manuscript more. My suitcases were packed for my predawn departure, so I opted to see if Maja was still up in her room. We analyzed the entire past week, marveling at the power and glory of God. We were practically jumping around the room, like two kids racing to open Christmas presents.

Chapter Twenty-Eight

*". . . Blessed are those who hear
the Word of God and keep it!"*

—Jesus says in Luke 11:28

Now settled in my own private bungalow in Hawaii, I carefully removed the crystal cross and dove sculpture that I hand carried to give to my new friend. I relished the opportunity to present the gift and learn more about business, philanthropy and life. My grand teacher, astute and driven, was a person I hoped to emulate in many ways, well before I reached my eighties. She had high standards, valuing truth above all else. She strove for excellence and loved life, embracing every moment of it.

I didn't have to swim in the ocean or be surrounded by lush tropical trees and flowers to know I was in a paradise of the heart and spirit. The very first morning of my visit, my new friend invited me to her room as she worked. Sitting on her bed, she was surrounded by her friendly and playful dogs, and piles of papers. She offered me a seat with them.

The French Open was on the television, in the background. I was pleasantly surprised at my comfort level in this personal setting. If the majority of people I knew invited me to such a situation, I would become immediately uncomfortable. Instead, I felt at ease. I was accustomed to being accepted unconditionally by God, but it was completely different for me to become so engaged with a person so quickly.

God was telling me, "This is why you flew over the ocean—for My love, power, healing and prosperity to grace you." The cherished atmosphere was beyond anything I could have set up on my own. During the discussions about tennis, life, business, philanthropy, family and friends, I boldly entered into even deeper territory.

"In all your years, what philosophies have held the most importance?" I asked.

With no hesitation whatsoever, she replied. "So often telling the truth isn't applauded; nonetheless, it should never be swayed from. There have been times where I voiced the truth and people became upset. Honesty has always been my policy regardless of people's reactions. The other area I feel is essential to living a full life is to honor and take care of true friendships made along the way."

I reflected on my mentor's candor, appreciating the wisdom she was imparting to me. We stayed in the bedroom, because it was where we could comfortably share stories while dogs leaped, barked and slid down ramps around us. My mentor was not frail or inactive. She skied, exercised daily and kept a schedule that many healthy thirty-year-olds could not keep up with.

She asked, "Have any tennis players donated to help your children's cause?"

I answered, "Oh yes! John McEnroe was the first person who ever donated. He has been such a staunch supporter and, more importantly, he has been one of my best friends. Andre Agassi has said yes anytime that I asked for his help. Pete Sampras has contributed enormously. Do you know he even pulled over on the side of the road once during a tournament so he could talk to this teenaged boy named Brandon? I called Pete explaining the doctors said how Brandon didn't have much time left because of a brain tumor and asked if he could call and cheer up the boy while he was staying at the ranch. He did, with no hesitation whatsoever, making sure the phone connection wouldn't be interrupted. Pete understands the importance of the programs on a very close level because his coach, Tim Gullickson, died of a brain tumor, a type similar to the one my dad has been battling for over a year."

She said, "I am sorry to hear about your father. How is he doing?"

"Not well," I answered, "The doctors didn't expect him to last this long, as he was diagnosed at stage four."

I continued listing tennis professionals who have donated money to the foundation: "Stefan Edberg, Michael Chang, Todd Martin, Jim Courier, Goran Ivanisevic, Mark Philippoussis, Mark Woodford and Todd Woodbridge have all donated to sponsor children's programs."

I was brimming with pride in how certain players made such an impact. "Gabriela Sabatini was the first female player to ever donate sponsorship funds to support the children's programs. She has always stepped up in ways that have made a great difference. I barely knew her when I asked if she would help, and she ended up donating a very large amount. You can really tell she cares so much about helping children. Behind those Grand Slam wins is not only a talented player, but someone with a heart of gold. Do you remember watching Pam Shriver at Wimbledon?"

She answered, "Of course. Has she been helpful?"

I said, "Pam has a huge heart to help people, and we have been fortunate to have had her contributions over the years. Lindsay Davenport usually buys up the major auction items when we have fund-raisers, whether she needs the items or not. Nicole Arendt has sponsored children every year. Monica Seles came to visit the children in Aspen. Do you ever visit the U.S. Open Grand Slam event?"

She answered, "We watch it on television. Wimbledon is the only tournament we have been visiting for the past thirty years."

I shared, "Well, you would have loved this one New York City/U.S. Open program we put together. For years we have run sessions where we bring kids to the U.S. Open tennis matches, take them to plays, go on private shopping sprees at Toys R Us where we pick up the tab, and a lot more. At every U.S. Open program, caring players visit with the children, signing autographs, answering questions and hanging out with our group. Pete Sampras, Andre Agassi, Steffi Graf, Gabriela Sabatini—when they used to play— and Anna Kournikova have participated in these festivities at all the tournaments in which we have run programs without ever missing a year of helping—Wimbledon and the Lipton event included.

"During the 2001 U.S. Open program, Anna agreed to attend a luncheon that was specifically arranged for a foundation contributor and his friends to help us raise money. Anna went to great lengths, flying from Florida to New York, since she was injured and not playing in the tournament, to help us guarantee a successful event."

Before I could continue sharing stories of other noble professional tennis players and other people who had contributed, my host announced, "I know how much you are trying to help children. I am going to give you a donation to support your efforts. You will have the contribution next week." The amount announced would be the fourth largest donation the foundation had ever received.

The surprise announcement grabbed hold of my heart. I didn't want the donation to be forced. We were enjoying each other's company, watching the French Open and sharing our own unique tennis stories. To ensure the donation was God's purpose for me to help children, instead of reacting in a purely professional manner, I asked quietly, "Are you sure? I came to visit you to say thank you."

The years of experience flowed from the teacher. "You need to raise money to help the children. I know that and I would like to help. In fact, I wish I could give more so you wouldn't have to worry about your funding needs. Now let's plan your visit. Do you have any friends in Hawaii or special sightseeing requests while you are here?"

Thrilled and greatly appreciative of God's and the generous woman's contribution, I decided the best course of action would be to say thank you and then answer the request. I said, "I don't know anyone in Hawaii, other than you and your assistant. I arranged with the local children's hospital to bring gifts on my birthday, June 4, for all the cancer patients. Other than that, the only plans I have involve working in my room. If you like, I could help you with chores."

She chuckled and then took on the role of social director with great enthusiasm. In a span of five minutes she had planned all my activities and meals, including picking mangos, side by side, in her yard.

The adventure in Hawaii also included a special tennis outing with a U.S. Open veteran from the 1940s. The experience of going down tennis's memory lane even further was a surprise addition to an already blessed few days.

While I was in Hawaii, other gifts were arriving at my home in Aspen. Peter Vegso sent me a bouquet of birthday flowers. There was also a warm and informative birthday message on my cellphone voicemail from Peter saying that HCI was interested in the book and that they would be sending me a contract.

My time in Hawaii was drawing to a close. I would miss our morning ritual of sitting on my friend's bed as we discussed a variety of subjects. When our last conversation took place there, I looked around the room one last time to make sure I took in every detail. My spirit directed me toward the dresser. It was filled with photos of family, friends and beloved pets. Also in full display was the crystal cross and dove I had given my friend. I hugged my beautiful host with an appreciation that would always be remembered. The drive to the airport could have been a sad occasion as the miles increased between me and the people I had come to love so much. But God made sure the journey of His blessings would continue in its miraculous capacity.

Looking at the road ahead, I stared at the car in front of me. The license plate on it, GVJ777, shouted out at me: "God Victory Jesus." And the number seven is listed over six hundred times in the Bible, often representing completeness. Lining up with God's purposes had brought a response from Him of released healing, restoration, prosperity and blessings. I felt like a prodigal daughter: once lost, now found. I pulled out the words to "Amazing Grace," by John Newton. As my driver focused on getting me to the airport, I softly sang the song's verses.

Soon after I arrived back in Aspen, the first of Silver Lining's summer sessions began. The children's arrival on June 6 was, like all other previous sessions, exciting and heartfelt. Orientation, medical check-in, rules, schedules and fire drill activities proceeded without a hitch.

It wasn't until nightfall that I knew we were entering a new phase. I had a dream that night, provided by God, that was full of vivid and colorful details. There was a large gathering of people, children and adults, young and old. They were standing in a circle, several layers deep. The attention was focused on a few of the many individuals involved.

I stood in the center of the circle and was cackled at and ridiculed by a couple of nonbelievers. They were shouting obscenities against God, my dedication to following the Bible and my relationship with God. The other onlookers seemed appalled by their actions.

The ranting continued, increasing in volume and ferocity, and

then someone slung slimy material at my face and body. Instead of
ducking, I kept a tall, peaceful and calm stance. At the peak of the
outlandish tirade, I reacted. From inside my shirt collar I pulled out
my cross. I brought it out for the entire audience to see and then I
smiled, recognizing the power and peace believing in the Cross of
Christ brings. The believers in the crowd responded by allowing
their spirits to be enhanced even further by the strength and security God brings to every follower.

The rebellious people in the massive crowd were silenced, and
they sauntered away. I awoke, refreshed by this new installment in
my life. It was apparent that my fellowship and walk with God was
not going to be openly received by everyone. There would be resis-
tance from people as God reconfigured my life, other lives and the
children's programs to incorporate the Word of God.

God gave a stern warning and direction in that dream, that if ever
someone forces issues in defiance to God, keep hold of the Cross of
Christ. Holding onto God would release victory, healing, blessings,
protection and favor. It wouldn't matter who was against our efforts in
standing on the truth of God. We would herald victory as long as we
kept our focus on God. Accusers would have their judgment day, ultimately, before God. In the meantime, we were not to get distracted.

The year 2003 also brought a miracle demonstrating what God
was uncovering for us all. One day we had a white-water rafting
trip scheduled. It was a great experience for the participants on a
number of levels. The children participating in the Foundation's
program would discover Colorado's beauty on a river. Rowing
together would require teamwork and courage. Our river guides and
staff understood the water—its currents, eddies, whirlpools and
hidden dangers. They also knew that the rapids eventually gave way
to more tranquil and serene waters.

Each boat had been carefully assigned a mixture of adults, children and nurses. Four boats were in relatively close proximity to

each other. The conversation in my boat centered on sharing feelings having to do with cancer, treatments, hopes for the future and tools everyone could gain from listening.

During one of the discussions, I noticed an extremely large, glowing white figure above and to the left of us, settled into the mountain. Having been down the river for over a decade numerous times every summer, I knew this was no ordinary sight. On every raft trip we play a game of trying to spot nature's creations. Ospreys, bald eagles, deer, geese, goslings, jumping fish, marmots, squirrels, birds of all shapes and sizes, and butterflies all made the list. This object, however, was definitely not from the animal kingdom. For at least thirty seconds, the figure stood glowing down on us. Sure of its presence and purpose, I pointed to it above and asked the children in my raft what they thought it was.

Everyone was silent for a moment. Ironically, one of the adults in the boat couldn't see it, yet all of the children found its location. I decided to ask one boy in particular what he thought it was. He was the biggest Boston Red Sox fan of all time. His journey with cancer was a difficult one, with many mountains before him yet to be climbed. The prognosis from his doctors was not stellar, but his spirit was.

In previous discussions in and out of the raft, his usual reply to my queries was, "I don't know," in an adorable New England accent. I looked directly at him and asked curiously, "What do you think it is?"

Loud, concise and clear, with no hesitation, the boy replied, "I think it is an angel." The young girls behind agreed. An adult counselor piped in, "It looks like a gigantic polar bear." The consensus: an angel.

God did it. He brought an angel into full view. From the minute I saw it, I had an overwhelming sense that it was sent to watch over and protect us. It was a sign that we were entering a new phase, revealing to all participants that we were standing on the Word of God, and in doing so, it would enhance the programs by helping people, especially children, to achieve a renewed and heightened relationship with Him.

I was excited to have witnesses to God's supernatural power. So often, the miracles, dreams, visions, signs and wonders I experienced in partnership with God were not seen by others. This time, that wasn't the case.

Just as in my dream, God was showing blessings to a welcome audience of His believers and followers. The other boats did not see the angel. It was a strong reminder that we still had a way to go in our quest to bring the enriching efforts of God's love and salvation to everyone we knew.

Chapter Twenty-Nine

Do not touch my anointed ones,
And do my prophets no harm.

—Psalms 105:15

I had come face to face, more often than I wanted, with the lesson that cruelty toward others is often rooted in a lack of knowledge and understanding, and in the fear of something or someone being different. The Bible references this concept throughout the Old and New Testaments. Jesus began His preaching at the age of thirty. Throughout His teaching, He was ridiculed for standing on the Word of God and for following the truth it revealed. At the age of thirty-three, Jesus was killed by His critics. Crucified at the hands of people possessed of fear and disobedience to God, Jesus was nailed to a cross in the hopes that their problems would be solved.

The power of God broke through. Jesus' death did solve problems, but not in the way His persecutors thought they would be fixed. The hate- and fear-filled individuals assumed wrongly that Jesus would stay buried with His body. His resurrection after the third day proved that Jesus' followers were correct in believing who Jesus was, thus forever changing the world.

Throughout history, talented individuals from all walks of life have been met with criticism for their innovations. Whether it includes an idea, invention, obedience, product, faith or creative art form, many brilliant, talented people have been met with hostility for their new and different ideas, only to be lauded long after their deaths for their genius and insight. But God is aware of all of His servants, saints, followers and believers around the world. They are protected and sealed in the Book of Life.

I had the amazing good fortune to meet one of the world's shining beacons of light. It was in 1999 on a clear August day with a hint of fall in the air. I was in Aspen, at a service station, filling my gas tank, when my cell phone rang. "This is the security team for Mr. Nelson Mandela. Is this Ms. Jaeger?"

"Yes," I said, as I immediately stopped what I was doing.

"Nelson Mandela would like to visit your Benedict-Forstmann Silver Lining Ranch. We would like to come over in the next fifteen minutes to discuss security with you."

I grabbed the receipt for my gas, called Heidi to organize our more than qualified team and high-tailed it back to the ranch. A short time after the initial phone call, Mr. Mandela came through the restricted entry gate and walked through the ranch's front door. We discussed methods of caring for children and how Mr. Mandela used the twenty-seven years he spent in prison for reflection.

He had an amazing sense of peace and liquid eyes that seemed to hold a universe of thoughts. I thought of his last remarks at his Rivonia trial: "I have fought against white domination, and I have fought against black domination. I have cherished the ideal of a democratic and free society in which all people live together in harmony and with equal opportunities. It is an ideal which I hope to live for and to achieve. But if needs be, it is an ideal for which I am prepared to die."

After that statement Nelson Mandela was sentenced to life in prison. In 1990 he was released. Born in 1918 in South Africa, Nelson Mandela would give up his own life if he had to, to fight for the freedom of others. He grew up attending Christian missionary schools. It is no surprise that he went on to receive the Nobel Peace Prize.

Mr. Mandela moved gracefully through the ranch tour. During our discussions, as we ventured from one room to another, Mr. Mandela exuded a presence that commanded respect and reflected wisdom gifted from God. It was a tremendous experience to share with him ideas and thoughts about how children less fortunate could benefit from the care and support of world leaders.

"You have done remarkable work in helping the children. Has this always been a dream of yours?" he asked.

"Yes," I enthusiastically replied. "I feel God has called me to help children. It is a gift I am thankful to have received." Maja, who was trying to film the historic occasion, was within arm's reach. I grabbed her and whispered in her ear. "Please tell Heidi I need her in the arts and crafts room immediately." Maja raced off faster than I had ever seen her move.

Heidi arrived in less than a minute, responding to Maja's alarming message as if perhaps something had happened to Mr. Mandela. The moment Heidi appeared, I announced, "Mr. Mandela, this is Heidi Bookout. We started the Silver Lining Foundation together." Mr. Mandela extended courtesies to Heidi.

I then asked, "Would you mind, after our tour, taking a picture with the entire staff?" Mr. Mandela kindly agreed. Heidi wanted me to do the tour solo to keep the meeting more private and to avoid extra people because the security team was accompanying us everywhere. I felt that Heidi should be extended the honor of touring with us and that the entire staff should be able to meet Mr. Mandela.

In the arts and crafts room I asked Mr. Mandela, "Would you like to sign the wall? As you can see, children before you and special visitors have left their imprint in this unique way." The walls were nearly full with children's and invited guests' artistry, signatures, messages and words of encouragement.

Mr. Mandela answered positively and with joy as he took a black marker to leave his permanent declaration of visiting the Benedict-Forstmann Silver Lining Ranch.

Now when I think back to his visit, I reflect on the scriptures describing how peacemakers have a gifting from God. Matthew 5:9 states, "Blessed are the peacemakers, for they shall be called sons of God."

God has appointed certain people to serve as peacemakers and they take on a great burden. A peacemaker is like a big bulldozer that plows through something first for the benefit of others. Would Nelson Mandela command the same respect if he spent twenty-seven years in jail angry at those who convicted him, hoping to kill them if he was ever released from his cell? Most definitely not.

Mr. Mandela put his life on the line for the freedom of others. He fought for that freedom. Through his battles, Nelson Mandela found peace. He left prison spreading love, forgiveness and peace, not bitterness, resentment and hatred. Mr. Mandela exemplified true ambassadorship to the purposes and calling placed on his life. Heidi and I saw the passion he had for people in his eyes. We felt it in his heart and heard it in his words.

Leaders like Nelson Mandela endured suffering to help advance the kingdom of God. Peacemakers like Nelson Mandela fight for peace; they live for peace, and in many cases these exceptional people die fighting for peace. Suffering, persecution, hardship and pain do not stop the peacemakers of God. Their work, will and triumph will always help advance God's Kingdom.

Learning from such leaders and taking direction from God has answered the question, why have a program such as Little Star that goes beyond helping children with cancer? It is because we are to instruct children—including those afflicted and oppressed by all diseases, hardships, plights and abuses—in the ways of God. This includes the benefits of having a relationship with God and the importance of having prayer in their lives.

So many children in the world are suffering in ways so varied and numerous that it is difficult to even imagine. And most of those children can't speak or fight for themselves. It should come as no surprise that having worked with children for years in their rawest, most vulnerable moments, I have become more passionate and more focused about standing up for their rights. My early attitudes about abortion, for instance, changed 360 degrees when the enormity of the numbers involved really sunk in: In America alone, nearly forty-five million babies have been aborted to date. The statistics for sexually assaulted and abused children are also extraordinary—and simply unacceptable: By the age of eighteen, one in four girls and one in seven boys has been sexually assaulted. That is nearly one-fifth of the U.S. population.

In Africa, fourteen million people live at the starvation level, and half of those are children. Africa also has almost thirty million people living with AIDS/HIV. By 2010, orphans will account for between 15 and 25 percent of all children in Africa.

In Southeast Asia, there are over sixty-five million orphans. In developing countries around the world, 150 million children are malnourished. Three hundred million people in India alone live in poverty. God has called us to help children worldwide, one child at a time, because every child matters to the Kingdom of God. After reviewing these statistics and other program research materials, it became more evident to me why God stated that funding would have to be increased in order to accomplish the goals He has set in place for us to achieve.

I started playing tennis events in South Africa at the age of thirteen, and with every trip I came to love the country, people and children more. I made a promise on my first journey there that when I grew up I was going to help South African children. The living conditions of so many children there are dire, making statistics on their needs almost incomprehensible. Before Nelson Mandela left the ranch, I agreed that in the not too distant future, one of our programs would start providing support to the children in South Africa. That work has already begun.

We also had another very special visitor at the ranch. One very gallant servant of God, who puts himself on the line every day to help others, is New York City Mayor, Michael Bloomberg. Michael could have sat at home enjoying his fortune, not once worrying about people who were suffering. Instead, he decided to serve God by running for mayor of New York City to try and make a difference. His generous donation of millions of dollars to New York and other causes—in a three-year span alone he gave over $350 million—does not even touch the surface of the humanitarian efforts that Michael accomplishes anonymously.

Before Michael succeeded Rudy Giuliani as mayor, he graced the halls of the Benedict-Forstmann Silver Lining Ranch, signing the arts and crafts room wall for all visitors to see.

Another famous visitor was Oprah Winfrey. Oprah reminded me a bit of Nelson Mandela in the way she proceeded to ask questions and tour the facility. Oprah took in the images of the wall of life, the colorful and playful murals, the enormous details involved in building such a venture, and the messages of children and guests from the arts and crafts room wall, through her heart and spirit. It was as if she went back in time to her own childhood, and was thankful that here, at this home, these children had the opportunity to be protected, cared for and supported in ways she had not been in her own childhood environment.

It is so easy to see Oprah's smile, confidence and effervescence. Still, those and more incredibly special qualities arrived after trauma and abuse had enveloped her as a child. We never talked about the impact the visit at the ranch had on her but, like Nelson Mandela, she made a choice to turn her pain and suffering into bringing love, light, joy, comfort and support to millions of people around the world. It doesn't mean her pain and suffering have been forgotten. Instead, she rose above them, refusing to succumb to them, and for that she has helped millions more than she can ever imagine. Healing and wholeness is a daily process, and it is one in which God is ready and willing to take part.

After the tour, Oprah and I stood outside the ranch admiring its striking architecture. "Andrea, thank you. What a beautiful thing you have done for the children," she said. Her silence before and after spoke even more than her words.

Every decision in support of God's commands affects the lives of people. Sometimes we never see what the bigger picture of obedience entails; other times God shows us the results. We do the best we can, praying along the way about the areas we do understand and certainly for those that we do not. One time when we followed God's orders—and thereby initially disappointed children and parents—the big picture revealed itself later. We learned, yet again, why obedience is so important.

There was only one time, in all the years of running children's cancer programs, that I cancelled a session. It was the summer of 2000. For years, I had been providing programs and gifts for children from England and Wales because of the warm hospitality I received there during my tennis-playing years. Even though we had no financial support from this geographic region, we forged ahead and were incredibly successful in bringing fun and laughter to the children.

The summer sessions were going full throttle with great success and the departure for the Wimbledon program was less than a week away. The Silver Lining Foundation headquarters trio, Heidi, myself and Chris, had built up our year-round staff. We added the talented and very capable Jennifer Lamb in the extremely important program coordinator position. Maja Muric left the pro tennis circuit to work for us full-time on our international and nationally based domestic programs and video projects. Candis Tai joined us to help with our administrative needs. And Petra Crimmel gave us support helpful to the organization. Beene, Kate and Mary, now all married and with growing families, kept their participation active in an advisory capacity along with yearly visits.

We already had seen what all of our hard work and common goals could accomplish together. It was a unit that performed beyond the typical nine-to-five, forty-hour-a-week schedule. I didn't expect anyone to match the hours Heidi and I were putting in, but I did look for a team that cared about the Foundation in grand ways.

With the Wall of Life cheering us on daily, and the filing cabinets full of thousands of heartfelt thank-you letters from children, parents, family and community members, hospitals and generous well-wishers, we gave our best every day.

A previous Wimbledon Ranch on the Road trip was met with tremendous success. Christopher Gorringe, the All England Club and Grand Slam Chairman and Director, was tremendously supportive. The very same guards, press liaisons, pass department individuals and transportation coordinators from when I played at the prestigious event were now welcoming, with open arms, our group of locally based children with cancer, as well as me and a few members of our staff.

The children were thrilled with the opportunities placed before them, as a ticket to attend the Wimbledon Tennis Championships is a prized possession sought out by people worldwide. We had everything in place. Center court tickets, player area lunch passes, Wimbledon memorabilia and an entire afternoon of watching tennis at its best on the green grass court surface.

Then it rained. Matches were postponed. We sat in our covered seats staring at tarps and raindrops. The children were trying to keep their spirits up, but once again disappointment was coming into their lives. I refused to be part of that so I went into action. With medical and adult supervision in place, I sprinted to the players' lunch room.

Michael Chang and local hero Tim Henman were eating. I received promises from them that they would meet with the children later that afternoon. I bumped into Steffi Graf in a hallway, and she gladly agreed to visit with the children. Standing outside the men's locker room area, Pete Sampras was peering out to check on the weather. As always, he happily arranged a secret meeting spot to share tennis stories and sign autographs for the children.

Things were looking up. Still, the tennis the children were waiting to watch included Andre Agassi and Monica Seles. They were nowhere to be seen. I ran around the entire grounds with no sighting of them or their support teams. I knew that both players were probably trying to conserve their energy so they would be prepared to jump into competition as soon as the skies cleared. I stared at the international cell phone I rented for the program. I remembered Andre's remark, "Andrea, call me anytime you need my help." The anytime reverberated in my mind. I dialed. On the other line Andre Agassi picked up. "Hello?"

"Andre, it's Andrea Jaeger. Remember the 'anytime I need your help I can call' comment you made?"

"Yes."

I continued, "Well, as you know it is raining. The kids are sitting at center court in amazing seats staring at the rain and dark skies. It would be incredible if I could bring them to you for a surprise visit. It won't only make their day or tournament, it will secure a spot as one of their favorite memories of all time. What do you think?"

"Andrea, I think it is a great idea. I am at the house I rented. Bring them over," he said.

"Are you serious?" I asked, incredulously.

"Absolutely. Let's show them a great time."

Andre proceeded to give me his address and I bolted to beg and plead with Christopher to allow me a transportation van for a few hours. As if Christopher didn't have enough going on, I offered up my last eight club passes for life, tennis lessons and the few English pounds in my pocket.

He refused to take any of my offers, actually kindly trying to hide his amusement that this was so important I would give everything past players cherish in order to help the children. Christopher replied, "Head the group over to the transportation venue in fifteen minutes."

I casually approached the children, many of whom had visited our ranch programs in Aspen, and I said, "Well, it looks like we won't be watching tennis for awhile so let's go into town and grab some lemonade. Sorry, kids."

No one grumbled or complained or looked at me like I had failed. Instead, they came over and hugged me, saying, "Andrea, we know you tried your hardest. Thanks. It was fun being with you."

I was touched nearly to tears by their generosity of spirit during what I knew was a very disappointing experience. We walked with umbrellas to the transportation area. They all assumed that was it for their Wimbledon experience as our tickets were only for that day.

As a coordinator pointed out which direction to go in, we all turned in unison. A driver and a balloon-covered van awaited us. Christopher had come through. We piled in and I gave the driver the address. A short time later we arrived at a house. The kids looked at me, and I said, "There is a tiny TV in this place. If the matches come on we can watch from here." It was the only thing I could think of as the surprise had to be hidden for a few more minutes; besides, the remark was true.

Coach Brad Gilbert met the van as we continued up the driveway. His smile was classic as he knew what fun was in store for the children. And then, out walked Andre in his Nike warm-up suit.

The shrieks and excitement coming from the van certainly announced we had found the right place. "Oh my God! That is Andre Agassi. He is walking toward us." The kids were screaming and scrambling to get to the front of the van. As if on cue, the moment Andre walked out, the rain stopped. He hugged and engaged each and every child in conversation. Andre and Brad played host with such enthusiasm and love. After taking pictures, signing autographs, and answering questions, our gracious hosts were thanked by the children and we climbed back in the van.

The children were so busy sharing their joy with each other they barely noticed that we had arrived at another house. Monica Seles had also granted permission for the children to visit her. Andre and Monica's grand slam trophies and top-ranked tournament prizes were so vast, they wouldn't have been able to fit in the van.

I explained to the children, "Well, I was telling you the truth. We are going to get some lemonade. Let's go grab some." Mrs. Seles greeted us and passed around lemonade while the next surprise came down the stairs. The kids stared, their eyes getting bigger with every step closer Monica took.

Monica's gentleness provided the atmosphere for everyone to hang out in the living room as if we were there for a family gathering. And the day still provided more blessings. The skies cleared, the other players kept their promises and the matches were played. Even the center court guards had little candy bags for the children upon their return to their seats.

With all those memories and stories still in mind, all of a sudden, in 2000, God talked to me in a loud, clear voice: "You need to cancel the overseas England program." I was extremely disappointed. I had lived my life on the principle that I would never promise a child something and then take it away. Instead of immediately canceling the program, I waited to see if God would give me a confirmation. The same day and the next day, I received affirmations in a concise voice from God that I should cancel the program.

I went to Heidi and explained the situation. We knew the youngsters would be terribly disappointed so we held a meeting and came up with a great alternative. We would cancel the London Ranch on the Road session and invite all the children to Aspen for a session. It would cost us more money to accomplish that change in direction, but being obedient to God's command was imperative. All the children were even more excited about the opportunity to come to the United States and take part in our Aspen-based programs.

During the rearrangements, on the exact day that Maja and I would have been flying overseas from Denver to London, Maja inexplicably became very ill. She went to her local doctor and then was rushed to the hospital. Maja was fortunate to have been minutes away from the hospital. Her blood pressure, for some odd reason, dropped dangerously low. If it had not been stabilized immediately, as she says, "I may not have made it through the London flight." Not only could Maja have endangered her life, but she could possibly have compromised the children's already weakened immune systems. I had no idea why we were to cancel the session, other than God wanted me to. Heidi and I were not guaranteed a favorable outcome, but we were secure in standing on God's Word through our faith and obedience. Although I did not have the complete picture, the urgency from God to respond demanded our attention and obedience. It is how we try to run the foundation's programs every single day.

It is difficult enough to run operations as it is, so there is certainly no way in the world we would ever venture out without God's permission. God's protection and provisions are critical. We thank Him profusely for allowing us in on the pieces of information that are revealed to us, as well as giving us the understanding that there is always a bigger picture we don't see.

The Silver Lining and Little Star Foundation's programs work because God has brought forth those that help according to their purposes and callings. Certainly, watching God's servants fulfilling their purposes awakens the gifts in all of us. Joined together, the prospect of making the world a better and brighter place for children and adults is possible when people care enough to search their souls, enable their spirits and contribute according to what God places in their hearts and spirits.

It is about one person caring enough to make a difference, because that one person can. Collectively, the miracles take shape.

Chapter Thirty

And we know that all things work together
for good to those who love God, to those
who are the called according to His purpose.

—Romans 8:28

For years, Heidi and I had a staff member videotape little pieces of the children's session events, so that the children would have a memento to share with their family members. Anna Levin, a gifted counselor from New York City, first took on this duty with determination and expertise. The kids and staff affectionately called her "Anna Spielberg." Anna captured precious moments, put in fun music and pulled it all together in time to give a sneak preview to the participants at the ranch before sending the videos off to their respective families.

Maja eventually assumed these duties and the video screening and completed project became an added bonus to a great week. As the project evolved, we decided to give the children the opportunity to share a message in their own words. This section of the video is called "Words of Wisdom." All selections were to be from a child's heart— not an adult's perspective.

Kids have shared thoughts such as: "This ranch is the best place.

Anyone stuck in a hospital—don't give up; this is the coolest place, so keep fighting and don't give up," "Mom and Dad, I love you. Thank you for everything," and "I caught seven fish at Kevin Costner's place," along with other personal, heartfelt words.

Sarah was ready for her turn on the video and she sat in the chair, like so many children before her, preparing to leave her own signature words in video form. Throughout the week, kids eagerly chatted away about what they would say, with others retreating to their rooms to craft their messages alone.

With Sarah's announcement completed, we headed to Kevin Costner's ranch with the entire group to continue with the week's schedule of fun-filled activities. Actor, director, Oscar winner and, more importantly, caring father, Kevin Costner made strides for us beyond the normal fund-raising doors.

As Kevin so aptly remarked, "Helping your program and the children gave my home a higher purpose." Kevin, like so many divinely appointed crusaders doing God's work, decided it wasn't enough to open his home for family, loved ones, associates and friends. He decided to make his home a sacred refuge for strangers. Those strangers included children with cancer, Heidi, me and the staff from our cancer programs. We are invited to fish, canoe, have lunch, relax and take in the majestic mountain scenery in great company. Kevin comes out and fishes with the children, making for an unforgettable afternoon.

The Costner family—Kevin, daughters Anne and Lily, son Joe, Kevin's fiancée Christine—and a variety of friends of the family have hosted us for more than five years, as if they are receiving royalty. During this particular 2003 summer season of children's sessions, Kevin took Heidi and me aside to reveal his dreams. Further excavation on Kevin's property had begun to give the children we bring all summer long an even nicer and bigger refuge. Kevin told us, "This is where they can find their own private fishing spot. The athletic field will be over there. A larger and better-equipped luncheon spot will be to the left. I really think the kids will love it."

Heidi and I marveled at the construction, which had already started. We replied, "Kevin, the other location has been great. This beautiful chosen area is even more spectacular. Thank you!"

Kevin enthusiastically continued his tour. "See that shaded area? That will be perfect for the children who want to stay out of the hot sun. I am also making sure that fishing nooks will be made all around the pond, and of course I will stock the water with fish, too."

The area is paradise. Nestled against private forest land with mountain views in a variety of directions, the tall pines and Colorado landscape are at their finest in this area on the outskirts of town. Kevin's help has been heaven sent, and we are thankful for God lining us up with the entire Costner family.

As I continued to pursue the servanthood of God with a passion, I saw how He brought things full circle. In August 2003, we were once again blessed with Ted Forstmann making one of his return trips to the ranch to visit the children. Throughout Ted's life, he has successfully commandeered an army of donors to reach further in their hearts and pockets to help children. God was still calling on Ted to lend his hand with the Silver Lining Foundation and Ranch and our umbrella and follow-up Little Star programs.

Now God wanted Ted to sit back and enjoy what had been built over the years. It wasn't only about the ranch. Ted was about to glimpse a tiny fraction of what his long-term support had made possible. The last talent show of the 2003 summer sessions had counselor James Myers exuberantly emceeing the show as if he was running the Oscars. The stage was alive in God's glory.

∞   ∞   ∞

The Divine encounters God has appointed for me, through Heidi, Ted, Michael, Pat, Ms. Anthony, John, Beene, Chris, Maja, KC and a plethora of other people, have brought unusual miracles and blessings of epic proportions that have greatly helped the children and blessed me on my calling. Divine encounters and relationships with people are felt in the spirit immediately. These unions are created by God, and they can last an entire lifetime or fill a purpose meant to last a minute. They are perfectly timed experiences that change circumstances forever, for the better, and leave a joyful, lasting impression etched and secure in the heart and spirit.

These heaven-sent partnerships can bring a variety of miracles. They can rescue us from danger. They most certainly bring laughter and unparalleled, unlimited joy.

Divine encounters tell the truth, regardless of the consequences, and they set the stage for salvation, freedom and blessings. They catch tears and bring hugs. Their existence can whisper and shout support, stand guard, and get a person back on his or her feet. Divine relationships orchestrated by God can arrive suddenly, captivating the chosen spirits as they harmoniously connect, playfully dancing as if time and space have no barriers, only love, laughter, light, peace, joy and energy—all heaven sent.

These sacred bonds, God-packaged gifts, change lives for the better for those who are willing to receive and open them. The individuals who embody divine relationships long to see a person soar into their calling and live their purpose to the fullest. Becoming more complete, wiser, kinder, gentler, and living up to receiving and opening God's blessing and gifts are certain results of divine encounters. They teach how to give fully and receive more easily, how to knock down the wrong boundaries while constructing the right ones.

Divine encounters create a voice that will get heard. They bring energy, light, love and laughter that raises the spirit. They connect together in the same ways that a sunset delicately touches an ocean—providing a glimpse of the glory of God that is present in all of us. Divine relationships are felt forever. Divine encounters will never be understood fully, because they were not created by man's instruction but are intricately choreographed by God.

I may not even have understood all the love, wisdom, guidance and support God's appointed angels have bestowed upon me at the time of delivery, but all the blessings and gifts have found their way in by playing pivotal roles in my life.

Divine encounters are discovered in the messengers. Their purposes draw them forth to help others. The spirit's agreement to receive is then passed along as the purposes live on, generated always by God's everlasting, unconditional love.

For all my past, present and soon to arrive Divine encounters and heaven-sent relationships, I am eternally grateful.

EPILOGUE

Words of Wisdom from the Children

Therefore, brethren, be even more diligent to make your call and election sure, for if you do these things you will never stumble.

—2 Peter 1:10

This is a day like many others that Heidi, I and the rest of the staff have experienced. The sun is shining, the sky is blue. The Colorado mountains are as majestic as ever. But not all is picture perfect.

The Proctors and the Prados lost their son this past weekend. Kaleb Proctor—"Special K," as we affectionately called him—never lost his spirit even as he lost his life to cancer before he graduated from high school. The Colorado native had a smile that went from ear to ear, beaming on everyone he met. In a Colorado

307

newspaper article titled, "Teen Teaches Life Lessons," the reporter shares some touching sentiments:

> *He faces life as it has been given to him. That includes tremendous pain from tumors and surgeries, incessant nausea from chemotherapy, and an uncontrollable lethargy that comes from his immune system being under constant attack.*
>
> *More than anything, Proctor wishes he could do the things other people his age [sixteen] do. He wants to play baseball, he wants to go to school, he wants to hang out with his friends and be a little reckless.*
>
> *But he can't. He has no control over the normalcy of his life. . . . "The only good thing about all of this is that he's gotten to meet a lot of great people," said Proctor's mom, Dixie. Caring, selfless people have given Proctor experiences he might not otherwise have had. He's been to Atlantis in the Bahamas, he's vacationed in Hawaii, he's even ridden in a Ferrari.*
>
> *However, none of these experiences compares to the week he spends each year at the Silver Lining Camp in Aspen. "The best times I've had are with those people," he said. "Up there, we forget about cancer and chemo. . . . It doesn't sound like much, but to the people dealing with cancer it means everything. Up there it is heaven."*
>
> *Proctor has been to the camp for children with cancer for three years. It's where he rejuvenates the spirit and acquires the courage he needs to make it through the life waiting for him back home.*
>
> *"Don't ever lose faith," he [Kaleb] said. "Stick it out, through thick and thin. And no matter what happens, don't give up. Failure is not an option."*

Kaleb went on to talk about the pain that kids in his high school cafeteria caused him when they picked up their trays and moved to the other side of the room when he was first diagnosed.

"That hurt," Proctor said. "I don't think any of them had any idea how much that hurt me." It is a pain that can't be treated with surgery or chemotherapy or radiation. It's one that has to be treated with knowledge, understanding and compassion.

"Cancer doesn't change a person," he [Kaleb] said. "They're no different. They just have more to deal with. They don't need people to make fun of them. They need people's help, and they need people to be nice to them."

Kaleb kept teaching even in death. His last wishes involved giving back, helping others and being nice to children with cancer. At Special K's request, his X-Box, video games and other play items were to be donated to the Silver Lining Ranch so other kids could enjoy them. For his funeral, he requested that people donate to the Silver Lining Foundation rather than send flowers in his memory. As for that smile and his beautiful spirit, they will both forever remain in our hearts.

Everyone who came in contact with Pete, a San Diego boy, benefited from his short time on Earth. Pete led by example. Laughing, loving, sharing, he brought joy to all who crossed his path. Never did one of his numerous relapses get him down. His hugs lasted a lifetime. As with Special K and Pete, or when any child dies, whether through cancer or not, their spirits carry on with God's loving embrace.

Each child born into the world represents a whole, regardless of background or health status. The children I have had the privilege and honor to help never balked at supporting their own peer group of children with cancer, or assisting and teaching others in need. Their cancer diagnoses may have set their ships on a different course—one which adults could never comprehend—but these children never lost sight of what was really important in life.

The children watch over their family, friends and loved ones in ways many of us are only beginning to understand. Their wise spirits live on, even if their bodies do not allow them to grow up to become women and men, perhaps mothers and fathers themselves. Their time on Earth may be short, but their influence will carry on for generations.

When an eight-year-old says, without remorse but matter-of-factly, "Candy doesn't taste the same since chemotherapy," as David remarked to me before he passed on, it imparts a special kind of pain—but never a sense of bitterness or anger. Even at his tender age, David kept others on their path despite his own hardships.

Lauren had her head stapled together after brain tumor surgery. Sometimes she left it uncovered for everyone to see. She wasn't ashamed. Instead, what had blossomed in her was a sense of comfort with the knowledge that she was still whole. Every activity she undertook was done with genuine enthusiasm for life. Back home, as seasons passed by, Lauren told me she was picking out makeup, clothes and music, not for the prom, a graduation ceremony or a party. At fourteen years of age, she was picking out the items for her funeral service. Her last words to me were, "I don't have millions of dollars to give you or time to raise money, but somehow I will help." At Lauren's memorial, a request was made for donations to be sent to Silver Lining in lieu of flowers. Years after Lauren's death, family, friends, loved ones and a caring community continue to give in her memory.

Rhea loved her foundation duties, one of which was to find other children in Chicago who might enjoy our programs. She found Keith and his family and loved them immediately, as we all did and still do. Keith laughed playfully as we entertained him, never once getting angry when he had to be carried piggyback style because of the cancer's progression. Keith's bright smile is still in our hearts.

All the children share and express themselves in their special ways. While the cancer may take away parts of them, and in some cases even more than that, they always make sure that cancer never wins the war by stealing away their laughter, love and light.

Shayna tossed water balloons with great accuracy, laughing at her team's victorious results, never once thinking of her last days, which would come soon. She wrote, "Thanks for being the best friend I ever had. For the gifts, too."

Susannah gracefully skied down the mountain, owning the carvings the entire way. She would have very few more of these moments on the slopes, but she opted to use them to teach others the fine art of skiing. In one of Susannah's visits she shared, "I thought I was done with cancer. Then I relapsed at fifteen years old. Even through all the bad things I have gone through in my life, I am so thankful for everyone in my life. I couldn't ask for anything more."

Camper James relished the opportunity to allow his gentle demeanor to take leadership roles during sessions. During his last days, he painted a gift for us: a teddy bear with a cross necklace. It graces the wall of the ranch's activity floor, forever showing others where his faith rested—in God.

Melinda never became depressed even throughout six relapses or while planning her last birthday party at the ranch. Her engaging personality took hold of people's hearts. She said with tears in her eyes, "I feel very special being a part of groundbreaking for the new ranch."

Melinda wrote out instructions on what to do with her remains. She asked for some to be brought to her grandparent's place in Florida and the rest to us at Silver Lining for a specific send-off.

As the snow delicately fell on a Thanksgiving holiday afternoon, Melinda's parents came through the front door of the ranch, handing me Melinda's box of ashes. As we walked to Melinda's favorite spot along the river, we reminisced about the ways Melinda unconditionally gave to and loved others. We know she is taking good care of other children above.

Andrew kept his faith throughout his battles, holding firm with God even at the rough end. Inspiring words and actions were his constant steps in life.

Carolyn brought charm and wit, holding her wisdom out for the taking. She always provided a measure of balance that sheltered others.

Michelle longed for her eyes to stay open. Drifting in and out of consciousness days before she would be released from cancer's hold to live on forever in spirit in the heavenly realm, she would slightly squeeze my hand.

Even during conversations, partnering up and connecting with children during their last moments in their physical state, children still make sure everyone else is doing okay.

During our hospital visit, Michelle made sure that the squeezes on my hand reminded me that I must keep helping other kids given similar fates.

The hospital time together would last for eternity.

Brandon cheered on his fellow campers. His caring smile stayed strong even though doctors told him he didn't have much time left. He was the boy who received a big boost when a call from Pete Sampras came in to the David Koch-sponsored health center at the ranch. He appreciated the gesture with such joy, and even to the end he never let his spirit succumb in the ways his body did.

Iraniza came from New York trembling from her cancer diagnosis. She was hesitant to try any activity. By the end of the fun-filled week, she was prepared to teach other people to conquer their fears. Years later, we know she is in a place with no pain, where the cancer can't hurt her anymore.

Kate became a spokesperson for how courageous kids fighting

cancer have to be. Thanks to Ross Greenburg's producing efforts during an HBO Sports feature, Kate had the opportunity to share with the world how she felt. Her first remarks were appreciative words for how our long-term support programs were making a difference in her life.

As Kate's voice choked up with emotion, she continued sharing, "You learn to appreciate things more and you realize how precious life is. And that every day you have to take as, you know, a gift. You have to say, 'This is a wonderful day.'" The mural at the ranch painted with Kate, other children, Cindy Crawford, her husband Rande Gerber, the staff and talented artist Ben Brown, captured Kate's session in full radiance. It has since been visited fondly by Kate's relatives from her hometown of Boston.

As Josh's parents described, "Josh beat this awful disease in the only way he could; Josh was lifted up by angels to eternal life. Thank you for everything you did for Josh."

Josh and his family, like so many other children and families we have come to know, represent in countless ways the glory of God and how pain and suffering, although felt deeply, never destroy the spirit.

Sonia battled many different surgeries, relapses and treatments with courage and prayers. Although her lungs, leg and brain felt the surgeon's scalpel—her leg eventually had to be amputated—it never deterred her compassion and her desire to spread her vibrant appreciation for life. Her only tears at the ranch were expressions of joy and care for her friends battling cancer and the nurturing staff. Days after she died, a reminder of how deep her love went appeared in a special care package. More poems and letters and a handmade glass replication of her handprint with her initials arrived at the ranch for placement in their permanent home.

Moments before her death, Kimberly, a little girl lying in a hospital bed, spoke through an oxygen mask, wanting to make sure everyone knew how special they were and how much she loved them. She recorded a message saying her thanks and hopes to see her friends and loved ones in heaven eventually one day. She held on long enough to make sure the message was made. Her heart and spirit, like other children before and others after her, found the strength in life and death to serve, to help and to ease the pain and suffering of others. Often, the foundation's work goes past providing fun and laughter to the children; this time, helping with funeral expenses was an effort we know Kimberly would have appreciated.

Pam came to our Aspen programs carrying news that her doctors gave her zero percent chance of survival. She didn't use her time to be hateful or bitter, or to live without purpose and appreciation. Pam danced, played and, with amazing creativity, created stylish and glamorous headwear to camouflage the after-effects of her chemotherapy treatments. She had a colorful personality and a bold sense of style. Pam's favorite way to address me is captured in one of her many notes. "Hey there, chickadee, what chya up to? Just thought I would drop a note to say HI! Hope you're having fun. Talk to ya later." A drawing of a heart and "Always, Pam" ended her note. Although gone in one way, Pam and the other children are never forgotten.

Like all the thousands of children we have met, helped and learned from, Pam lived life to the fullest, never once refusing to stop and smell the flowers. These children, whose lives are often cut so short, have lived deeper, appreciated more in their brief time than many adults do in their entire lives. Whether the children have days, years or decades remaining to share their beautiful hearts and spirits, they taught this same important lesson: Make the most of today and your life by living according to God's purposes and callings, which will also support those God has put in your life to help. It is a choice that lasts well beyond the gift of tomorrow.

Here are a few of the ways children we know are making an effort to care from their hearts.

Sarah lives overseas. Through her more than five-year battle with cancer, numerous brain tumor surgeries and loss of sight, she has resolved to make a difference by trying to fund-raise for us. Her goal? To run a marathon in hopes of raising money to sponsor children from her area.

Allison was ten when she first visited the ranch. She brought incredible energy and enthusiasm to everyone. When she returned home she began making greeting cards to help us raise money. As her mom explains proudly: "Allie started designing the cards to show her appreciation for all that everyone at the ranch did for her and other children fighting cancer." Allison is now thirteen and is still creating cards for us from her home.

Lindsay recently wrote a paper titled "Life with Lindsay." It starts, "I was only twelve when I initially got sick. This memory is so fresh in my mind, I still get chills when I think about the day I was told that I had brain cancer." Despite countless relapses and new tumor occurrences, Lindsay decided that she wanted to help others and she applied to attend a college social work program.

The update came with loving comments of how we all helped formulate her decision by the ways we gave fully, along with a request for Heidi and me to write a recommendation letter for her application. Happily she was accepted, not because of our words, but because anyone could see upon meeting Lindsay that she has a purpose and calling to give back, teach and help others. These qualities are always brimming in the children.

Katie visited the ranch at age ten, after losing one eye and a leg to cancer. Now, at sixteen, she is a terrific host who continues to enthusiastically race around with grace, agility and laughter.

Brian's mom wrote us a letter titled "Angels among Us." It states:

> *I wanted to write this letter to let everyone know how incredibly wonderful this foundation is. Andrea Jaeger and all the foundation workers are angels on*

Earth. They have reached out and touched so many of God's children and made their days a little brighter and their lives a little richer. However, the giving doesn't end after the week at camp. . . .

Our family owes a debt of gratitude to these blessed people that can never be repaid. They gave our son one of the best times in his life at one of the worst times in his life. Brian's first plane ride was to Aspen. His first horseback ride was at Aspen. The first time he went white-water rafting was at Aspen. He met his first movie star [Cindy Crawford] at Aspen. He will be graduating college this week because of the generosity of the Silver Lining Foundation.

We were strangers brought together by cancer and now our lives are intertwined forever. We humbly give thanks to these angels and offer up their names and their foundation in prayer to God, that He will continue to bless them and their work as they continue to bless others. Again, thanks for the many blessings you have bestowed, not only on our son and family but for all the children and families all over the world that have been touched by the work of the Silver Lining Foundation.

With great love, JoAnn

Brian was one of countless education- and faith-minded individuals from our Silver Lining programs who received our Jeff Crawford College Scholarship Award. Newly graduated, Brian serves as a youth minister and is on our advisory board. His love for God and sharing God's Word is his walk, talk, calling and purpose, which he takes on with tremendous joy.

Nicole, who we welcomed over the years, attended culinary school on the East Coast. She was another of our college scholarship award recipients. After graduation, she flew across country to prepare a special meal for a big group—the children at the Benedict-Forstmann Silver Lining Ranch.

Under the ranch's roof, Asal gave inspiring speeches as a counselor extraordinaire. Her bout with cancer left more than physical scars, it gave a sense of purpose to care and help others in need. A February 2004 reunion trip for past children participants, now young adults, was organized and arranged by Asal's passion to continue our long-term support programs. Her little steps in wanting and choosing to help others have grown to huge strides of making a difference.

After Rhea left to teach us from heaven and the stars, Alicia took over the newsletter reins with thanks and appreciation. As Alicia battled her cancer as an adolescent, her main priority was to bring happiness to children in their later stages of cancer. Her efforts were met with great success.

Tripp fought courageously for his life throughout numerous relapses. As he shared, "Though I was very sick for two years, I do not regret getting sick. I have never once asked why. I know why. I'm a person who doesn't give up." Tripp's thank-you hugs, given with such appreciation over the years, lasted much longer than the moment; they will last forever.

Now stronger, older, bigger and in remission, Tripp chooses to spend his time serving the United States of America in protecting innocent people. Tripp is now serving our country in the U.S. Army.

Abby kept us all entertained. Her appreciation for life changed tears to laughter. At the Aspen airport on the day of departure, instead of using all her saved-up dollars for souvenirs, Abby chose to give us a twenty-dollar bill and a handwritten note stating, "I want every cancer patient to experience this and this is my way of helping. Thank you so much!"

Amy uses her poor prognosis days as a catalyst to care for and bring happiness to others. Despite having only one leg, she is the first one at the hospital, on the support hotline, with prayerful words and packages for her dear friends also fighting cancer. Amy helped pick the picture for this book cover by pointing out her favorite picture from the ranch's Wall of Life.

As Amy says, "It is much easier to go through everything that happens if you have a good attitude. You need to take it a day at a time and never faster. Take things as they come to you and don't worry about things you don't need to, or let someone else worry about them for you. I went into every chemo, surgery, radiation treatment as this is doing me good and it will help me in the long run. Whenever I would hear bad news, I would say to myself, 'I can do it.' 'I can handle it.'"

Amy's faith in God is so strong. She has become an intercessory prayer warrior for countless children. Like all the children, Amy is more than a tribute to life; she is a servant and tribute to God.

Tommy stood among his peer group, foundation staff and dozens of reporters as he was chosen by Pete Sampras to ask the first question at a U.S. Open press conference. Nervous but not shaken, and hopeful that the tennis hero before him would be as legendary of a person as he was on the tennis court, Tommy took charge of the interview. The result was what can be expected when Pete is asked to help out children—a class act going well beyond his record Grand Slam titles. Partnered up, Tommy and Pete made a great team.

Sunny sang of praise and worship to God in all activities beyond the talent show. Sunny's goal is to become a missionary for God. She is well on her way in training, but the main part we saw is already 100 percent there—her declaration to serve God in every and any way He asks of her.

Rob summed up his grit, wisdom and determination in fighting cancer, "I think of all the other horrors that plague the world besides my cancer like war and famine, and in comparison to all of these, my illness appears to be so insignificant. If people have the strength and courage to end wars and put an end to famine, surely I have the power and courage to fight and beat cancer."

∞   ∞   ∞

The following youngsters found their own trademark thoughts and words of wisdom. The children spoke and lived these words and they made sure their spirit shined on others to receive the same messages of love and support.

"Cancer has shown me that you need to cherish every second you are living, live life to the fullest, because one day you will be gone. The day I was diagnosed, I thought I was going in for a blood test; a half hour later they are telling me I have cancer. Cancer gave me some of the best friends in the world, and so did going to the ranch. I will never forget anything that went on at the ranch."

—Michael, 15

"Cancer taught me that there are great people in this world who have to leave all too soon."

—Sarah, 15

"I think that cancer taught me to love others and tell them you love them every day because you don't know what tomorrow will bring."

—Adam, 15

"When I found out I had cancer, I was eleven years old. I think cancer has showed me how valuable my life is. I don't think cancer took anything away from me. But it gave me so much more."

—Nellie, 15

As with all the children we have been blessed to know, Anna has a special and gifted spirit. A frequent foundation participant, Anna's source of love, life and faith rests in the mighty Lord above. A Christian since age two, Anna chooses to provide insightful resources to help us develop our new daily devotional program. Anna has declared, along with her doctors, it is a miracle that she is still alive. Anna's conclusion, "God has a purpose for me. Prayers make a difference. Jesus is my Savior. I rest all my days on Him."

This story comes from Anna's mom, sharing a tiny glimpse of what life has been like since her daughter's cancer diagnosis. The family lives in Chicago and traveled to a New York City hospital in hopes of finding specialized treatment that could help.

So . . . we wait again. Welcome to our world.

Take elevator A, push the third floor button—the cancer button ("Can't I push another button—four, five?"). The doors open to parked wheelchairs and stroller upon stroller. Clinic: Chaos. Loud video on TV. Cell phones. Coffee. Averted eyes. Tears. Clowns. Valium. Bald, bald, balder. IV pole riding. Cheerful nurses. Tired parents. Numb. Disbelief. Healthy siblings throwing tantrums. Frail and pale kids fighting for their lives.

Day hospital means chemo and antibody treatment— it is a very strange world, a world where pain is good because it means they haven't made HAMA yet, so the antibodies must be getting to the disease. Or the hives are good—the antibodies are not being destroyed by HAMA and must be getting to the cancer.

A world of adorable kids and screams from every room. But strangely enough, you get used to it. You know it all means hope. A concentration camp where some kids win. The first couple of days, while Bob

> *[Anna's dad] was still with us, I walked into day hospital, heard the screaming and, in anticipation of Anna's treatment passed out . . . twice. Anna promptly sent me home. Fortunately, by the time Bob left I got comfortable with the familiarity of this surreal setting. No more fainting . . . I guess you can adjust your idea of normal to the familiar. . . .*
>
> *Thank you all so much for praying us through this marathon.*

Nic challenged the other children and adults with his summer ranch visit, asking, "Do you think God has a purpose for you?" He was thirteen years old at the time and had been through many brain tumor surgeries and hospital visits. Now, at an even wiser fourteen years of age, baptized to serve God to the fullest, he has answered his own question. In his recent interview with me on his school project, "My Hero," he asked many defining questions. The one posed back to him, provided a clear, adamant and confident statement. "My purpose to serve God includes helping run the Silver Lining Foundation."

With playful enthusiasm, he added, "And to feed bacon to the ranch mascot dogs Lola and Cortez."

His purpose has received a head start. The devotional program Little Star is sponsoring for Silver Lining includes Scripture and Bible materials and stories written by the children, for the children.

Every child we have met has a place in our spirits, hearts and memories, and there are more than enough inspirational and heart-warming stories to fill a library of books. Each child we have crossed paths with is unconditionally, completely and equally loved by God. Over the decades, across the continents, God has called

upon us to help thousands of children, one child at a time. We have
gladly obliged. God continues to challenge us to reach our
purposes. Again, we are committed 100 percent to helping children
in every way God has instructed us. One hundred percent of my
proceeds from writing, editing and promoting *First Service,* goes to
helping children.

Pediatric hospitals, abuse shelters, juvenile delinquent programs,
rape and sexual molestation support programs, suffering children
all around the world, as well as children in general, will benefit
from proceeds of this book.

I thank God for entrusting me with a God-serving team of people
to support such a noble purpose in equipping children with the
Word of God. Children are precious, priceless treasures to be protected, supported, cared for, loved and equipped according to God's
instructions.

For us, it matters not only what we do, but how we do it. Success
is measured by God ordaining the results. Children have a great
capacity to teach us the ways of the Father. Their innocence, purity,
truth, appreciation for life, giving nature, generosity of spirit and
honesty need to be preserved, protected, equipped and supported
with the Word of God.

Generously, and perhaps to prepare me, God has given me a
small viewing of future things to come in the purposes He wants me
to continue in helping children worldwide. It includes the entire
Rancho Milagro building project being completed, which includes
the much anticipated Children's Prayer Center Complex—and the
endowment, building and program funding needs being met; film
and television projects; a newspaper column; more books and
signs, wonders, blessings, miracles and divine relationship
encounters.

How and when God decides to release those and other exciting
things, I am sure will be revealed to me—on His schedule. Who is

the next person I want to have a Divine relationship with arranged by God and His appointed angels? The very person I am supposed to meet, by the orchestration of God, for every path crossed is not random, it is for a purpose. I know priceless treasures, blessings and miracles exist for all of God's children to experience, and they come in a variety of packages. God leaves the choice to His children about how they receive and open the gifts He so lovingly prepares, provides and delivers.

Meanwhile, I will continue my lifelong dedication and calling of helping children around the world. I hold fast to the three beliefs that have brought me this far in my purposes, calling and great appreciation of how all God's children are a gift, and in my becoming a joint heir and co-laborer in the kingdom of God: God loves everyone and that includes me. . . . God always knows the bigger picture. . . . and . . . Hold on to the Cross of Christ whatever you do, wherever you go.

Being of service to God is as much about letting go as holding on. The ultimate level of service comes in stepping out in faith, in wanting a relationship with God. The journey—life—isn't meant to be experienced alone. Every step, each moment, is an opportunity for purpose ordained by God to be released. In serving God, healings, blessings, peace, love, joy and gifts from above are released, and from that we and all of God's children can benefit as the Kingdom of God advances.

More About
The Silver Lining Foundation

A question I'm frequently asked is: "Why did you choose to pursue working with children who have cancer?" During my years on the professional tennis tour, visiting children in hospitals was one of my favorite things to do at tournaments. Children are models of hope and courage. Watching children fight for their lives on a daily basis inspired the premise on which the Foundation is based: Kids will have an opportunity to regain some of their missed childhood—a childhood stripped by the harsh realities of cancer.

The Silver Lining Foundation is a magical world created for children with cancer. Participants exchange a sterile hospital environment and rigid medical schedule for white-water rafting, horseback riding, gondola rides up Aspen Mountain, skiing and making friends. Children with cancer endure losses that extend far beyond their disease. They lose much of what healthy youngsters can take for granted. Education is disrupted; participating in sports becomes a wish. Normal, everyday opportunities for developing independence, self-reliance and a strong self-image are diminished. In the midst of doctors, therapies and hospital stays they tend to lose the sense of being in control of their lives. At the Benedict-Forstmann Ranch, youngsters with special needs don't have to sit on the sidelines. Independence is encouraged, and campers often try adventures that they normally would not attempt. Engaging in new activities helps the children gain self-esteem. Cancer can isolate children and their families from others. By sharing experiences, the children give encouragement, understanding and comfort to each other. Bonds of friendship are formed. Renewed in spirit, they are ready to face the challenges of their everyday lives.

Other custom-made programs involve extensive follow-up with the children that include college scholarships, family retreat sessions, employment opportunities, medical assistance and out-of-state activities. Fun, education and adventure are instrumental to our programs, which are designed to last a lifetime.

We welcome you to celebrate life with these wonderful children. The growing world of our Foundation needs your help to maintain and build toward our successful future in helping children—a future that is bright with limitless possibilities. If you would like more information about the Silver Lining Foundation log on to *www. firstservicebook.com* or *www.andreajaeger.com*.

Helping One Child at a Time—
First Service and Little Star

In an effort to help children around the world, a portion of the proceeds from this book will go to the Silver Lining Foundation, Little Star programs and other domestic and international children's programs. Founded in 1990, the Silver Lining Foundation serves children affected by cancer and other life-threatening, life-changing conditions. At the Silver Lining Ranch, campers with cancer exchange a sterile hospital environment and rigid medical schedule for white-water rafting, horseback riding and skiing. Here, fun and adventure are part of the healing process: Children are allowed to be children, they make lasting friendships and acquire the emotional strength to endure present and future challenges. Little Star supports Silver Lining programs as well as children afflicted by other diseases, abuse and other life-threatening and life-altering conditions:

International Programs bring supplies to various hospitals and programs in Africa, the Middle East, England, Germany, Croatia, Italy, France, Australia, Switzerland and Bosnia.

The Jeff Crawford Scholarship Program helps defray education costs so that teen-agers battling their illnesses can continue their education.

The Medical Relief Program assists when insurance does not meet the child's needs.

Other custom-made programs involve extensive follow-up with the children that includes family retreat sessions, employment opportunities, out-of-state activities, daily devotional support and other assistance. Little Star also supports the entire family and caregiver system and provides educational materials and supplies promoting the importance of protecting, helping and equipping children with the Word of God.

You can join Little Star's efforts by donating funds and/or new copies of *First Service*. All contributions are tax deductible. Federal Tax ID #86-0947944.

If you would like more information about Little Star log on to *www.firstservicebook.com* or *www.andreajaeger.com*. P.O. Box 11569, Aspen, CO 81612.

PROCEEDS BENEFIT

Children's

CHARITIES

I would like to help children with the amount of:

❏ $25.00 donation
❏ $50.00 donation
❏ $100.00 donation
❏ $250.00 donation
❏ Other amount $_____
❏ $1,000.00 donation (This entitles you to receive a limited-edition leatherbound copy of *First Service* autographed by Andrea Jaeger.)

_____
NAME

_____
ADDRESS

_____
CITY   STATE   ZIP CODE

_____
PHONE NUMBER

Please send your tax-deductible donations to:

Little Star
P.O. Box 11569
Aspen, Colorado 81612
www.firstservicebook.com
Federal Tax ID is: 86-0947944

PROCEEDS BENEFIT
Children's
CHARITIES

"Once you're through the [ranch] gates you have no worries, no fears, and nothing in life can add up to this feeling—knowing you're problem-free and there's nothing you can't do."

—Edward, 15

"Cancer has taught me that you need to cherish every second you are living and live life to its fullest."

—Michael, 15

"[The ranch] is a place where dreams come true and the friends that are made will never be forgotten. The supportive and loving staff makes each camper feel like a part of the family, and camp becomes a second home."

—Erica, 15